The Mourning After

Postmodern Studies 40

Series
edited by

Theo D'haen
and
Hans Bertens

The Mourning After

Attending the Wake
of Postmodernism

Edited by
Neil Brooks and Josh Toth

Amsterdam - New York, NY 2007

Cover design: Pier Post

The paper on which this book is printed meets the requirements of "ISO 9706:1994, Information and documentation - Paper for documents - Requirements for permanence".

ISBN-13: 978-90-420-2162-4
©Editions Rodopi B.V., Amsterdam – New York, NY 2007
Printed in The Netherlands

To Danica and to Claire, David, and James

Contents

Mourning and Praying at the Wake

Acknowledgements

The support and guidance of many people have made this project a possibility. We would like to offer explicitly our sincere gratitude to Laurel Mitchell for her excellent copy-editing and Clay Dion for his creative input. Thomas Carmichael, Tilottama Rajan, Ramona Lumpkin, Trish Fulton, Jef Clarke, Joseph Buttigieg, Jim Collins, Cecily Nicholson and Stephen D'Arcy are all colleagues who have provided us with both insight and inspiration. Many thanks need to go out, also, to Theo D'haen, Hans Bertens and Marieke Schilling at Rodopi for their kind encouragement and to our contributors for their excellent papers, their goodwill and their positive feedback. Finally, the support of our families has been constant and invaluable.

Permissions and Illustrations

John D. Caputo's "The Weakness of God: A Theology of the Event" is an altered version of a chapter originally published in Caputo's *The Weakness of God: A Theology of the Event* (Bloomington: Indiana University Press, 2006). It is printed here with the permission of Indiana University Press.

Introduction: A Wake and Renewed?

Josh Toth & Neil Brooks

> [M]ourning also wants to get rid of the past, to exorcize it, albeit under the guise of respectful commemoration. To forget the dead altogether is impious in ways that prepare their own retribution, but to remember the dead is neurotic and obsessive and merely feeds sterile repetition. There is no 'proper' way of relating to the dead and the past.
>   –   Fredric Jameson, "Marx's Purloined Letter"

In her brief epilogue to the 2002 edition of *Politics of Postmodernism*, Linda Hutcheon seemingly placed the final nail in postmodernism's coffin: "it's over" (166). According to Hutcheon, "the postmodern moment has passed, even if its discursive strategies and its ideological critique continue to live on – as do those of modernism – in our contemporary twenty-first century world" (181). On the one hand, Hutcheon seems to wash her hands of the whole thing. Postmodernism is dead, no more, finished, passed, past. Yet, on the other hand, she seems to suggest that postmodernism persists, that it "lives on" (at least in part). What does this mean, though? In what way is postmodernism both past/passed and present? What parts of it have managed to "live on"? Are these parts, these "discursive strategies" (like parasites), "living on" something else, some other epochal trend? If so, what new "episteme" (if we loosely employ Foucault's terminology) carries this burden, this inheritance, this debt? Or, put differently, what new period of cultural production is this that seems (quite necessarily) to be defined by its commitment to an inevitable work of mourning, a work of mourning the passing (on) of an epistemological trend that defined the past 50 years of cultural and theoretical production? What or who, then, is witness, here (now) at this wake of postmodernism?

Of course, Hutcheon has arrived somewhat late to this seemingly on-going wake – or rather, this ongoing *work* of waking, of enduring the wake, of *waking*, of waking *up*.[1] The "wake" began, it would seem, as early as the mid-eighties. More specifically, and following a writer like Raymond Federman,[2] we might argue that the first symptoms of some terminal epistemological illness became irrefutable on December 22, 1989 – the day Beckett died. In the mid to late-eighties, in fact, a number of events seemed to herald the end of postmodernism as the reigning epistemological dominant: the journal *Granta* published an issue dedicated to American "dirty realism;" neo-realist writers like Raymond Carver rose in status; Tom Wolfe published his "Literary Manifesto for the New Social Novel;" Paul de Man's youthful association with National Socialism was uncovered; Donald Barthelme (along with Beckett) died; Derrida seemed to suddenly shift his attention to distinctly ethico-political issues; religious thinkers, like Emmanuel Levinas, began to garner significant critical attention; and the Berlin Wall fell, suggesting the final triumph of capitalism. Although all of these events seemed to signal a (new) period of mourning, the fall of the Berlin wall is, we think, of particular significance.

Given that postmodernism is typically defined by its opposition to all latent utopian impulses, the fall of the last viable political alternative (i.e. the utopian promise of communism) seemingly speaks to the victory and hegemony of a distinctly postmodern, or late-capitalist, ideology. Not surprisingly, then, it is at the very moment when this victory is imminent – that is, when postmodernism seems to have become the very thing it aimed to destroy – that we begin to see signs of an emergent cultural trend, or "epistemological configuration." Put differently, the fall of the last overtly utopian discourse seems to effect the dissolution (also) of a postmodern, or hegemonically "counter-Enlightenment," epoch. In *the wake of socialism*, postmodernism's increasingly dogmatic rejection of all utopian discourses began to seem totalitarian, if not dangerously utopian. The result, it would seem, was a renewed interest in (or an overt willingness to mourn) the utopian, the teleological, the religious, etc. An example of this "renewed interest" might in fact be Derrida's apparent "ethical turn." It seems hardly coincidental that Derrida published (and presumably wrote) his first overtly ethico-political works – i.e. *The Force of law, The Other Heading, Specters of Marx, Politics of Friendship*, etc – just as the world was experiencing the dissolution of the Soviet Union. As such texts mark the beginning of Derrida's interest in the arena of ethics, justice, and the messianic, we would argue that they represent the first stages of a period of mourning, a period of mourning for viable political/utopian alternatives that marks (more broadly) the dissolution of the postmodern episteme. Simply put, this emergent epoch seems to "mourn" the apparent loss of the very idealistic alternatives that postmodernism strove to efface. Moreover, and if we recall Derrida's own take on mourning, this period can be defined by its desire to get over – or, rather, to finally lay to rest – that which came before.

Of course, many might view our locating some shift in the zeitgeist with the fall of the Berlin Wall or any other late twentieth-century signifier we might choose as misleading (if not simply erroneous), as the most obvious marker of a new cultural dominant must certainly be the terrorist attacks in New York on September 11, 2001 and the culture of fear they initiated. After all, what has been enabled by those events has done much to shape the way in which postmodernism has been either rejected or re-fashioned. Quite simply, a culture demanding a shared sense of "moral outrage" doesn't seem reconcilable with a sustained rejection of metanarratives and a demand for stylistic experimentation. So, indeed, if postmodernism became terminally ill sometime in the late-eighties and early-nineties, it was buried once and for in the rubble of the World Trade Center.

Still, what we want to highlight here is that a particular *work of postmodern mourning* began sometime in the early-nineties; in the nineties critics began making claims about the fact that the "high-tide" of postmodernism had finally begun to crash[3] and that a new form of realism had begun to emerge in its wake. Indeed, with the "First Stuttgart Seminar in Cultural Studies" – a conference in 1991 that included writers like Ihab Hassan, John Barth, Raymond Federman, William Gass and Malcolm Bradbury, and that was aptly titled "The End of Postmodernism: New Directions" – critics began to formally confirm an apparent shift in aesthetic and theoretical focus. Since then, or so it would seem, we have been engaged in a process of mourning, a process that sees us trying to break (finally) with postmodernism – or, at the every least, to break (finally) with postmodernism's apparent solipsism and irresponsibility, its ethical and social vacuity. After all, since the beginning of the nineties, the suggestion has been that, for one reason or another, postmodernism failed and that its demise (via a certain *re*turn to ethics, religious and realism) was inevitable. Put differently, critics (some of whom have contributed to the following collection) have increasingly stressed the fact that the basic imperative that animated postmodernism paradoxically necessitated its demise. This may require some clarification.

In the 1983 *Granta* issue (entitled "Dirty Realism: New Writing in America"), Bill Buford argued that a "new" type of realism had emerged in response to the pretensions of postmodernism. While introducing the issue's contributors – such as Jayne Anne Philips, Raymond Carver, Frederick Barthelme and Tobias Wolff – Bill Buford positioned, what he referred to as "dirty realism," in direct contradistinction to both traditional forms of realism and the metafictional devices of postmodernism:

> It is not heroic or grand: the epic ambitions of Norman Mailer or Saul Bellow seem, in contrast, inflated, strange, even false. It is not self-consciously experimental like so much of the writing – variously described as 'postmodern', 'postcontemporary' or 'deconstructionist' – that was published in the sixties and seventies. The work of John Barth, William Gaddis or Thomas Pynchon seems pretentious in comparison. (4)

The sense we get from Buford is that this new form of realism is a type of realism that remains inflected by the lessons of postmodernism: "This is a curious, dirty realism about the belly-side of contemporary life, but it is realism so stylized and particularized – so insistently informed by discomforting and sometimes elusive irony – that it makes the more traditional realistic novels of, say, Updike and Styron seem ornate, even baroque in comparison" (4).

This revival of (some type of) "realism" was further solidified by the American writer Tom Wolfe in his 1989 "Literary Manifesto for a New Social Novel." Rejecting the claims of postmodernism as decedent and elitist, Wolfe argued that only the realistic novel – i.e. realistic in the journalistic tradition of a writer like Zola – has the ability to be socially pertinent and captivating: "It is not merely that reporting is useful in gathering the *petits faits vrais* that create verisimilitude and make a novel gripping or absorbing, although that side of the enterprise is worth paying attention to. My contention is that, especially in an age like this, they are essential for the greatest effects literature can achieve" (55). Not surprisingly, Wolfe holds up his own book, *The Bonfire of the Vanities*, as an example of his specific brand of neo-realism, a form of narrative that rejects postmodern strategies as overly and unjustly privileged by academia. By 1989, then, the demise of postmodernism seemed to be, for most, an inevitability. And, by the mid-nineties, the phrase "after (or beyond) postmodern" was to be found on the cover of any number of critical works.[4]

Of course, and as the above list of significant "events" suggests, this recent shift in stylistic privilege – from ostentatious works of postmodern metafiction to more grounded (or "responsible") works of neo-realism – seems to echo the recent ethico-political "turn" in critical theory, a turn that is, as we suggested above, most obvious in Jacques Derrida's later work on Marxism, friendship, hospitality, and forgiveness. Along with a later Derrida, though, we might also include the likes of Jean-Luc Nancy, Jean-Luc Marion, John D. Caputo and Slajov Žižek in a list of theorists who seem to have broken "the postmodern mould." For the most part, and by turning their attention to issues of community, religion and ethical responsibility, such theorists do not (if we us Žižek's phrasing) fall "prey to any kind of 'post-modernist' traps (such as the illusion that we live in a 'post-ideological' condition" (7). In line with this theoretical turn, then, and in the *wake of postmodernism*, a growing body of cultural and literary criticism has dedicated itself to the careful recovery of various "logocentric" assumptions, assumptions that postmodernism seemed to think it could finally do without. Recent essay collections – such as Jennifer Geddes' *Evil after Postmodernism: History, Narratives, Ethics* and John D. Caputo and Michael J. Scanlon's *God, the Gift and Postmodernism* – might stand (for the moment) as prime examples of this shift in critical concern.

The suggestion is that the narrative and theoretical production that is typically read as the effect of a subversive and nihilistic epistemological trend has been undermined by a new discourse that is no longer compelled to *focus on* (or endorse) the impossibility of the subject (or author) and the need to avoid a grounded, or situated, commitment to the ethical, political and/or religious. In a recent article

– i.e. "Recent Realist Fiction and the Idea of Writing 'After Postmodernism'" – Günter Leypoldt succinctly articulates the nature of this "shift" (especially as evidenced in recent narrative and stylistic rejections of postmodernism). In *The Man Who Wasn't There*, the protagonist, Ed Crane (played by Billy Bob Thornton), after being accused of murder, is defended by an attorney named Freddy Riedenschneider (played by Tony Shalhoub). A satirical representation of the typical postmodern hero, Riedenschneider is so convinced that reality is nothing more than an effect of contingent representations he attempts to defend Crane by arguing that what "really happened" can never "really" be known, for the "The more you look, the less you really know." Riedenschneider, though (and this is Leypoldt's point), loses the case, and Crane is "really" sentenced to death. As Leypoldt argues, "Riedenschneider's fixation on uncertainty recalls the playful skepticism of the metafictional tradition, but in contrast to the heroically self-reflexive philosopher narrators of classic postmodernism, he is portrayed as moronic, vain, and ultimately feckless" (20). For Leypoldt, the presence of a character like Riedenschneider in a Hollywood film speaks to the way in which "the metafictional and fabulist devices lost their subversive edge and began to seem less interesting, less 'progressive'" (26).

From the perspective of a writer at this wake of postmodernism, then, postmodernism (at least as it was understood in the mid-eighties) has failed. Its failure is, in fact, two-fold. On the one hand, its self-affirmation as an anti-ideological discourse, a discourse that privileged individualism and solipsism over the illusion of communal bonds, religious faith. ethical claims, and the possibility of communication, seems (quite naturally) to parallel the progress of modernization. Consistent with the trajectory of modern "avant-garde" movements, postmodernism's value as a subversive discourse ends when its dominance appears evident. Not surprisingly, and as we suggested above, this moment for postmodernism is heralded by many critics of aesthetic production *after postmodernism* by the fall of the Berlin Wall and the end of the Cold War – or, rather, the end of the last viable utopian ideal/impulse. On the other hand, the postmodern withdrawal from public and/or social discourse – that is, the postmodern imperative to be inaccessible, *to expose* as illusory the ideal of shared experience and communal understanding – becomes itself a very public (because dominant) claim. In other words, an aesthetic that aimed to dismantle binary distinctions, that attempted (more specifically) to destabilize the opposition between high and low culture, becomes (itself) a vacuous and in-effectual aesthetic of the elite. It is, after all, the "elitism" of postmodernism that most critics identify as its most glaring failure. Thus, postmodernism's increasingly emphatic insistence on inaccessibility – on, that is, the utterly private nature of all discourse (or, rather, the futility of the social or public text) – became a dominant ideal, a hegemonic standard in both academia and the artistic community

Put differently, we might say that postmodernism "failed" because it *continued to speak*, because it continued to make (and privilege) *truth claims* about the impossibility of making such claims (while, for the most part, failing to overtly articulate the fact that such claims were necessarily and ironically animated by the latent belief that the truth could finally be expressed). In short, postmodernism failed *because it didn't die* (as it should have). Instead, its increasingly loud movement toward silence and/or the absolute denial of objective truth claims became dogmatic, institutionalized and programmatic. Thus recent critical and theoretical work (including much of the following) seems to highlight the past hegemony of high-postmodernism and the need for a form of cultural production that is no longer confined by a corrosive and socially impractical imperatives (however paradoxical and self-reflexive such imperatives might have been). In brief, if somewhat crudely, our current work of mourning – and, thus, of "waking" – is (to a certain degree) a work of *getting over* the apparent hegemony of postmodernism, of postmodern aesthetic and theoretical imperatives, of (perhaps) imperatives generally.

As a result of postmodernism's pervasiveness – or rather, as a result of its hegemony – we see (in works of literature and film like that of the Coen Brothers) a type of mourning, which is also (and of course) a type of resistance. However, this resistance remains, to some degree, postmodern. Indeed, like the theorists mentioned above, the writers and directors whose work defines (what we might think of as) a still emergent period of "renewalism" seem to carry on a certain postmodern project while (all the while) critiquing elements of that project as ineffectual, irresponsible, dangerous, absurd, "feckless," etc. That said, and while extrapolating on the suggestions made in the following chapters (and elsewhere), we might view the following as a tentative list of renewalist writers and directors: David Foster Wallace,

Jonathan Franzen, Russell Banks, Richard Powers, Lorrie Moore, David Lynch, Sophia Coppola, Wes Anderson, Paul Thomas Anderson, Maxine Hong Kingston, Mark Z. Danielewski, Darren Aronofsky, Nicholson Baker, Dave Eggers, Jared Hess, etc. Obviously, such a list will always be fraught; and we will not attempt to defend the veracity of this particular list here. However, those listed all share a certain affinity with postmodernism; at the same time, though, they all seem to move beyond the parameters of a specifically postmodern project. Many of them, in fact, seem unabashedly nostalgic and "realistic" (if not, perhaps, openly logocentric, humanistic and/or onto-theological).

Ultimately, then, it would seem that (at the wake of postmodernism) we are not seeing a simple "knee-jerk" reaction to the dominance of a seemingly nihilist and socially irresponsible cultural trend. Attending the wake of postmodernism is not a matter of blind and reactionary repudiation. As the following essays make clear, postmodernism – or, at the very least, *the ghost of postmodernism* – has much to teach us (yet). What we have inherited from postmodernism cannot be simply denied, or rejected outright. To a certain extent, then, attending the wake of postmodernism is also a matter of *awakening* postmodernism, of *awakening* it to all of those issues postmodernism in its reified form seemed so anxious to circumvent: issues of faith, ethical responsibility, politics, community, etc. As Klaus Stierstorfer recently pointed out in his introduction to *Beyond Postmodernism: Reassessments in Literature, Theory, and Culture* (and as several of the contributors here also suggest), this (re)turn to seemingly pre-postmodern ideologies remains very much tempered by the lessons of postmodernism:

> Whether it is the more universal interest in the possible foundations of a general or literary ethics in a world of globalisation, or the more specific and local issues of identities, scholars and writers alike nevertheless continue to find themselves in the dilemma of facing the deconstructive gestures inherent in postmodernist thought while at the same time requiring some common ground on which ethical agreements can be based. Hence some form of referentiality, even some kind of essentialism is called for. (9-10)

In terms of the apparent shift to a type of neo-realism,[5] then, we might say that some form of mimesis is called for – that is, some type of renewed faith in the possibility of what postmodernism narrative has repeatedly identified as impossible: meaning, truth, representational accuracy, etc. But as Stierstorfer suggests, this shift to some type of "renewalism" is not simply a backlash in response to postmodern cultural production; it is neither a reactionary return to the (ethical) imperatives of modernism nor a revival of the traditional forms of realism and ethical discourse that proliferated in nineteenth century. What comes after postmodernism, then, is (perhaps) best described if we recall the ethical paradoxes explored by Derrida in his most recent work; this period of renewal, of renewalism, is, in other words a period of "faith without faith," of "religion without religion," of "mimesis without mimesis," etc, etc. In short, Postmodernism, to a certain degree, persists. We, undoubtedly, continue to mourn. What follows, then, are attempts to understand and negotiate this often difficult (if inevitable and necessary) process of mourning…

The first section of this book looks at the ways in which postmodernism has responded to and been altered by recent events, from the attack on the two towers to the re-election of George W. Bush. In "Postmodernism in a Fundamentalist Arena," Paul Maltby examines fundamentalism within American political and cultural discourse, a fundamentalism often ironically empowered by its seeming rejection of other forms of fundamentalism. This new fundamentalism alters how postmodern theory and writing is received or can be efficacious. Robert McLaughlin, in "Postmodernism in the Age of Distracting Discourses," then examines how the proliferation of twenty-first century discourses seeking legitimation can be understood as a product of postmodernism well also being navigated successfully through a renewed understanding of the ethical component latent within postmodernism. The final two essays of the opening section go on to locate and discuss this ethical component. Jennifer Geddes analysis of suffering, in "Attending to Suffering in/at the Wake of Postmodernism," suggests that new articulations of postmodern thought can awaken and develop a latent emphasis not only on justice, but on compassion; Jane Flax, in "Soul Service: Foucault's 'Care of the Self' as Politics and Ethics," uses Foucault's writing to argue that the conscience of postmodernism does not need to be invented, merely uncovered as we remove the over-simplifying interpretations and look at the inspirations and motivations of figures such as Foucault, Lyotard, and Derrida.

The second section examines specific cultural productions and trends. In "Mood Swings: The Aesthetics of Ambient Emergence," Katherine Hayles and Todd Gannon examine important parallels between recent writing and recent architecture and argue that a new aesthetic has arisen not only as a result of changes on the cultural-political landscape but also as a result of changes in the very way technology allows us to process "material." Their characterization of "ambient emergence" provides an avenue to understanding through an enhanced attentiveness to the very ambient influences a fundamentalist culture ignores if not destroys. This essay is nicely complemented by Gavin Keulks' "New York, Los Angeles, and Other Toxicities: Revisiting Postmodernism in Rushdie's *Fury* and *Shalimar the Clown*" and William Little's "Nothing to Write Home About: Impossible Reception in Mark Z. Danielewski's *House of Leaves*." While Keulks examines how attention to the urban setting in the recent work of Salmon Rushdie can help explain Rushdie's re-assessment of postmodern techniques, Little explores the ways in which Mark Danielewski's *House of Leaves* requires that the reader simultaneously invoke and reject the sorts of self-referential knowing attitude that the reader of many postmodern novels is positioned and expected to take. This line of argumentation is approached from yet another perspective in Robert Rebein's "Turncoat: Why Jonathan Franzen Finally Said 'No' to Po-Mo." In analysing Jonathan Franzen's recent work, Rebein considers the ways in which "postmodern" and "realist" aesthetics can no longer be held as simply oppositional even if the emergence of the latter seems on the surface to be the death knell of the former. And, just as Hayles and Gannon's work parallels literature with architecture, Clayton Dion's paper – "Serving *Pi*(e) at the Wake of Postmodernism: Mathematics and Mysticism at the End of the 20th Century" – looks at this new "realist" aesthetic within the context of how the changing notion of the mathematical "real" has paralleled and influenced similar trends within both literary study and mainstream religious discourses.

Following on the heels of Dion's discussion of the recent marriage of mathematics and mysticism, the final section of the book examines the re-emergence of ethics and religion in contemporary theoretical discourse. Returning to some of the issues of the opening section, Dawne McCance's "Derrida and the Ethics of Mourning After" elaborates upon the Derridean concept of "mourning;" looking both backwards and forwards, McCance places the current cultural moment as one of "mourning" infused with both loss and possibility. Clayton Crockett, in "Postmodernism and the Crisis of Belief: Neo-Realism vs. the Real," takes the issues of "realism" and representing "the real" (issues central to the essays of the second section) and examines the crisis of belief engendered by the neo-liberal strains of postmodernism thought, suggesting, like Flax, that the solution to this crisis and the escape from debilitating fundamentalisms can be found by revisiting and not simply rejecting the continental philosophy that underpinned postmodern ideals. Finally, John Caputo's "The Weakness of God: A Theology of the Event" offers us a sustained example of a type of theoretical discourse that is no longer constrained by the dogmatics of postmodern anti-foundationalism, a discourse that can speak openly about a sincere need and desire for God while understanding and accepting that need and desire as an essential and animating effect of responsible (or better, *postmodern*) doubt.

In the end, then, these papers come together to work a certain work of mourning. They come together, that is, here, at this wake of postmodernism. They work to awaken postmodernism while they work to escape the dogmatism and violence of its wake. They struggle with the burden of inheritance while they point to and embrace the possibility of a future (after). These are, in short, works of renewal. These papers take into account a certain postmodern failure, or limitation. In one way or another, they struggle with the fact that postmodernism has lost its efficacy and relevance in a period of rampant fundamentalism, moral righteousness, and political conservatism. Yet, in calling for reappraisals and critical re-engagements, these papers ask us to endure the wake, to attend to it, to respect it. If we are indeed experiencing a period of renewalism in the wake of postmodernism then we must be wary of reactionary and conservative blindness, of irresponsible rejections of critical and theoretical doubt, of nostalgic returns to unchecked idealism. If we can no longer appeal to the "spirit of postmodernism" in its utopian sense, we must nonetheless continue to respect the fact that the ghost of postmodernism is essential to the future of our critical discourse. Postmodernism might be dead, but it still has much work to do. And for that work, it would seem, we must now take responsibility.

Q. of Theory in times of reaction
of the Theory symposium Critical Inq?

Notes

[1] A fact, of course, that Hutcheon herself admits: "For decades now, diagnosticians have been pronouncing on [postmodernism's] health, if not its demise" (*Politics* 165).

[2] See Federman's "Before Postmodernism and After (Part One)" and "Before Postmodernism and After (Part Two)," both of which he delivered in 1991 at the "First Stuttgart Seminar in Cultural Studies" – i.e. "The End of Postmodernism: New Directions"

[3] Klaus Stierstorfer describes the situation like this: "in a much-quoted survey Lance Olsen reported an astounding increase in occurrences of the term 'postmodern in American newspapers from 1980 through 1984 to 1987 at a ratio of 2: 116: 247. In his turn, Hans Bertens charted a 'history of the debate on postmodernism from its tentative beginnings in the 1950s to its overwhelming self-confidence in the early 1990s'. From the later 1990s onwards, however, this narrative of the progress of postmodernism appears to lose direction. Although no statistical data are available, the quantity of references to postmodernism in scholarly publications as well as in the daily press seems to decreases, as does the heatedness of the debate" (1).

[4] Along with those discussed above, some examples might include: José López and Garry Potter's *After Postmodernism: An introduction to Critical Realism*; Robert Rebein's *Hicks, Tribes and Dirty Realists: American Fiction After Postmodernism*; and Klaus Stierstorfer's *Beyond Postmodernism: Reassessments in Literature, Theory, and Culture*.

[5] For several useful examinations of the emergence and significance of neo-realism after postmodernism please see *Neo-Realism in Contemporary Fiction*, a collection of essays edited by Kristiann Versluys.

Works Cited

Buford, Bill. "Editorial." *Granta 8: Dirty Realism* (1983): 4-5.

Caputo, John D. and Michael J. Scanlon, ed. *God, the Gift, and Postmodernism.* Bloomington: Indiana UP, 1999.

Coen, Joel, dir. *The Man Who Wasn't There.* Perfs. Billy Bob Thorton, Frances McDormand and James Gandolfini. Good Machine, 2001.

Derrida, Jacques. *Force of Law: The "Mystical Foundation of Authority." Acts of Religion.* Trans. Mary Quaintance. Ed. Gil Anidjar. New York: Routledge, 2002. 228-98.

—. *The Other Heading.* Trans. Michael B. Naas and Pascale-Anne Brault. Indiana UP, 1992.

—. *Politics of Friendship.* Trans. George Collins. London: Verso, 1997.

—. *Specters of Marx: The State of the Debt, the Work of Mourning, and the New International.* Trans. Peggy Kamuf. New York: Routledge, 1994.

Federman, Raymond. "Before Postmodernism and After (Part One)." *The End of Postmodernism: New Directions.* Proc. of the First Stuggart Seminar in Cultural Studies 04. 08. – 18. 08. 1991. Dir. Heide Ziegler. Stuttgart: M & P Verlag für Wissenschaft und Forschung, 1993. 47-64.

—. "Before Postmodernism and After (Part Two)." *The End of Postmodernism: New Directions.* Proc. of the First Stuggart Seminar in Cultural Studies 04. 08. – 18. 08. 1991. Dir. Heide Ziegler. Stuttgart: M & P Verlag für Wissenschaft und Forschung, 1993. 153-170.

Geddes, Jennifer, ed. *Evil after Postmodernism: Histories, Narratives, and Ethics.* New York: Routledge, 2001.

Jameson, Fredric. "Marx's Purloined Letter." *Ghostly Demarcations: A Symposium on Jacques Derrida's* Specters of Marx. Ed. Michael Sprinkler. New York: Verso, 1999.

Leypoldt, Günter. "Recent Realist Fiction and the Idea of Writing 'After Postmodernism.'" *Amerikastudien/American Studies* 49. 1 (2004): 19-34.

López, José and Garry Potter, eds. *After Postmodernism: An introduction to Critical Realism.* London: Sage, 1994.

Rebein, Robert. *Hicks, Tribes and Dirty Realists: American Fiction after Postmodernism.* Lexington, KY: UP of Kentucky, 2001.

Stierstorfer, Klaus. "Introduction: Beyond Postmodernism – Contingent Referentiality?" *Beyond Postmodernism: Reassessments in Literature, Theory, and Culture.* Ed. Klaus Stierstorfer. Berlin: Walter de Gruyter, 2003. 1-10.

Versluys, Kristiaan, ed. *Neo-Realism in Contemporary Fiction.* Amsterdam: Rodopi, 1992.

Wolfe, Tom. Stalking the Billion-Footed Beast: A Literary Manifesto for the New Social Novel." *Harper's Magazine* 279. 1674 (Nov. 1989): 45-56.

Žižek, Slavoj. *The Sublime Object of Ideology.* London: Verso, 1989.

2

Postmodernism in a Fundamentalist Arena

Paul Maltby

Polling statistics for the 2004 US presidential election showed that nearly one in four voters were white evangelicals. Alienated by the liberal values of the coastal metropolises, their electoral mobilization tipped the balance in Bush's favour, with almost 80% voting Republican (Freedland 5). This outcome prompted observations about a clash of cultures, in particular, Christian conservatism versus secular liberalism. Simon Schama, speaking of the "Divided States of America," identified a "Godly America" hopelessly estranged from a "Worldly America" (19-20). Yet, within this cultural divide, we can distinguish an even more dramatic polarization, one that can be framed in epistemological terms, between fundamentalist and postmodern paradigms of knowledge. Usually, postmodernism is understood in relation to another paradigm, the secular paradigm of Enlightenment humanism. We are familiar with accounts of postmodernism as a set of critiques whose objective is to expose those submerged forms of metaphysical thinking that linger in what Enlightenment humanism assumed to be a full-fledged *post-metaphysical* order of knowledge. Yet, today, we are witness to a pre-Enlightenment strain of thought that has asserted itself in key domains of national life, that is, the metaphysics of Christian fundamentalism.[1] Inspired by their faith and emboldened by their connections in the White House, fundamentalists are actively shaping legislation designed to attack the secular basis of everyday life (education, medical research, and sexuality are among the primary targets). Under these circumstances, postmodernism, as a radically anti-metaphysical mode of critique, may be welcomed as a robust adversary of fundamentalist thought. Indeed, the political advance of fundamentalism supplies an eminently practical context in which to appreciate the adversarial potential of postmodernism. At the same time, a confrontation of the two paradigms will be seen to reveal limitations of postmodernism, which were not apparent in its earlier engagements with secular philosophies.

The Fundamentalist Arena

North American fundamentalist Protestantism emerged haphazardly in the late 19th Century as a hostile reaction to modernist (or "irreligious") tendencies in mass culture and thought, and to the influence of liberal theology and ecumenism. It grew out of older religious traditions (evangelicalism, revivalism, millenarianism) and did not achieve a distinct identity until around 1910. This essentially conservative movement sought to counter modernist and liberal influence by stressing adherence to five basic doctrines as "fundamental" to Christianity: (1) the inerrancy of the Bible; (2) the Virgin Birth of Christ; (3) his substitutionary atonement; (4) his bodily resurrection; (5) the authenticity of his miracles. Approximately 40% of fundamentalists also hold to the doctrine of premillennialism. Where an older postmillennialism held that Christ would return only *after* Christians had created the one-thousand-year Kingdom of God on earth, premillennialism, lacking faith in the redemptive potential of "man-made institutions," postulates the any-moment coming of Christ and an End Times schedule of events: the Rapture, the rise of the Antichrist, the Second Coming, Armageddon, and, finally, the dispensation of Christ's millennial reign on earth.

Since the 1970s, fundamentalists – in the same way as pentecostalists and charismatics – have been counted as a subset under the vast canopy of Evangelicalism. George Marsden opens his classic study, *Understanding Fundamentalism and Evangelicalism*, with the proposition, "a fundamentalist is an evangelical who is angry about something" (1). He adds, "an American fundamentalist is an evangelical who is militant in opposition to liberal theology in the churches or to changes in cultural values or mores, such as those associated with 'secular humanism'. In either the long or the short definitions, fundamentalists are a subtype of evangelicals and militancy is crucial to their outlook" (1).

Taking the "born-again" experience as the criterion for measurement, estimates of the numbers of evangelicals in the US widely vary, ranging between 90 and 126 million (30-42% of the population).[2] But exactly what percentage of evangelicals may be counted as fundamentalist is unclear. Two additional criteria help distinguish fundamentalist from non-fundamentalist evangelicals. First, fundamentalists are biblical literalists: they believe *inter alia* in the doctrine of Creationism and in the End Times prophecies of Revelation. A Gallup Poll of 1995 shows that 57 million evangelicals take the Bible as the literal word of God (Johnson, Table 2). (Conversely, evangelical interpretations of the Bible are also tempered by a critical hermeneutics that takes account of socio-historical contexts and metaphorical language.) Second, fundamentalists actively support programs for imposing Christian conservative values via state and federal legislation, such as prohibition of same-sex marriage and abortion. This cohort – self-described as "conservative evangelicals" – constituted 40% of Bush's electorate in 2000 (Kaplan 3) and 51% in 2004 (Lieven 7). (Yet, we should note that African-American and Latino evangelical communities do not endorse the hardline policies favoured by most white Republican evangelicals, while the Sojourners of Washington D.C. espouse a distinctively leftist politics.) In the absence of firm statistical data but building on the preceding figures, I shall work with an estimate of 50 million fundamentalists - a figure that amounts to roughly 17% or one in six of the US population and at least 40% of all evangelicals. Finally, many of the writers quoted below are in the habit of referring to fundamentalists simply as "evangelicals," and fundamentalists, mindful of the media's negative image of fundamentalism, prefer to call themselves "conservative evangelicals" or just "evangelicals." This erosion of the distinction dogs much commentary and scholarship, while the coinage of "fundagelism" is popular across the blogosphere (Sutherland).

In the Bush era, an opportunistic alliance with neo-conservatives has enabled fundamentalists to achieved an influential, though by no means hegemonic, position in the sphere of policy formation. Richard Land, a top executive and lead lobbyist of the 16-million-strong Southern Baptist Convention (a church hijacked in the 1980s by evangelicals and then purged of its liberal leadership) has observed that "More born-again Christians work in [Bush's] administration than in any other in modern history" (qtd. in Waldman A5). Together with George Bush, who became a born-again Christian at 40, conservative evangelicals who serve or have served in his administrations include such senior figures as former Attorney General John Ashcroft, former House Majority Leader Tom DeLay, head speech writer Michael Gerson, Senate Majority Leader Bill Frist, and a host of officials assigned to key positions in Health and Human Services, the State Department, and the Justice Department. In 2004, the seven highest-ranking Senate Republicans (Bill Frist, TN; Mitch McConnell, KY; Rick Santorum, PA; Bob Bennett, UT; Kay Bailey Hutchinson, TX; Jon Kyl, AZ; George Allen, VA) each received a scorecard of 100% from the right-wing Christian Coalition for voting 100% of the time with coalition supported bills (Theocracy Watch). Anatol Lieven notes that, in 2001, "29 senators out of 100 and 125 House members out of 435 – that is, more than a quarter of the members of both houses of the US Congress – voted 100 per cent of the time in accordance with the Christian Coalition's principles" (7).

Fundamentalist leaders who enjoy direct access to Beltway lawmakers include: James Dobson, Chairman of the family-values media conglomerate Focus on the Family and Christian radio host; Ralph Reed, former Christian Coalition director and Southern regional chairman of the 2004 Bush/Cheyney re-election campaign; Pat Robertson, founder of the Christian Coalition and Christian Broadcasting Network; and Jerry Falwell, founder of the Moral Majority. Bush aides will often consult with, and seek the approval of, fundamentalist leaders when formulating policies. For example, Elliott Abrams, the National Security Council's top Middle East aide, has conferred with the Apostolic Congress to ensure that Bush's policy on Israel conforms with evangelical prophecy about the role of Israel in its End Times scenario (Perlstein).

Thus, vigorously represented in the White House and empowered in their capacity as a vital constituency of the governing party, conservative evangelicals have played a major role in the formulation of both domestic and foreign policy. Suffice here to note the appointment of more anti-abortion judges to federal benches; new limits on stem cell research; bans on cloning; programs to teach sexual abstinence in schools; the prohibition of same-sex marriages; proposals that empower religious institutions to disburse federal money for social welfare; a push for legislation that would give students the right to sue professors who insist that evolution is a fact. In the domain of foreign policy, fundamentalist apocalyptic beliefs have produced self-proclaimed "Christian Zionists," estimated at 20 million in the US (Lampman 15), who give vociferous and financial support to the continued expansion of illegal settlements until Israel reaches her Old Testament boundaries (Zunes; Engel).[3] Fundamentalists are also strong advocates of the war with Iraq, a state they see as the modern-day embodiment of Revelation's wicked city of Babylon.

Control over policy-making is critical to the theocratic agenda of Reconstructionism, a powerful wing of fundamentalism. Leading advocates of the latter, like Gary DeMar, Gary North, and the late R.J. Rushdoony, invoke what they believe to be a biblical mandate to "take dominion" over all secular institutions in order to usher in the millennial Kingdom

The extent to which conservative evangelicals drive policy-making today is evidence of a highly mobilized and well-coordinated movement with enormous grassroots appeal. Their beliefs are promulgated far beyond the pulpit via the strategic presence of Christian conservatives on town councils and school boards, via hundreds of TV and radio stations controlled by fundamentalist media moguls like James Dobson, via vast, well-financed publishing houses such as Tyndale, publishers of the *Left Behind* novels. The fundamentalists are waging a war of position, exercising their electoral and propagandizing power in a hard fight for cultural supremacy.   *cp. Reagan's admin ?*

Apocalypse and the Warrior Jesus

Fundamentalists have fabricated a grand eschatology by cobbling together dispersed passages from the Bible. According to their millennialist view of history, the Second Coming, which they say is imminent, is conditional upon Israel occupying *all* the lands within God's grant to Abraham (i.e. "from the river of Egypt to...the river Euphrates" – Genesis 15:18) and the conversion of the Jews. Then Russia will wage war on Israel, initiating a great struggle between Godly and Satanic forces. Meanwhile, all "true believers" will be "raptured", that is to say, they will suddenly be stripped of their clothes and rise to heaven, where they will join God. (There is some debate at the Pre-Tribulation Research Center, in Dallas, as to whether the raptured would also be stripped of their contact lenses and false teeth.)[4] And from up on high, they will witness the Great Tribulation down on Earth, whereby those left behind, i.e. all infidels, will in true biblical fashion suffer the excruciating torments of God's wrath. Finally, Christ will make a glorious return and overpower the forces of Satan in the valley of Armageddon. His victory will mark the start of a new Christian millennium.

This is the future which, according to a "literal" but, in fact, highly tendentious reading, is foretold in the Book of Revelation. Polls indicate that 15-18% of US voters belong to churches that subscribe to this account of the End Times (Monbiot). According to a *Time/CNN* poll of June 2002, 36% of Americans claim to follow the news in the context of biblical prophecies about the end of the world. Esther Kaplan cites a survey conducted by the Pew Forum on Religion and Public Life, which found that "63 percent of white evangelicals believe Israel fulfills the biblical prophecy about Jesus' second coming" (25-26).

The Reverend Tim LaHaye and Jerry Jenkins have propagated this End Times doctrine in their *Left Behind* novel cycle. It is estimated that, as of January 2005, with twelve novels in print, over 65 million books from the series have been sold. The figure rises to 75 million if we include the graphic novels and children's editions, not to mention 10 million spinoff products such as screensavers, postcards, calendars, and boardgames ("Book"; see also Kidd 18). And the series is still growing with five more novels on the way. The extraordinary success of these books, several of which have hit number one on the *New York Times* and other best-sellers' lists, easily outselling the likes of John Grisham and Michael Crichton, has induced Jenkins to claim, "God was in this...[it would be] folly to take any human credit for it" (qtd. in Safer). (Alas, as we shall see, the prose does not bear the imprint of divine inspiration.)

LaHaye and Jenkins have given voice to a remarkably violent and vindictive eschatology; their fiction abounds with gruesome and sadistic images of torture and slaughter in the war between the righteous and the forces of the Antichrist. In *Glorious Appearing* (2004), the authors imagine Jesus as a warrior, emerging from the clouds on a white stallion (203), and taking revenge on the infidels below, who "writhed as they were invisibly sliced asunder. Their innards and entrails gushed to the desert floor...their blood pooling and rising in the unforgiving brightness of the glory of Christ" (226); and "Even as they struggled, their own flesh dissolved, their eyes melted, and their tongues disintegrated" (273). In *Apollyon* (1999), thousands of infidels desperately attempt suicide after being stung by demonic locusts but, as punishment, they must survive so that their agony is prolonged: "...no one died. They just lived in torment" (342). And lines from Revelation prophesying retribution against non-believers are frequently cited, as in 6:8, where power is given Death on his pale horse "'over a fourth of the earth, to kill with sword, with hunger, with death and by the beasts of the earth'" (*Tribulation Force* 60). Clearly, the hundreds of passages in the New Testament that preach mercy, compassion, and forgiveness count for nothing against a few selected verses from Revelation. Ted Haggard, president of the 44-million-strong National Association of Evangelicals, has endorsed the warrior image of Jesus promoted in the *Left Behind* novels: "In our stained-glass windows and our popular culture, Jesus is a kind of marshmallowy, Santa Claus Jesus, which is not at all in keeping with the gospels" (qtd. in Kirkpatrick 6). LaHaye blames liberalism for "twisting" the image of Jesus into someone "loving and wimpy," when Jesus is really a warrior who "slays the enemy with the sword, that comes from his mouth, which is the Word" (qtd. in Safer).

This belligerent form of Christianity easily meshes with the militaristic nationalism of Bush's administrations. As LaHaye puts it, "I think if [Jenkins] and I were cut, we'd bleed red, white and blue. We believe that God has raised up America to be a tool in these last days, to get the gospel to the innermost parts of the Earth" (qtd. in Safer). Indeed, thousands of missionaries from the Samaritan's Purse, the Southern Baptist Convention and other churches have followed the US military into Iraq, seizing the opportunity to evangelize among subdued Muslim populations (Kaplan 14-15). And we can see in this surge of missionary activity, this crusade to "save" the "benighted" souls of "natives," not just a replication of the racist ideology of late 19th-century Europe, but also a reflection of the neo-imperialist ideology which is currently fashionable among revisionist historians, like Niall Ferguson and Andrew Roberts, and "national security" advisors of the PNAC stripe. The latter ideology holds that non-westerners would benefit from the imposition of western ways, such as programs for privatizing public assets and opening foreign markets to western capital. Today, Christianisation helps pave the way for free-market colonization of Third World economies.

The *Left Behind* books exemplify fundamentalism as a literary genre, whose themes and aesthetics are, typically, patriotic, triumphalist, traditionalist, melodramatic, eminently didactic, and supernaturalist (in that solutions often take the form of miraculous interventions and the world operates according to a divine plan). The superhero action comic supplies the conventions for much of the writing. Jesus, the Macho Messiah, is the principal superhero. Then there's the "Tribulation Force", comprising airline captain Rayford Steele, his daughter Chloe, pastor Bruce Barnes, and journalist Buck Williams. (The hackneyed, not to say kitschy, names conjure up characters from 1950s adventure comics.) Their mission is to challenge the forces of Satan during the Tribulation period prophesied in the Bible. Their determination to do good cannot be doubted:

> They moved through the terminal toward the parking garage, striding four abreast, arms around each other's shoulders, knit with a common purpose. [They]...faced the gravest dangers anyone could face, and they knew their mission. The task of the Tribulation Force was clear and their goal nothing less than to stand and fight the enemies of God during the seven most chaotic years the planet would ever see. (*Left Behind* 468)

They must defeat the evil European, Nicolae Carpathia, who has become UN Secretary General and moved the UN headquarters to the rebuilt city of Babylon. Carpathia, "a rabid global disarmament proponent" (*Tribulation Force* 103) and advocate of greater power for the UN, is depicted as the incarnation of the Antichrist, a component of the story clearly consonant with the Bush administration's aversion to multilateralism. Furthermore, as an epic of good versus evil, which renders psychological exploration of character largely redundant, the narrative is plot-driven, a tendency to which we are at once alerted by the action-oriented subtitles of the novels, such as "The Destroyer Is Unleashed" and "The Cosmic Battle of the Ages." Finally, at the heart of this genre is the theme of the End Times, the dispensation toward which all events unfold according to a divine plan. Here lies the opportunity for the ultimate action narrative: catastrophe, war, and destruction on a cosmic scale. And for LaHaye and Jenkins, the suffering involved must be explained as God's vengeance on sinners, rather than as the failure of human institutions.

In a monograph on the fundamentalist "hagiopic," Pamela Grace identifies a film genre whose aesthetic and thematic features, point for point, could apply to LaHaye's and Jenkins' books:

> Conventional hagiopics are recognizable by their indulgence of regressive desires: longings for magical solutions, paternal protection, vengeance, and a feeling of moral superiority. These films invite the viewer to identify with the virtuous hero, who suffers but ultimately triumphs, and encourage us to enjoy the sadism and brutality that is usually directed toward both good and evil characters. Extreme suffering and even killing are made acceptable because they are part of a divine plan, the same divine plan that places us comfortably in our seats as we watch the torture and murder that usually occurs on screen. Conventional hagiopics try to convince us that we are still living in miracle-time, that a righteous and ever-watchful God, who shares our values, may intervene at any moment to make certain that we, and not our enemies or competitors, will have our wishes fulfilled. The feel-good ending of the conventional hagiopic assures us that even if good does not prevail in this world, it will in the next. (Grace 341-42)

Apocalyptic writings of the *Left Behind* type have long made the bestseller lists. Relatively recent publications include Jerry Falwell's *Nuclear War and the Second Coming* (1983), Grace Halsell's *Prophecy and Politics* (1986), and Hal Lindsey's *The Late Great Planet Earth* (1970), the last described by the *New York Times* as the "no.1 non-fiction best-seller of the decade." The phenomenal sales of these books have played a vital part in constituting the everyday metaphysics of popular culture in the Southern and Midwestern Bible Belts. Bush himself often speaks in apocalyptic terms. The day after the attacks of September 11, 2001, he framed the nature of America's response thus: "This will be a monumental struggle of good versus evil, but good will prevail". He has donned the mantle of the righteous warrior averring that "the light shines in the darkness, and the darkness will not overcome it" (qtd. in Zunes). In the 2002 State of the Union address, he invoked the "wonder-working power" of the American people in a time of danger, an allusion to a refrain from an evangelical hymn: "There is power, power, wonder-working power in the precious blood of the lamb" (qtd. in Cornwell).

The apocalyptic scenarios of all the above writers are derived from a literal reading of Bible prophecies, in particular, those of Revelation. In one of the sermons in *Tribulation Force*, Bruce Barnes challenges his audience and, by implication, the reader, to understand the account of the Four Horsemen of the Apocalypse in a purely literal sense: "If you have ever been exposed to such imagery and language before, you probably considered it only symbolic, as I did. Is there anyone here who still considers the prophetic teaching of Scripture mere symbolism?" (64-65). And readers are warned that scepticism results in being unraptured: "But those who had relegated this kind of teaching to the literalists, the fundamentalists, the closed-minded evangelicals, had been left behind" (67). For God's truth is revealed in the Bible and thus His Book requires no interpretation. That generations of schoolmen had argued over competing interpretations of biblical texts is immaterial to the fundamentalist reader. After all, the Truth is not arrived at: it's delivered. For David Cooper, Pastor at the Mount Paran Church of God in Atlanta and "strict fundamentalist," the Bible is "God's only inspired, inerrant and authoritative revelation of Himself to man in written form" (qtd. in Kaplan 26).

The fundamentalist practice of biblical literalism derives from a view of the writing that constitutes the Bible as not just a material inscription of the *logos* but its very embodiment; in other words, the Bible does not merely record God's voice but *speaks* it. Ed MacAteer, a founder of the Moral Majority, is explicit on this point: "The Bible does not contain the word of God....The Bible is the word of God" (qtd. in Simon).[5] Hence the fundamentalists' faith in the viability of a pre-interpretative reading of the Bible in which, so to speak, a signifier directly relays the reader to a fixed signified. Yet, quite apart from the old objection that biblical literalists overlook the semantic distortions that arise from translation and transcription errors, and the objection that all readings are necessarily historically or culturally situated, postmodern critique teaches us that meaning is always mediated, never purely itself. Indeed, "Jesus" *qua* signifier is deeply scored with traces of its existence in a multitude of divergent and conflicting texts, a condition which threatens any monological literalist reading of the New Testament. Reading Revelation, so pivotal to the fundamentalist credo, provides an egregious instance of how "Jesus" is destabilized by intertextual dynamics. The text speaks of "the wrath of the Lamb" (6:16), of enemies who "shall be tormented with fire and brimstone...in the presence of the Lamb" (14:10), of "the Lamb [who] will conquer [his enemies], for he is Lord of lords and King of kings" (17:14). And an elder tells the narrator not to weep, for Jesus is the fighting "Lion of the tribe of Judah" (5:5).

Thus, the lamb metaphor persists in Revelation but in the paradoxical form of a lamb with lion-like qualities. Yet, how are we to read this image of Jesus as a wrathful and conquering lamb, and even a warrior lion, in the light of the more familiar image of the gentle, sacrificial lamb described in John: "Behold the Lamb of God, who takes away the sin of the world!" (1:29)? (Cf. Hebrews 10:12).[6] Moreover, the interplay of texts does not stop with the books of the Bible. Surely no reader of Revelation can forget the contradictory images of Jesus supplied by generations of bible-story illustrations, paintings, and Hollywood biopics, with their stress on lamb-like gentleness and virtuous suffering, to say nothing of the West's most familiar icon, which depicts a near-naked man nailed to a cross with bowed head and bleeding wounds. LaHaye and his cohort may insist that liberals have "twisted" the image of Jesus into a meek, submissive being, but their fundamentalist reading can do its ideological work only by repressing the ongoing dialogical tension *within* Revelation's image of Jesus (the paradox of the leonine lamb) and *between* that and the counter-image projected by the Gospels and a multitude of other *pre-*liberal texts. Only the most elaborate exegesis which, by definition, would violate the practice of literalism, could begin to address the aporia of a "Jesus" that signifies both warrior lion and sacrificial lamb.[7]

Self-Reflexiveness Erodes Textual Authority

The fundamentalist paradigm of knowledge is premised on the pre-Enlightenment beliefs that: (1) Truth is divinely revealed; (2) the Bible is the primary medium for the delivery of that Truth; (3) Truth in the Bible can be immediately apprehended through a literal (pre-interpretative) reading. In short, the assumed authority of the Bible forms the foundation of this paradigm. And if we are to invoke a counter-paradigm, one whose critical resources are especially suited for contesting the former, it must surely be postmodernism, whose principal deployment, not to say *raison d'etre*, is, precisely, the delegitimation of textual authority. Of course, the practice of challenging the authority of texts is as old as philosophy itself. However, postmodernism has developed new critical tools specifically for this purpose, notably, deconstruction, the genealogical mode of historical philosophizing, more extensive forms of ideology critique, and the strategic use of particularizing (anti-totalizing) concepts (e.g. perspectivism, ethnicity, locality). Indeed, postmodernism promotes reading practices that work to dismantle rather than ratify meaning; practices that expose the contingency, uncontrollability and rhetoricity of meaning. What makes postmodernism look so subversive from a fundamentalist standpoint is the prospect, inherent in its very mode of critique, of delegitimation without end.

By "textual authority" I mean the authoritative status assigned to a text by a culture, whereby the text is frequently and ritually cited for the first principles or moral truths it is said to embody. In this way, some texts – be they sacred, legal, or literary – are institutionally empowered to interpret reality, to authorize the terms in which history is understood. (See also Giroux, "Reading" 67.) And the fundamentalist paradigm, insofar as it is built on faith in the unassailable authority of its paramount text, the Bible, throws into sharp relief the counter-tendency of postmodernism, summarized here as the delegitimation of textual authority.

To talk about how a fundamentalist text is vulnerable to delegitimation by means of a formal deconstruction would be to take this argument in a predictable direction. Besides, there are strands of postmodern theology which have already addressed the confrontation between deconstruction and Christian faith. Suffice it here to note the work of Thomas Altizer, which deconstructs theology as textual production and, proceeding from Nietzsche's death-of-God thesis, reconstructs theology as the study of non-existing entities.[8] I shall focus, instead, on the role of postmodern fiction in cultivating the delegitimating mindset. Indeed, the point at which postmodern critique, with its deconstructive tools, and postmodern fiction, with its eminently self-reflexive techniques, most clearly converge is precisely this goal of delegitimation. Both pursue strategies that undermine the authority assigned to a text whose claim to truth is believed to rest on its assumed mimetic or metalinguistic powers, on its assumed naturalness or purity or authenticity.

By means of its programmatic use of self-reflexive writing techniques, postmodern fiction supplies a user-friendly version of many elements of postmodern critique. My premise is that postmodern fiction induces postmodern readings of other texts. In particular, its ostentatious use of self-reflexive devices has helped to forge an interpretive community, which is suspicious and sceptical of any claim to textual authority. And the size of this community must be quite substantial given the roll-call of conspicuously self-reflexive postmodern writers who have achieved best-seller status and/or canonization: Kurt Vonnegut, Thomas Pynchon, John Barth, Joyce Carol Oates, William Burroughs, Kathy Acker, Vladimir Nabokov, Tim O'Brien, Carol Shields, Paul Auster, Ishmael Reed, Mark Leyner, and E.L. Doctorow among others.

Self-reflexive writing techniques are, of course, not exclusive to postmodern fiction but they are far more common and obtrusive among postmodern writers than among their predecessors. These techniques draw attention to writing as a set of conventions and, hence, serve to critique textual claims to naturalness or mimesis or truth. Among the techniques used to this end are: (1) a foregrounding of the practices of plotting, troping, and naming so as to expose their arbitrary nature and highlight the artificial processes of a text's construction; (2) a conspicuous and often parodic use of the narrative structures and stereotypes of mass-market genres, myths, and folk tales in order to show how the literary text is intelligible only in relation to other texts (intertexts), not in relation to reality; (3) casting a writer or an artist-surrogate as protagonist so as to heighten our awareness of how the truth of writing is delimited by the writer's geo-historical situation, institutional function, cultural status, and pressure to meet readers' expectations; (4) the deployment of metatextual devices, such as authorial intervention or typographic experiments, which work to "break the frame" and thus shatter the illusion of the text as a self-sufficient voice; (5) hybridizing strategies, such as genre-splicing or mixing heterogeneous styles, which prompt the reader to question the assumption that the formal purity of a literary text is a criterion of its validity or truth; and (6) pointing up the indeterminacy or fragility of meaning by impeding narrative closure, confusing ontological levels, or using floating signifiers.

It seems reasonable to propose that nearly fifty years of postmodern self-reflexive fiction have created a savvy readership with a raised awareness of how the laws that govern the narratives of texts are different from the laws that govern reality; of how the generic formulas, rhetorical devices, and mythologizing tendencies of narratives produce truth-effects rather than Truth; of the historicity of the standpoint from which a book is written; of the institutional controls that constrain the way we interpret a text; of the unstable and contaminated nature of the signs on which we depend for meaning. The payoff for recognizing these limits and distortions as they inhere in narrative, language, and the reading process is a salutary demystification of textual power and an enhanced sense of the contingency of textual authority. And this demystifying focus can be trained on fundamentalist beliefs in the purity, intrinsic sanctity, and closure of hallowed texts and the totalizing knowledge claimed in their name. In short, the self-reflexiveness of postmodern fiction may be valued as a resource that facilitates or promotes a critical attitude towards *any* text-based truth-claims and, in particular, towards the overbearing textual authority of fundamentalism.

To further our understanding of self-reflexiveness as a form of critique, we need to situate it within the larger context of that broad tendency, which emerged in the 1960s and which continues to this day in an intensified form, namely, a radical questioning of the quotidian and dominant frames of intelligibility. This is the moment of a host of counter-institutional inquiries into the ideologies of consumption (Marcuse, Lefebvre), schooling (Illich, Freire), patriarchy (Millett, Friedan, Ellmann), racism (Fanon, Malcolm X), psychiatry (Goffman, Szasz, Foucault), mass culture (Frankfurt School, Situationists). It is the moment of what has been called the "adversary culture" (Daniel Bell) or the "Counter Culture" (Theodore Roszak), of which the anti-Vietnam war movement and the campus insurgencies were only the most visible expressions. And the marked shift to self-reflexive fiction in the Sixties may be seen as part and parcel of this pervasive spirit of critique. Only, here, the target institutions are, on one level, literature – most often, realism's pretensions to objectivity and truth – and, on another level, language itself, in particular, the forms in which public communication is contaminated and degraded by ideology and popular myths, and the consequences of being trapped in the official narratives of, among others, nationalism, government, history, and science.

Thus, perhaps the chief cultural legacy of the Sixties is the delegitimation of authority in almost any form it takes - the unleashing of an interminable process of critique. In particular, self-reflexiveness, understood as a mode of critique, is an attitude that is now so deeply embedded in the everyday life of postmodern culture that the authority of any text is permanently under erasure.

Much of today's popular culture is manifestly self-reflexive. One thinks of the endless stream of movies conceived as parodies of genre films: the blockbuster *Austin Powers* and the *Scary Movie* series; the popularity of mockumentaries and playful retro-movies. We are accustomed to self-parodying TV commercials (recent examples include advertisements for Old Navy, Shout, and Mountain Dew) and music videos, such as those of Spike Jonze and Chris Cunningham. We see television-show hosts (Jay Leno, David Letterman) whose wisecracks and mimicry ironically target the boundaries and conventions of the role they are hired to play (e.g. "This is the point in the show where I have to get excited"). Think also of the frequency with which news magazine programs include segments that review media reports, especially stories of corruption and scandal in political office - that is to say, media coverage of media coverage. All these tendencies may be read as symptoms of a hyperconsciousness about how we communicate today; about our sense of entrapment in a media culture saturated with catchphrases, platitudes, factoids, and PR hype. There's a heightened suspicion that we can no longer speak authentically or innocently. Recall the note on "the postmodern attitude" in the "Postscript to *The Name of the Rose,*" where Eco observes that a man can no longer say to a woman, "I love you madly;" rather, he feels compelled to speak from an ironic distance so as to avoid a cliche: "As Barbara Cartland would put it, I love you madly" (530-31). If I may borrow Biyi Bandele's comment on postmodern culture, "things are becoming meta and meta."

This self-reflexive disposition to refuse any text an inviolable and sacrosanct authority has become an integral part of postmodern popular consciousness. And this delegitimation need not depend on familiarity with theories of textuality which, in general, have not extended far beyond academia. Instead, we may think of self-reflexiveness as a practical version of postmodern critique, which has been widely diffused through the mass media and the arts (especially Conceptual Art). The point is that we should value this popular delegitimating attitude as a powerful bulwark that ensures a limit to the spread of fundamentalist thinking. To reframe the issue slightly, it seems inevitable that once our focus shifts from the text-as-product to the *process* of its production, the text will be stripped of its mystique, its aura and its power.

Fundamentalist History, Postmodern Contingency

According to Charles Caldwell Ryrie, the pre-eminent theologian at the Dallas Theological Seminary, "Dispensationalism reveals the outworking of God's plan in the historical process in a progressive revelation of His glory" (37). This fundamentalist doctrine projects a model of history which depends on an abstruse numerology derived from archangel Gabriel's prophecy in Daniel (9:24-27). In what, from the start, has been received as a highly contentious interpretation that builds on the significance of the number 7, "seventy weeks of years" was elaborated into a system of history, whose time-frame extends all the way forward to the Christian millennium (see Marsden, *Fundamentalism* 52-54). The doctrine divides history into seven divinely administered epochs or "dispensations". We are currently living under the Sixth Dispensation, that of Grace, which followed that of the Mosaic Law, and which will end at the second coming of Christ, giving way to the dispensation of the Millennium

As I suggested above, this conception of history is entirely based on faith in, and a literal reading of, biblical prophecy.[9] "'Bible prophecy is history written in advance,'" says a pastor in *Left Behind* (214). Indeed, all the novels in LaHaye and Jenkins' cycle include lengthy quotations from, and commentaries on, prophecies recorded in selected biblical texts, notably Revelation, Daniel and Ezekiel. (LaHaye, according to the covers of his books, is a "renowned prophecy scholar".) In an interview on CBS's *60 Minutes* in 2002, Ed MacAteer, co-founder of the fundamentalist Moral Majority, said of the current conflicts in the Middle East: "I believe that we are seeing prophecy unfold so rapidly and dramatically and wonderfully and, without exaggerating, [it] makes me breathless" (qtd. in Simon). For John Hagee, a fundamentalist pastor and Christian television host, the al-Qaida attack on the US is a preliminary step toward the End Times: "We are seeing in my judgment the birth pangs that will be called in the future the beginning of the end. I believe in my mind the Third World War has already begun. I believe it began on 9/11" (qtd. in Rossing, *Rapture* 71). The invasion of Iraq is also welcomed as a step toward World War III (i.e. Armageddon), as more evidence that history is unfolding according to the dispensationalist schedule. Apparently, Revelation explicitly prophesied the invasion: "I heard a voice...saying to the sixth angel...'Release the four angels who are bound at the great river Euphrates.' So the four angels were released, who had been ready for the hour...to kill a third of mankind" (9:13-16).

Biblical prophecy implies belief in history as the outworking of God's plan which, here, means events occurring in accordance with the timetable of the dispensations. In this divinely ordered world, there is no place for accident, for chance occurrences that may initiate chains of events with unpredictable consequences which diverge from God's purpose. (Human agency cannot forestall the apocalyptic sequence of events; it can only prepare humans for it.) As Bush remarked in a speech on the first anniversary of the 9/11 attacks: "We do not claim to know all the ways of Providence. Yet we can trust in them, placing our confidence in the loving God behind all of life, all of history" (qtd. in Cornell). In short, the dispensationalist history, as derived from a literal reading of the prophecies recorded in (chiefly) Revelation, is a one-way, God-centred process, in which all decisive events are governed and connected by a single, purposive *telos*. Yet, such a model of history could not be more dramatically at variance with the postmodern model of an incoherent multiplicity of random micro-events. Here, for instance, is Foucault's account of the latter model: "The forces operating in history are not controlled by destiny or regulative mechanisms, but respond to haphazard conflicts. They do not manifest the successive forms of a primordial intention and their attraction is not that of a conclusion, for they always appear through the singular randomness of events" (*Language* 154-55). And, for good measure, here's Joseph Heller's postmodern cynic, Bruce Gold, for whom "History was a trash bag of random coincidences torn open in a wind" (78).

Thus, where a fundamentalist history is inclined to seek a necessary link between 9/11 and the war in Iraq – a view that conforms to the dispensationalist model of a uniform and predetermined chronology – a postmodern history, premised on the contingency of events and rejecting any singular plot-line, desists from a search for links and, instead, thinks in terms of a coincidence of microhistories. For example, Bush told Palestinian president Mahmoud Abbas that "God told me to strike al-Qaida and I struck them, and *then* he instructed me to strike at Saddam, which I did" (qtd. in Zunes). I emphasize "then," the use of which implies a divinely ordered *sequence* of events. (And, as we have seen, Ed MacAteer and

John Hagee, among other fundamentalists, have endorsed this view of God working his purpose out in the Middle East.) Yet, as has been widely noted, "regime change" in Iraq had been planned long before 9/11. In the classified but leaked "Defense Policy Guidance" draft of 1992, Paul Wolfowitz, then-Under Secretary of Defense For Policy, outlined plans for US intervention in Iraq to assure, among other things, "access to vital raw material, primarily Persian Gulf oil" (qtd. in Kirk). A PNAC document of September 2000 discussed a plan to take military control of the Gulf region as part of its "blueprint for maintaining global US pre-eminence" (Mackay). And, though, months earlier, advised by the CIA that "there was no evidence that Saddam Hussein was connected to the September 11 attacks" (Weinberger 9), Bush announced the end of major combat in Iraq saying, "The battle in Iraq is one victory in a war on terror that began on September 11th, 2001" (qtd. in Milbank A18). In fact, the only link between the 9/11 attack and the invasion of Iraq was that the former was exploited by neo-conservative hawks as a pretext for the latter (see Kirk). Otherwise, the two events may be understood as a convergence of unrelated plots: one by Islamic fundamentalists seeking revenge on the US for its support of the corrupt and repressive House of Saud, and one to remove a non-compliant dictator as part of a long-term strategy for regional dominance. Moreover, in conformity with the postmodern paradigm, the consequences of this conjuncture of events have proved truly haphazard: an exacerbation of Jihadist activity, as the illegitimate war mobilizes pan-Islamic radicals; the emergence of Iran as a regional hegemon facilitated by a US recoiling from the strategic catastrophe of its occupation of Iraq; social breakdown in Iraq as the state fragments into zones controlled by warring sectarian, ethnic, tribal, and criminal groups. Here history looks far more like a chaotic entanglement of contingent forces with unpredictable outcomes than a dispensationalist plan unfolding in an inevitable line of development.

The postmodern perception of truth as relativized and delimited by geo-historical contingencies prompts inquiry into the time and place at which dispensationalism emerged as a discourse. If the doctrine could, as it adherents claim, be traced back to the apostles (van Deventer), it might seem inevitable and natural to Christianity, ratified by two millennia of continuity. However, dispensationalism is a relatively recent and localized phenomenon, which arrived and flourished under historically specific and fortuitous conditions. In fact, the doctrine is barely 170 years old: its origin pinpointed to the 1830s. It had no place in the creed before then. Its progenitor, John Nelson Darby (1800-1882), was an Irish-born lawyer living in England, who later became a leader of the Plymouth Brethren. Darby saw the Established Church as corrupted by Erastianism and clericalism. He charged it with abandoning the teachings of the apostles in favour of "man-made doctrines." He railed against the increasing latitude by which the Church allowed freer (i.e. non-literal) interpretation of the Bible. (The Higher Criticism of the Tubingen School applied Hegelian historicism to the study of Christianity. In investigating the sources of biblical texts to determine dates, place of composition, and authorship, it undermined traditional claims to a unified Scripture of divine revelation.) Hence, in an endeavour to reaffirm the authority of the Bible's account of Christian history and combat the secularizing effects of liberal thinking, Darby called for a return to a fundamentalist respect for biblical literalism. Dispensationalism was the theory he developed for the purpose of this counter-attack.

Proceeding from a "literal" interpretation of Scripture, Darby proposed that Jesus would return without warning to rapture the church of "true believers" *before* the seven-year Great Tribulation, and that he would return a second time, *after* the Tribulation, to defeat Satan's forces at Armageddon and, only then, establish his millennial kingdom. While not quite a wooden literalism altogether insensitive to figures of speech, Darbyite dispensationalism elides the generic distinctions between gospels, prophecy, epistles, and parables, thereby losing sight of the specific cultural and historical contexts in which they were formulated. For example, Barbara Rossing of the Lutheran School of Theology in Chicago, in an historicist vein, has shown how dipsensationalist theology is derived from a misconstrual of "prophecy" in its biblical usage. "Prophecy" does not signify prediction but God's word of "timely warning" of the dire consequences of worldly power (*Rapture* 88). She explains that Revelation was written in the context of the rival forces of militaristic empire and "Lamb power": "Revelation aims to convince us that Jesus' model of Lamb power is a model of victory more powerful than Rome's model of *nike* as military conquering" (120). Rossing reminds us that the meaning of "apocalyptic" is "unveiling," rather than a prophetic disclosure of God's plans for the future (81). The purpose of

Revelation was to "unveil" the vision of an alternative, Godly life for the churches oppressed by the Roman Empire: "Revelation's proclamation of an impending 'end' referred not to the end of the world but to the end of Roman rule" (87). Revelation sought to bring a message of hope to Christians in an age of imperial violence. Prophecy necessarily relates to the time in which it was written.

Insofar as Darby's tours of North America coincided with the Civil War and its aftermath, his theology - with its focus on the cataclysmic events prophesied in Revelation and the imminent return of Christ - must have resonated with communities devastated by what was "widely interpreted as 'a true Apocalyptic contest'" (Marsden, *Fundamentalism* 11). (The conflict claimed 650,000 lives in a population estimated, in 1870, at under 40 million.) Ernest Sandeen has argued that it was the "millenarianism" of the last half of the nineteenth century which "gave life and shape to the Fundamentalist movement" in the US (xv), while "World War I greatly stimulated interest in the second advent of Christ and the interpretation of prophecy" (233; see also Marsden 145-46).

Darby's American followers were also alarmed by the rapid advances of liberal theology in the US from the 1870s onward. However, conservative Christians were no longer contending only with historicist and rationalist criticism; evolutionary naturalism and a growing interest in fossil records also posed a serious challenge to Scriptural authority. Postbellum American protestantism was polarized between conservatives striving to defend "the fundamentals" of the faith and modernizing liberals. Thus, dispensationalism was adopted as a militant reaction to the incursions of liberal theology and naturalism; it was the product of an historically conditioned struggle of ideas, rather than, as Darby claimed, "a rediscovered truth."

The popularity of the Scofield Reference Bible, published in 1909, proved to be the critical factor in the spread of dispensationalism among American Protestants. This version of the King James Bible, which has sold over 12 million copies (Couch), printed commentary directly inspired by Darby's theology beneath the Scriptural text. As Rossing has observed, these annotations acquired authority simply by virtue of appearing in a Bible when, in fact, it is just Cyrus Scofield speaking, not the Bible ("God so Loved"). Later in the century, dispensationalist doctrine would be promulgated not only by pastors preaching from the pulpit and by its vocal proponents at the

Dallas Theological Seminary but also by radio programs (many sponsored by the Moody Bible Institute of Chicago); by Christian television such as the Trinity Broadcasting Network and the Christian Broadcasting Network; by the phenomenal output of the doomsday publishing industry, notably Hal Lindsey's *The Late Great Planet Earth* and *There's a New World Coming*, with combined sales exceeding 20 million copies and, currently, the *Left Behind* books, described by Jack Van Deventer as "recycled Darbyism." *The Chronicle of Higher Education* refers to recent polls in which "upwards of 40 percent" of Americans "believe that Bible prophecies detail a specific sequence of end-times events" (Boyer B10).

The attraction of dispensationalism, in recent decades, derives from the revulsion felt for what fundamentalists see as the profanations of postmodernism, especially its "debased" media culture, from the disruptive effects of an ever-modernizing capitalism, and from the continuing appeal to an apocalyptic/millenarian mindset of Darby's core concept of the pre-Tribulation Rapture, which could occur at any moment given, as Darby argued, that Christ's return is imminent.

We can see, then, how dispensationalism emerged and flourished in a web of historically and culturally specific contingencies: a punctual reaction to the first wave of 19th-century liberal theology; a misreading of "prophecy" in its Scriptural context; dissemination thanks largely to a run of books with sales almost unrivalled in publishing history; the receptivity of a culture given to periodic bouts of millenarianism. In spite of its universalizing pretensions and claims of apostolic pedigree, dispensationalist doctrine has distinct local and historical limits.

Election Versus Radical Democracy

Perhaps the most effective political challenge to fundamentalism will come from moderate Republicans, who feel that the hijacking of party policy by the Christian Right will, eventually, prove an electoral liability. John Danforth, a former Senator for Missouri, has spoken in the *New York Times* of his party as "transformed...into the political arm of conservative Christians". Chris Shays, Republican Representative for Connecticut, has conceded that "This Republican Party of Lincoln has become a party of theocracy" (qtd. in Theocracy

Watch). Other sources of opposition include traditional Christian ministries, for whom fundamentalists have betrayed the Gospels' message of compassion and forgiveness, and the liberal press (see especially Schwartz), which alerts its readers to the dangerous politics of a movement that believes its agenda is divinely sanctioned. Postmodern critique can also play the part of a political adversary though, to be sure, it does not amount to a counterforce that can match the political clout of fundamentalism. As an enterprise, it rarely evokes the passions generated by religious belief; it cannot mobilize the kind of fighting response which, in 2004, brought millions of evangelicals to the polls and enabled their political gains. Nevertheless, postmodernism's commitment to radical democracy serves as an ideal by which to critique the undemocratic tendencies inherent in fundamentalism.

First, we should note that postmodernism's adherence to radical democracy logically follows from its pluralist epistemology. In his 1962 monograph, *Nietzsche and Philosophy*, Gilles Deleuze promoted Nietzsche as the philosopher of pluralism, for whom there is "nothing beyond multiplicity" (23). Recall Nietzsche's assault on systems of thought founded on an all-unifying, final totality and his substitution of "a necessary perspectivism by virtue of which every force center – and not only man – construes the whole rest of the world *from its own point of view....*" (qtd. in Kaufmann 264). Here we have a readiness to theorize difference on its own terms, without recourse to a grand synthesizing scheme; a proto-postmodern logic of non-totalizable multiplicities. Matei Calinescu chiefly defines postmodernism as a "pluralist renaissance," wherein "our consciousness exists in a multiplicity of (actual and possible) worlds in perpetual 'chronotopical' change" (284). And, finally, Lyotard has argued that the discontinuities between ever-increasing "*petits recits*" (little narratives) – each like an autonomous language game that plays by its own rules – can no longer be resolved by appeal to the consensus and closure of an overarching metanarrative; hence, "Postmodern knowledge... refines our sensitivity to differences" (xxv).

The collapse of the metanarratives of modernity facilitates the development of a micropolitics of identities, minority rights, and single-issue movements. Henry Giroux has developed a critical pedagogy grounded in this kind of pluralizing agenda. He embraces "the postmodern emphasis on the proliferation of local narratives, the opening up of the world to cultural and ethnic differences, and the positing of difference as a challenge to hegemonic power relations parading as universals" ("Modernism" 40). He believes in "the emancipatory promise of plurality and heterogeneity as the basis for new forms of conversation, solidarity, and public culture...." ("Postmodernism" 222). And Chantal Mouffe, speaking specifically of radical democracy and its recognition of the "irreducible plurality" of subject positions, "welcomes [postmodern philosophy] as an indispensable instrument in the accomplishment of its goals" (44).

Insofar as advocates of radical democracy recognize the plurality of political identities and respect the autonomy of their fights for civil rights, they tend to think and act strategically within the confines of local struggles and single issues; the talk is of piecemeal change rather than wholesale social transformation. Informed by postmodernism's heightened sense of the limits imposed by cultural differences, ethnicity, and locality, radical-democratic theory refuses macro-political or universal solutions. Then, in extreme contrast to this realistic appraisal of the limits that constrain programs for change, consider the fundamentalist paradigm's haughty and utopian disregard of *any* limits in its conception of an ameliorative history. Its End Times scenario, as exemplified in the books of LaHaye/Jenkins and Lindsey, implicates all humanity; its millennial vision is premised on faith in the Second Coming as a miracle of universal significance. Where postmodern politics thinks within the modest frame of conjunctural limits, fundamentalist politics is guided by belief in a dispensation unfolding on nothing less than a cosmic and eternal scale.

For Mouffe, the "task of radical democracy is indeed to deepen the democratic revolution and to link together diverse democratic struggles" (42); a "principle of democratic equivalence" must be established for the diverse struggles of workers, women, minorities and others (42). However, respect for diversity is fiercely rejected by fundamentalists as an essentially unchristian value. Thus, the following words are given to Nicolae Carpathia, the Antichrist of the *Left Behind* novels, who becomes the head of the world government:

> One of the hallmarks of my administration is tolerance. We can only truly be a global community by accepting diversity and making it the law of the

land....Religions that saw themselves as the only true way to spirituality now accept and tolerate other religions that see themselves the same way....Under the unity of the aptly named Enigma Babylon One World Faith, all the religions of the world have proved themselves able to live harmoniously. All, that is, save one....It is the sect [the fundamentalists] that claims roots in historic Christianity.... Indeed, they say, Jesus blew a trumpet and took all his favorite people to heaven, leaving the rest of us lost sinners to suffer here on earth. I do not believe that accurately reflects the truth of Christianity as it was taught for centuries. My exposure to that wonderful, peace-loving religion told of a God of love and of a man who was a teacher of morals. (*Apollyon* 104-105)

Evidently, for fundamentalists of the LaHaye/Jenkins stripe, a conventional Christianity that advocates tolerance of diversity and an administration that governs on behalf of all faiths and communities are simply agencies in the service of satanic power.

This antipathy to diversity and multiculturalism is not just an isolated quirk of fundamentalism; rather, it is best understood in the wider context of the resurgent nationalism so central to the neo-conservative ascendancy. Here, for example, Samuel Huntington writes as an advocate of "robust nationalism":

Non-conservatives [e.g. liberals] tend to degrade national identity either in favor of ethnic, racial, gender or other sub-national identities, or in favor of identity with supranational institutions and ideals....In the broadest sense, American national identity is under challenge from a multiculturalism that subverts it from below and a cosmopolitanism that erodes it from above. (3-4)

A "robust nationalism" also inspires the ethnocentric vision of an Americanized planet articulated as the Project for a New American Century. The neo-conservatives who, in 1997, formulated the PNAC manifesto and who advise Bush on "defense" policy, call for a return to Reaganite levels of military spending in the name of "a foreign policy that boldly and purposefully promotes American principles abroad" and in preparation for multiple theatres of war against "regimes hostile to our interests and values" ("Statement of Principles").

The belief, dear to US fundamentalists, that America is God's chosen nation induces the Christian Right to support the imperialist objectives of the current administration as divinely sanctioned. Moreover, the ultra-nationalist ethos of neo-conservatism infuses missionary activity with renewed confidence. In 2002 alone, more than 60,000 American evangelicals went abroad to "save" the souls of non-white infidels, a program which leads many to conclude that the Evangelical church is "the new face of western imperialism" (Sikand).

Where a postmodern politics seeks to enlarge democracy by extending it to subaltern and subnational groups, fundamentalism promotes the doctrines of a creed whose model of salvation is profoundly *un*democratic. In the final stage of their violent eschatology, as illustrated in the *Left Behind* novel cycle, only "true believers" will be elected to the millennial paradise; the rest of humanity will be left to suffer the horrendous tortures inflicted by a wrathful God. One paradigm is committed to the goal of broadening and deepening democracy as far as possible; the other is committed to policies that usher in the cataclysmic events of the End Times, after which, salvation will be the lot only of the faithful, tribulation the lot of infidels. One paradigm generously seeks to be inclusive by recognizing diversity; the other is relentlessly *ex*clusive, saying to Jews, Muslims, and others, "think like us or be damned." Suddenly, in the harsh light of the fundamentalist arena, postmodernism – so often dismissed as the socially irresponsible pastime of idle academics and self-indulgent artists – looks rather attractive.

However, we should not be too smug in assuming postmodernism's capacity to embrace diversity. Cornell West has identified the "narrowly Eurocentric" limits of postmodernism's "discourse of otherness" (391), given the dependence of its pioneering theorists on the European philosophical tradition of Nietzsche, Heidegger, and their successors. Similarly, Jane Flax, observing the lack of attention to feminist issues in the work of the same theorists, concludes that "postmodernists are unaware of the deeply gendered nature of their own recounting and interpretations of the Western story and the strategies they oppose to its master narratives" (423). And even though postmodern critique aligns itself with other progressive efforts to acknowledge the claims to respect and equality of communities marked as "Other" – e.g. a postmodern pedagogy that promotes "border crossing" (Giroux, "Postmodernism" 248); the heteroglot expressions of a postmodern art that promotes hybridized identities – fundamentalists remain obdurately "other" to the postmodern mind. This is not just a matter of the polarization between a militantly religious and an intransigently secular paradigm, which makes dialogue, less still transculturation, between the two impossible; postmodernists also recoil before the "otherness" of a community whose beliefs they find reactionary, offensive, weird, and grotesque. Yet, here is a truly popular, grassroots movement for change; a constituency, at least 50-million-strong, of working- and middle-class Americans with which postmodernism – aspiring to radical democracy – cannot in the least identify. Here is a type of diversity that postmodern pluralism cannot accommodate, a political agenda that has no place in the victory imagined for other communities in their struggles for recognition and rights. This unyielding alterity of Christian fundamentalism exposes an embarrassing limit to the postmodern dream of a non-exclusionary democracy.

Conclusion: Disenchantment without End

Fundamentalism developed out of a series of 12 pamphlets, *The Fundamentals* (1910-1915), whose essays sought to defend the 'fundamentals' of Christian faith (see above) against modernist culture and liberal theology. According to George Marsden, "...fundamentalism was originally a broad coalition of antimodernists. From the 1920s to the 1940s, to be a fundamentalist meant only to be theologically traditional, a believer in the fundamentals of evangelical Christianity, and willing to take a militant stand against modernism" (*Reforming* 10). And insofar as we understand pre-World War Two fundamentalism as, in large part, a strategic reaction to modernism, we may think of today's right-wing fundamentalism as an alarmed response, a dialectical counter-swing, provoked by the diffusion of postmodern secularism through the mass media, the arts, and academia. Postmodern attitudes of scepticism, cynicism, irreverence, and self-reflexiveness have virtually institutionalized an untiring practice of critique, in such forms as demystification, demythologization, desacralization, decentering, and delegitimation. Postmodernism has created a culture of disenchantment, to which today's extremist variant of fundamentalism has responded with a belligerent re-affirmation of belief in the transcendent, the sacred, and textual authority.

Many of us who respect the critical agenda of postmodernism will have been astonished by this dramatic resurgence of Christian fundamentalism. Any satisfaction we derived from that "post" prefix, insofar as it seemed to align us with avantgarde developments in thought, has been weakened by the striking political and cultural advances of, paradoxically, a *pre*modern current of thought. The latter appears to the postmodern mentality as regressive, alien, and just plain bonkers. Bluntly stated: how do we come to terms with the fact that, in the 21st Century, in the world's most scientifically advanced society, tens of millions fervently subscribe to belief in the Rapture, dispensationalism, and biblical prophecy? Here, I want to consider how a newly confident fundamentalism can disturb our complacency about the value of postmodernism. This problem is most visible vis-a-vis antithetical attitudes to transcendentalist thinking. Where fundamentalism crucially depends on belief in a transcendent authority, the central thrust of postmodernism lies in its critique of transcendentalist thought.

Postmodern critique is just the most recent successor to a long tradition of secularist assaults on ideas of the transcendent. Its most eminent predecessors include Darwinism, Dialectical Materialism, positivism, Freudianism, Behaviorism, and analytical philosophy. All have defined themselves by their anti-metaphysical credentials, by their determination to purge their discourse and methodology of transcendentalist assumptions. Postmodernism is as single-minded as its predecessors in the task of erasing all vestiges of transcendentalism, and the impact of this has been felt across the humanities and social sciences, across popular culture and the arts.

The proto-postmodern Nietzsche exhorted philosophers to root out residues of transcendentalism in post-Enlightenment thinking. Hence the project announced in *The Gay Science* whereby, after the death of God, "we still have to vanquish his shadow" (167). Richard Rorty seems to have had a similar project in mind when he called for a Wittgensteinian approach to language, whose effect would be to "de-divinize the world" (21). Foucault explained that his "essential task was to free the history of thought from its subjection to transcendence...to cleanse it of all transcendental narcissism." (*Archaeology* 203). In *Nietzsche and Philosophy*, Deleuze affirmed, "Philosophy is at its most positive as critique: an enterprise of demystification" (106). Finally, recall Derrida's programmatic assault on philosophy's ingrained transcendentalism; his critique of the role of self-certifying concepts ("transcendental signifieds" like God or

Telos) in arresting the disruptive "play" of those elusively present "traces" or counter-meanings that threaten the semantic integrity of any system of thought: "All dualisms, all theories of the immortality of the soul or of the spirit, as well as all monisms, spiritualist or materialist...are the unique theme of a metaphysics whose entire history was compelled to strive toward the reduction of the trace" (*Grammatology* 71).

In general, the postmodern insistence on the instability and contingency of language, whereby *any* text is necessarily denied a secure and final meaning, must be deeply offensive to Christian fundamentalism, given that it is founded on a discourse of Transcendent Authority. But this is not to say that postmodernism has had the last word in this clash of paradigms; indeed, critics who speak from a theological standpoint and who are conversant with postmodern theory have challenged the latter's secularist assumptions. Brian Ingraffia of Calvin College cogently argues that postmodern theorists can only deconstruct the God produced by *their own* accounts of Christianity, not the God of biblical revelation. Defining ontotheology as "theology based upon human imaginings about God," he concludes: "Ontotheology is the result of our attempt to formulate an understanding of god rather than the result of God's revelation toward us" (241). And the Islamist theorist, S. Parvez Manzoor, has proposed that we "desacralize secularism," arguing, in postmodern terms, that we deconstruct the factitious secular/sacred binary, invented by secularism itself; that we unmask the "secularist will-to-power"(545) behind secularism's claim to truth; that, above all, secularism has "turned itself into a faith: a faith in humanity and a faith in progress" (548).

Postmodern anti-transcendentalism finds expression in an unwavering scepticism and cynicism towards appeals to absolute criteria (God, the Good, Truth, History, etc.); from its enhanced sense of the cultural and historical particularism of meaning and value follow challenges to such appeals. (In Rorty's terms, postmodernism produces "ironists," people who acknowledge the contingency of their beliefs, in opposition to "metaphysicians," people who defend their beliefs as beyond time and change (xv).) This amounts to a radical and pervasive state of disenchantment. To be sure, disenchantment is desirable to the extent that, often, it is the sign of our liberation from belief in oppressive institutions which, typically, legitimized themselves in the name of some absolute or sacrosanct authority: Nation, Race, Empire, Reason, the Market, Heterosexualism, the Canon. Indeed, postmodernism has played a crucial (though by no means exclusive) role in divesting the "master narratives" of many of these institutions of their authority; in unmasking the operations of power and the rhetorical manoeuvres behind their discourses. In this respect, disenchantment is a welcome gain, the result of decades of critical activity. Yet, we must also reckon with something like a dialectic of disenchantment: for at the same time as the postmodern tendency to disenchant frees us from the myths and mystique of authority, it condemns us to a deep suspicion of authority in general, for which we pay a price. That price is an erratic and anomic kind of spirituality; often a "feel-good," self-focused experience without prayer, praise, or penitence. This is not to say that the postmodern subject is necessarily less spiritual than his/her fundamentalist counterpart; only that the spirituality of the former cannot be legitimized by appeal to any transcendent authority. Any sense of the sacred or supernal cannot be grounded in some universal or transhistorical criterion of truth or certainty.[10]10 In short, spiritual experience may be real enough for the postmodern individual but it cannot be integrated into any conception of the self beyond the here and now. Paul Auster, in a postmodern detective novella, sums up this conception of the self in manifestly non-transcendentalist terms: "In the end, each life is no more than the sum of contingent facts, a chronicle of chance intersections, of flukes, of random events, that divulge nothing but their own lack of purpose" (256). Fundamentalism enjoins its adherents to look for redemptive meaning beyond history, to engage continually in soul-building in preparation for The Second Coming. In stark contrast, the postmodern view of the subject as immersed in history, a history which, moreover, is conceived as purposeless and incoherent, disconnects us from myths of our place in some larger, salvational scheme. To cite Nietzsche again: "When the historical sense reigns *without constraint* and draws all its consequences...it uproots the future, because it destroys illusions...." (*Untimely* 95). But to be disabused of a transhistorical existence comes at a price: where the fundamentalist lives within view of eternity's values, the postmodern temporal self must live with the inconsolable prospect of its brute extinction.

High Modernism invoked art as a substitute for religion, an attitude dramatically evinced by the Rothko Temple. It believed in art as a redemptive force, extolled it for its visionary power, and *a la* Joyce, Yeats, Stevens, and others, exalted the artist as a God-like artificer. Then postmodernism rudely punctured this faith in a relentless process of demystification. In producing art which self-reflexively staged the processes of its own composition, postmodernism repackaged art as just a bag of tricks, not the inspiration of genius. It exposed the fictionalizing essence of all narrative forms (historical, scientific, philosophical), laying bare the fabricated nature of plotting, troping, and dependence on generic coding. It highlighted the derivation of art works from a matrix of past or contiguous discourses (rather than from the personal creativity or originality of the artist), thereby bringing into focus a patchwork of intertexts in place of a sense of the "purity" of artistic expression. In consequence, art in a postmodern culture can no longer serve as a vehicle for spiritual truth; in its post-auratic, decathected, depthless reincarnation, art is, perhaps, the most visible symptom of our postmodern disenchantment. (And it is this disenchantment with art which surely helps explain postmodernism's appreciation of kitsch and "trash aesthetics": the avant-pop writings of Mark Leyner and Mark Amerika; the self-celebrating schlock and banalities of Mike Kelley and Jeff Koons; the obsessive indulgence in B-movie conventions of Tarantino's *Kill Bill* movies or Burton's *Batman* movies.)

Disenchantment permeates not only the arts, mass media, and academia, but also political culture, given the postmodern impulse to delegitimize authority of any kind. Our ruling institutions – liberal-democratic government, legal systems, the Market – must constantly be defended vis-a-vis an increasingly disillusioned public. Indeed, Jurgen Habermas has identified a full-blown "legitimation crisis." Today, under "organized capitalism," when the state intervenes in the market to manage its dysfunctional side-effects, governments are continually under pressure to justify their policies. However, the contradictions of capitalist production coupled with rising expectations of welfare provision that cannot be met, creates an ever-increasing need for governments to secure mass loyalty. Hence, they employ "advertising techniques" to manipulate cultural beliefs and values and engineer public opinion. But, "There is no administrative production of meaning....The procurement of legitimation is self-defeating as soon as the mode of procurement is seen through" (Habermas 70). And while, for Habermas, this deficit in legitimation arises because of the unmanageable tasks the state must perform *qua* total capitalist, the diffusion of postmodern thinking across the public sphere – creating *inter alia* a media-savvy public, alert to the political exploitation of the news and the rhetoric of government PR hype – has greatly compounded the deficit, insofar as it enables many to "see through" the strategies of legitimation.

At the end of Don DeLillo's *Libra*, the mother of Lee Harvey Oswald, reflecting on her history, remarks, "I can't give facts point-blank. It takes stories to fill out a life" (453). The problem, today, is that many of those "stories," which give our lives meaning beyond the empirical data of our biological existence, have lost their credibility; postmodern critique has reduced them to myths or, in Lyotard's terms, has rendered us incredulous of the redemptive promise of modernity's grand narratives (xxiv). Perhaps many in postmodern society still cling to the pre-postmodern stories that "fill out a life," especially stories of transcendence through religious faith or artistic vision or utopian politics or belief in some preordained purpose to one's life. However, for over forty years now, these stories have been the fixed target of postmodern critique: deconstructed, decentred, delegitimized. While fundamentalist beliefs (creationism, dispensationalism, salvationism) can generate narratives that assign an elevated purpose and order to human life, the demythologizing impetus of postmodernism generates narratives that, *by comparison*, dramatically scale down the significance of human life; for in tandem with the emancipatory effects of critique comes a raised awareness of life as governed by chance and contingency (not to say defined by futility and waste). The problem is not just that disenchantment is not spiritually sustaining but that re-enchantment hardly seems like a viable option; either we have crossed the point of no return or it will surely take a good deal of theoretical labour to reinstate spiritual narratives of redemption in terms that are acceptable to the postmodern mind. Clearly, from a postmodern standpoint, the adherents to fundamentalist doctrines appear absurdly credulous. However, the striking fact of this kind of credulity could have the benefit of prompting us postmodernists to reflect on the consequences of our deep-seated incredulity.

Notes

[1]   To identify Christian fundamentalism as a pre-Enlightenment philosophy is not to overlook its rationalistic commitment to propositional truth. The credibility of fundamentalism depends on a clear and precise demonstration of the Bible as an "inerrant" text. (See Marsden *Fundamentalism* 56-57.)

[2]   John Sutherland, writing in *The Guardian*, refers to an "estimated 90 million evangelical Christians in the US." Larry Eskridge, of Wheaton College's Institute for the Study of American Evangelicals, concludes, after discussing the limitations of earlier surveys, that "a general estimate of the nation's population could safely be said to average somewhere around 35% of the population, or about 100 million Americans." Morley Safer works with the same figure in his CBS documentary on the *Left Behind* novels. Ron Suskind, writing in the *New York Times* (51) and Todd Johnson of the Gordon-Conwell Theological Seminary, both cite a 2003 Gallup Poll that gives the number of evangelicals as 42% of the US population (i.e. 126 million).

[3]   On January 5, 2006, Pat Robertson announced on his TV show, "The 700 Club," that the stroke which disabled Ariel Sharon was divine retribution for the leader's policy of withdrawing Israeli settlers from Gaza. Apparently, Sharon was guilty of "dividing God's land...." (CNN.Com).

[4]   George Monbiot invites us to click on www.raptureready.com and wryly observes that, "The infidels among us should take note that the Rapture Index currently [as of April 2004] stands at 144, just one point below the critical threshold, beyond which the sky will be filled with floating nudists."

[5]   This view overlooks the arbitrary role of clerical debate in deciding which texts would constitute the authorized version of the Bible and which would be excluded as apocryphal. The status of the Book of Revelation was, for centuries, the subject of a fierce polemic; the text almost failed the selection process.

[6]   I am indebted to Steve Moyise for his selection of New Testament passages in a discussion of intertextuality vis-a-vis Revelation.

[7]   The Rushdie Affair provides a notorious example of fundamentalist literalism in conflict with postmodern thought. Recall how, in 1989, the Ayatollah Khomeini issued a *fatwa* against Salman Rushdie, whose postmodern political novel, *The Satanic Verses*, became the target of Islamic fundamentalists. The latter, unfamiliar with postmodern games with fictionality, read the book too literally and concluded it was blasphemous.

[8]   Another strand of postmodern theology seeks to reconcile Christian doctrine and postmodern critique, insofar as the former, as Merold Westphal argues, can learn from the latter, in order to pursue the goal, common to both, of overcoming the God of onto-theology.

[9]   For example, a passage from 1 Thessalonians is read quite literally as predicting the Rapture: "And the dead in Christ will rise first; then we who are alive, who are left, shall be caught up together with them in the clouds to meet the Lord in the air...." (4:16-17). Barbara Rossing, a biblical scholar, has challenged this literal reading arguing that "the Apostle Paul is writing about resurrection" ("God so Loved").

[10] Elsewhere, I have contested the alleged "postmodern" character of the ecospiritual perception of "universal interconnectedness." See Maltby *Visionary.*

Works Cited

Altizer, Thomas J.J. et al. *Deconstruction and Theology*. New York: Crossroad, 1982.

Auster, Paul. *The Locked Room*. 1986. In *The New York Trilogy*. Harmondsworth: Penguin, 1990.

"Book Review: The *Left Behind* Series." Biblical Discernment Ministries. Jan. 2005. Accessed 12 July 2005. <http://www.rapidnet.com/~jbeard/bdm/Book Reviews/left.htm>.

Boyer, Paul. "John Darby Meets Saddam Hussein: Foreign Policy and Bible Prophecy." *Chronicle of Higher Education*, supplement, 14 Feb. 2003: B10-11.

Callinescu, Matei. "From the One to the Many: Pluralism in Today's Thought." In *Innovation/Renovation: New Perspectives on the Humanities*. Eds. Ihab Hassan and Sally Hassan. Madison: U Wisconsin P, 1983, 263-88.

CNN.Com. "Robertson suggests God smote Sharon." 6 Jan 2006. Accessed 1 Feb 2006. <http://www.cnn.com/2006/us/01/05/robertson.sharon/index.html>.

Couch, Mal. "History of the War Over Dispensationalism: Where We Stand Today, Part I." 17 June 2002. Accessed 1 Feb 2006. <http://www.conservative online.org/journals/06_17_journal/2002v6n17_id05.htm>

Cornwell, Rupert. "In God he trusts: how Bush infused the White House with a religious spirit." *Independent* 21 Feb. 2003.

Danforth, John. "In the Name of Politics." *New York Times* 30 Mar. 2005.

Deleuze, Gilles. *Nietzsche and Philosophy*. 1962. Trans. Hugh Tomlinson. New York: Columbia UP, 1983.

DeLillo, Don. *Libra*. 1988. Harmondsworth: Penguin, 1989.

Derrida, Jacques. *Of Grammatology*. 1967. Trans. Gayatri Chakravorty Spivak. Baltimore: Johns Hopkins UP, 1976.

Eco, Umberto. *The Name of the Rose*. 1980. San Diego: Harvest, 1984.

Engel, Matthew. "Meet the New Zionists." *Guardian* 28 Oct. 2002. <http://www. guardian.co.uk/israel/Story/0,2763,820528,00.html>.

Eskridge, Larry. "Defining Evangelicalism." April 2005. Institute for the Study of American Evangelicals. Accessed 18 June 2005. <http://www.wheaton.edu/ isae/defining__evangelicalism.html>.

Falwell, Jerry. *Nuclear War and the Second Coming of Jesus Christ*. 1983.

Flax, Jane. "Excerpts from *Thinking Fragments*." *A Postmodern Reader*. Eds. Joseph Natoli and Linda Hutcheon. Albany: State U of New York P, 1993. 419-25.

Foucault, Michel. *The Archaeology of Knowledge*. 1969. Trans. A. M. Sheridan Smith. New York: Pantheon, 1972.

—. *Language, Counter-Memory, Practice*. Ed. Donald F. Bouchard. Cornell UP, 1977.

Freedland, Jonathan. "Democrats Need Rebirth." *Guardian Weekly* 12-18 Nov. 2005: 5.

Giroux, Henry. "Modernism, Postmodernism, and Feminism: Rethinking the Boundaries of Educational Discourse." *Postmodernism, Feminism, and Cultural Politics*. Ed. Henry Giroux. Albany: State U of New York P, 1991. 1-59.

—. "Postmodernism as Border Pedagogy: Redefining the Boundaries of Race and Ethnicity." *Postmodernism, Feminism, and Cultural Politics*. Ed. Henry Giroux. Albany: State U of New York P, 1991. 217-256.

—. "Reading Texts, Literacy, and Textual Authority." *Falling into Theory*. Ed. David H. Richter. Boston: Bedford Books, 1994. 63-74.

Grace, Pamela. *Blockbuster Jesus: The Hagiopic, Fundamentalism, and Religious Violence*. Diss. New York U, 2004.

Habermas, Jurgen. *Legitimation Crisis*. (1973). Trans. Thomas McCarthy. Boston: Beacon Press, 1975.

Halsell, Grace. *Prophecy and Politics*. Lawrence Hill Books, 1986.

Heller, Joseph. *Good as Gold*. 1979. London: Corgi, 1981.

Huntington, Samuel P. "Robust Nationalism." *The National Interest* Winter 1999. Accessed 1 Feb 2006. <http://www.findarticles.com/p/articles/mi_m2751/is_1999_Winter/ai_58381619>.

Ingraffia, Brian D. *Postmodern Theory and Biblical Theology*. Cambridge UP, 1995.

Johnson, Todd. "USA Evangelicals/Evangelicals in a Global Context." Jan. 2006. Lausanne World Pulse. Accessed 31 Jan. 2006. <http://www.lausanneworldpulse.com/trendsandstatistics>.

Kaplan, Esther. *With God on Their Side*. New York: The New Press, 2004.

Kaufmann, Walter. *Nietzsche: Philosopher, Psychologist, Antichrist*. Fourth Edition. Princeton UP, 1974.

Kidd, Colin. "My God was bigger than his." *London Review of Books* 26.21 (2004): 15-18.

Kirk, Michael. "The War Behind Closed Doors." Frontline PBS. February 20, 2003. <http://www.pbs.org/wgbh/pages/frontline/shows/Iraq/etc/wolf.html>.

Kirkpatrick, David D. "Wrath and mercy: The return of the warrior Jesus." *New York Times*. Week in Review. Section 4. 4 Apr. 2004: pp.1, 6.

Krugman, Paul. "An Academic Question." *New York Times*. 5 April 2005: A23.

LaHaye, Tim & Jerry B. Jenkins. *Apollyon*. Wheaton, Illinois: Tyndale House Publishers, Inc., 1999.

—. *Glorious Appearing*. Wheaton, Illinois: Tyndale House Publishers, Inc., 2004.

—. *Left Behind*. Wheaton, Illinois: Tyndale House Publishers, Inc., 1995.

—. *Tribulation Force*. Wheaton, Illinois: Tyndale House Publishers, Inc., 1996.

Lampman, Jane. "Mixing prophecy and politics." *Christian Science Monitor* 7 July 2004: 15.

Lieven, Anatol. "Taking Back America." *London Review of Books* 26.23 (2004): 7-9.

Lieven, Hal and Carole C. Carlson. *The Late Great Planet Earth*. Zondervan Publishing House, 1970.

—. *There's A New World Coming*. Bantam Books, 1980.

Lyotard, Jean-François. *The Postmodern Condition: A Report on Knowledge*. 1979. Trans. Geoff Bennington and Brian Massumi. Manchester UP, 1984.

Mackay, Neil. "Bush planned Iraq 'regime change' before becoming President." *Sunday Herald* 15 Sept. 2002.

Maltby, Paul. *The Visionary Moment: A Postmodern Critique*. Albany: State U of New York P, 2002.

Manzoor, S. Parvez. "Desacralizing Secularism." *The American Journal of Islamic Social Sciences* 12.4 (Winter 1995): 545-59.

Marsden, George M. *Fundamentalism and American Culture: The Shaping of Twentieth-Century Evangelicalism 1870-1925.* New York: Oxford UP, 1980.

—. *Reforming Fundamentalism.* Grand Rapids: W.B. Eerdmans Publishing Company, 1987.

—. *Understanding Fundamentalism and Evangelicalism.* Grand Rapids: W.B. Eerdman's Publishing Company, 1991.

Milbank, Dana. "Bush Disavows Hussein-Sept. 11 Link." *Washington Post* 18 Sept. 2003. A18.

Monbiot, George. "Their beliefs are bonkers, but they are at the heart of power." *Guardian* 20 Apr. 2004. Accessed 6 May 2004. <http://www.guardian.co.uk/Columnists/Column/0,5673,1195727,00.html>.

Mouffe, Chantal. "Radical Democracy: Modern or Postmodern?" *Universal Abandon? ThePolitics of Postmodernism.* Ed. Andrew Ross. Minneapolis: U of Minnesota P, 1988. 31-45.

Moyise, Steve. "Intertextuality and the Use of Scripture in the Book of Revelation." *Scriptura* 84 (2003): 391-401.

Nietzsche, Friedrich. *The Gay Science.* 1882. Trans. Walter Kaufmann. New York: Vintage Books, 1974.

—. *Untimely Meditations.* 1873-76. Trans. R. J. Hollingdale. Cambridge UP, 1997. Perlstein, Rick. "The Jesus Landing Pad: Bush White House checked with rapture Christians before latest Israel move." *The Village Voice* 18 May 2004.

Project for a New American Century (PNAC). "Statement of Principles." <http//newamericancentury.org/statementofprinciples/htm>.

Rorty, Richard. *Contingency, Irony, and Solidarity.* Cambridge UP, 1989.

Rossing, Barbara. "God so Loved the World that He Gave Us World War III." Interview with John W. Whitehead. *Oldspeak* 1 July, 2004.

—. *The Rapture Exposed: The Message of Hope in the Book of Revelation.* Westview Press, 2004.

Rushdie, Salman. *The Satanic Verses.* Viking, 1989.

Ryrie, Charles C. *Dispensationalism.* 1966. Chicago: Moody Press, 1995.

Safer, Morley. "The Greatest Story Ever Sold." *60 Minutes.* CBS News. 13 Apr. 2004.

Sandeen, Ernest R. *The Roots of Fundamentalism: British and American Millenarianism 1800-1930.* U Chicago P, 1970.

Schama, Simon. "Onward Christian Soldiers." *Guardian Weekly* 12-18 Nov. 2004: 19-20.

Sikand, Yoginder. "The Evangelical Challenge: A New Face of Western Imperialism." Christian Aggression. 15 Mar. 2005. Accessed 18 Nov. 2005. <http://www.christianaggression.org>.

Simon, Bob. "Zion's Christian Soldiers." *60 Minutes.* CBS News. 6 Oct. 2002. <http://www.cbsnews.com/stories/2002/10/03/60minutes/main524268.shtml>.

Suskind, Ron. "Without a Doubt." *New York Times.* Magazine. Section 6. 17 Oct. 2004: 45-51, 64, 102, 106.

Schwartz, Walter. "The right of Holy Writ." *Guardian* 7 Apr. 1987.

—. "The stars of God's own soap opera." *Guardian* 6 Apr. 1987.

—. "With God on his side." *Guardian* 8 Apr. 1987.

Sutherland, John. "God Save America: the Race for the White House will be decided by Fundagelicals." *Guardian* 3 May 2004.

Theocracy Watch. "The Rise of the Religious Right in the Republican Party." 15 June 2005. Accessed 21 Apr. 2004. <http://www.theocracywatch.org>.

Van Deventer, Jack. "Darby's Dispensationalism." *Credenda* 13.5 (2001). <http://www.credenda.org/issues/13-5.php>.

Waldman, Peter. "Evangelical Christians coat US foreign policy with an activist tinge." *Wall Street Journal Europe* 26 May 2004: A5.

Weinberger, Eliot. "What I heard about Iraq in 2005." *London Review of Books* 28.1 (2006): 9.

West, Cornell. "Black Culture and Postmodernism." *A Postmodern Reader*. Eds. Joseph Natoli and Linda Hutcheon. Albany: State U of New York P, 1993. 390-97.

Westphal, Merold. *Overcoming Onto-Theology*. New York: Fordham UP, 2001.

Zunes, Stephen. "The influence of the Christian right on U.S. Middle East policy." *Foreign Policy in Focus* June 2004. Accessed 4 July 2004. <http://www.fpif.org/papers/0406christian.html>.

3

Postmodernism in the Age of Distracting Discourses

Robert McLaughlin

In May 2003, about the same time President Bush declared the war against Iraq a mission accomplished, Chris Hedges, a reporter for the *New York Times*, took the stage as guest speaker at the commencement ceremony at Rockford College in Illinois. His remarks, arguing against the war and against the efficacy of war in general, were greeted by the crowd of graduating seniors and their friends and families with boos, catcalls, and threats. Rockford College's website boasts that the institution is Jane Addams's alma mater and says, "We seek to create a world that is more just, more humane, and more democratic. Students at Rockford College today, like Jane Addams before them, think critically, act compassionately, and embrace the ideals of citizenship" ("Rockford College"). Hmmmm. In the aftermath of the commencement fiasco Rockford's president apologized – not to Hedges, but to the students for having invited him – and the *Times* reprimanded Hedges for letting the world know he has opinions.[1]

This episode strikes me as a particularly telling example of how language and the political intersect in our cultural moment, but how have we gotten to this moment? How can we reconcile what seemed to be the liberatory potential of the postmodern celebration of the multiplicity of discourses, the Bakhtinian notion that heightened heteroglossia – the dialogic interaction of a variety of languages – indicates a centripetal, decentered, pluralistic, multifarious society, the basic idea that the larger the number of a society's available discourses, the healthier its democracy, with the stubborn clinging to an idea of truth no matter the cost to social harmony or common sense, the belligerent intolerance of any idea that might challenge one's own, the simple refusal to listen to anything one doesn't already agree with and the insistence that this refusal to listen is a right that must be respected by others? If we live, as we seem to, in a society that's moving rapidly toward totalitarianism, has it happened despite postmodernism or, more frightening, has postmodernism contributed to it? And how, as Oedipa Maas wonders in Thomas Pynchon's *The Crying of Lot 49*, "had it ever happened here, with the chances once so good for diversity?" (181). Perhaps because it came of age during the sixties, postmodernism has been associated by many of us on the Left with freedom, liberation, progressive ideologies; but now, in the Bush years, I wonder if the Right does postmodernism better than we do, and, if they do, I wonder what use postmodernism can be in creating a socially progressive society.

A superficial look at contemporary society would suggest a Bakhtinian paradise: millions of voices in dialogue. There are hundreds of channels available through our TVs, thousands of books, magazines, and newspapers available at our local superstores and hundreds of thousands more via web stores, millions of web pages available through our computers, plus CDs, DVDs, cell phones, and so on. Thanks to technology, never has it been possible for us to listen to so many voices and never has it been so easy for the technologically savvy among us to make our voices available for others to listen to. But this seeming multiplicity of available discourses masks the centralizing forces operating beneath them. As Ben H. Bagdikian argued as early as 1983 in *The Media Monopoly* (which has been updated through several subsequent editions), the great majority of the many books, magazines, newspapers, cable channels, and major websites come from an increasingly smaller number of large, interlocking media conglomerates. Yes, there are small, noncommercial publishers, independent newspapers, public-access cable, and individual blogs, but the media conglomerates' interdependent components funnel their audiences' attention back and forth among them (e.g., the synergy among Time-Warner's magazines, websites, book publishers, book clubs, film studio, cable systems, and music companies – not to mention the clout it achieves through its advertising dollars – is frightening) to the point that, despite the multiplicity of discourses, a near complete social, corporate-consumerist, and ideological homogenization of culture results. In support of this, the growing influence of the media conglomerates makes possible the co-optation of alternative or dissenting discourses. Such protest and countercultural sixties anthems as "The Times They Are A-Changin' " and "In-A-Gadda-Da-Vida" are now used in commercials for financial firms (hey, the baby boomers are getting ready to retire!), and the urban discontent of rap music has been rapidly transformed into an advertising vehicle for the likes of Coke and McDonald's.

An even more important effect – perhaps a counter intuitive effect for those of us who placed our confidence in the health of our democracy in multitudes of discourses – of the technologically inspired explosion of voices is that there's just too much: too much to listen to, too much to take in and process, too much to follow. Mucho Maas anticipates the danger of this in a conversation with Zoyd Wheeler set circa 1970 in Pynchon's *Vineland*. In response to Zoyd's comment that sixties acid gave him the revelation that he was never going to die and that he'll never forget this, Mucho says,

> "Easy. They just let us forget. Give us too much to process, fill up every minute, keep us distracted, it's what the Tube is for, and though it kills me to say it, it's what rock and roll is becoming – just another way to claim out attention, so that beautiful certainty we had starts to fade, and after a while they have us convinced all over again that we really are going to die. And they've got us again." (313-14)

The sheer number of available discourses distracts us from the way they operate, from the way the great majority of them serve the hegemonic ideological agenda of the conglomeratized corporations and their conservative political collaborators. Instead of fostering democracy, the distracting discourses are in effect reactionary, maintaining and reproducing the status quo. With all this in mind, it becomes easier to see why the Rockford College commencement crowd reacted as it did.

The Rockford incident becomes still easier to understand and the role of the fallout of postmodernism becomes clearer if we link the dominance of distracting discourses with what at first might seem its opposite: a rising intolerance of dissent, but intolerance with a twist. Consider the following examples.

In March 2006 Jay Bennish, a high school teacher in a community outside of Denver, was put on unpaid leave after a recording of his comments in class the day after President Bush's

State of the Union address was played on a conservative radio talk show. He compared Bush's rhetoric to "the things that Adolf Hitler used to say." He criticized the violence at the heart of American foreign policy and called the United States "probably the single most violent nation on Earth." He set his remarks in the context of trying to get his students to think, rather than trying to get them to agree with him. Nevertheless, says a newspaper report of the incident, "Tustin Amole, a spokeswoman for the school district, said officials were investigating whether Bennish had violated a policy that says teachers may not intimidate students who hold political beliefs different from their own" (Riccardi 1: 4).

Laura Berg, a nurse at a VA hospital in Albuquerque, wrote a letter that was published in a local newspaper, criticizing the Bush administration in the wake of Hurricane Katrina. She wrote, "I am furious with the tragically misplaced priorities and criminal neglect of this government," and continued, "Bush, Cheney, Chertoff, Brown, and Rice should be tried for criminal negligence." After the letter appeared, VA administrators seized her computer to determine if the letter had been written on government equipment. When that turned out not to have been the case, the head of human resources at the hospital informed Berg, "The agency is bound by law to investigate and pursue any act which potentially represents sedition" (Rothschild, "Seditious Nurse" 14).

In his Feb.17, 2006 newspaper column, Cal Thomas attacked Al Gore for a speech the former vice president gave the previous week in Saudi Arabia. Gore criticized the Bush administration for its treatment of Arabs in the United States in the days following 9/11. Thomas goes on to list Gore's other criticisms of the president, including calling him "the most dishonest president since Richard Nixon." Thomas concludes,

> One definition of "treason" is: Violation of allegiance toward one's country or sovereign, especially the betrayal of one's country by waging war against it or by consciously and purposely acting to aid its enemies. (dictionary.com)
> By any objective standard, Al Gore's remarks in Saudi Arabia appear to fit the definition. (A6)

These three examples have something in common. In each case it was not the *content* of the utterance – Bennish's or Berg's or

Gore's criticisms of the Bush administration – that the reaction or reprisal ostensibly responded to. It was the *occasion* or the *form* of the utterance. That is, the responders don't make a case that answers the points of the critics, that argues that equating Bush's and Hitler's rhetoric is facile, that the response to Katrina was the best possible under the circumstances, that the roundup of Arabs in America after 9/11 was justified by events. Rather, they say that it's inappropriate for teachers to preach their political beliefs in the classroom in front of impressionable students, that a government employee should not use her position (or government equipment) to criticize her employer's policies, that a former senator and vice president should not speak ill of his country while in another country. Connected with this is something that the Bennish example has in common with the Rockford incident: the insistence on the auditor's right not to have to hear things that he or she disagrees with. In short, the right to free expression of our political beliefs is under attack not by those who would limit what we say but by those who would limit the occasion for discourse and assert the rights of listeners over those of speakers.

What's interesting and scary about this from the point of view of those of us who embrace the postmodern primarily for the liberatory potential it offers is that there's much about these Right Wing attacks on others' right to free expression that seems like a twisted version of postmodernism thrown back at us. After all, it's postmodernism – or at least one articulation of postmodernism – that has insisted on the primacy of discourse and discourse's construction of reality and that has refused to separate linguistic, rhetorical, and narrative form from the content it tries to communicate. It's postmodernism – or at least one articulation of postmodernism – that has critiqued the impulse to elevate one worldview over another as imperial hegemony and that has insisted on letting multiple narrative constructions of the same phenomena exist simultaneously and contradictorily. The postmodern watch cry of "respect others in their otherness" suggests that none of us has the right to call into question another's beliefs and practices. Thus when the Religious Right pushes forward Intelligent Design, insists that it be taught side-by-side with evolution, and parrots "Let's teach the controversy," do I have to hand over my postmodern credentials when I respond, "There is no controversy. Evolution is a fact"? Uh oh.

Light may be shed on the Right's use of postmodernism by a recent *New York Times* Op-Ed piece by Stanley Fish, written in response to the violent protests that broke out in the Islamic world after a Danish newspaper published cartoons depicting the Prophet Muhammad. Fish uses this incident as a club to beat on what he calls "the religion we call liberalism" and as a window to expose the transcendental belief – in this case freedom of speech – in the liberal system that claims to have no transcendental beliefs. He argues that liberalism's refusal to see the distinction between discourse and content is one of its problems. The editors who published the cartoons defended their decision with the principle of freedom of expression, but for Fish, this defense valorizes expression for the sake of expression and disregards the content of the expression. As he puts it, "The first tenet of the liberal religion is that everything (at least in the realm of expression and ideas) is to be permitted, but nothing is to be taken seriously" (4: 15). He dismisses the idea of respect, as in "respect others in their otherness," writing, "The thing about respect is that it doesn't cost you anything; its generosity is barely skin-deep and is in fact a form of condescension: I respect you; now don't bother me" (4: 15). He concludes by showing the fatuousness of a reliance on dialogue among discourses if, on one side, there is the liberal faith in discourse qua discourse and, on the other, a deep-seated belief in content:

> The belief in the therapeutic and redemptive force of dialogue depends on the assumption (central to liberalism's theology) that, after all, no idea is worth fighting over to the death and that we can always reach a position of accommodation if only we will sit down and talk it out.
> But a firm adherent of a comprehensive religion doesn't want dialogue about his beliefs; he wants those beliefs to prevail. (4: 15)

Fish wouldn't like this reduction, but one way to think of this is as a conflict between true believers in discourse versus true believers in content.

For Fish's "liberalism," I read "postmodernism" – or at least one articulation of postmodernism. I keep saying that, but what do I mean by it? I mean that it's an articulation of postmodernism in which reality is a linguistic construct, in which truth-value is indeterminate and all utterances are equally valid or invalid, in which, as Agnes Heller puts it, the message is "anything goes." She explains,

"'Anything goes' can be read as follows: *you* may rebel against anything you want to rebel against but let *me* rebel against the particular thing I want to rebel against. Or, alternatively speaking, let me not rebel against anything at all because I feel myself to be completely at ease" (503). In this articulation postmodernism is a reactionary movement in that it takes the form of rebellion but its dismissal of content, its privileging of discourse over truth-value, its emphasis on dialogue, negotiation, and contingency over principle, its general oh-well-what-the-Hell-ness subvert actual rebellion based in such values as justice, equality, and freedom.

This articulation of postmodernism has reasonably widespread currency. It seems to have much in common with Fredric Jameson's argument that postmodernism, by replacing historical depth with pastiched surface, is one of the devices contributing to the dominance of late capitalism. More persuasive to me is David Foster Wallace's take on how the liberating aspects of sixties postmodernism have trickled down into post-eighties popular culture to take politically heinous forms. Wallace explains in an interview with Larry McCaffery,

> Irony and cynicism were just what the U.S. hypocrisy of the fifties and sixties called for. That's what made the early postmodernists great artists. The great thing about irony is that it splits things apart, gets up above them so we can see the flaws and hypocrisies and duplicities. . . . Sarcasm, parody, absurdism and irony are great ways to strip off stuff's mask and show the unpleasant reality behind it. The problem is that once the rules for art are debunked, and once the unpleasant realities the irony diagnoses are revealed and diagnosed, *then* what do we do? Irony's useful for debunking illusions, but most of the illusion-debunking in the U.S. has now been done and redone. . . . All we seem to want to do is keep ridiculing the stuff. Postmodern irony and cynicism's become and end in itself, a measure of hip sophistication and literary savvy. (146-47)

Interestingly, Wallace links this poisonous postmodernism to one of its most effective practitioners, Rush Limbaugh, a model "of postmodern irony, hip cynicism, a hatred that winks and nudges you and pretends it's just kidding" (147). By now, thirteen years after giving this interview, Wallace would have more evidence linking the Right to the kind of postmodernism he finds so destructive. In the examples we looked at earlier, the Right is using the forms of postmodernism with a clearly nonpostmodern agenda. That is, they make their attacks not by insisting on the truth of their position or rightness of their claims but by gestures toward rhetorical situations, dialogism, and respecting others in their otherness. But, as Wallace suggests in reference to Rush, they are not, to use the terminology from my Fish reduction, true believers in discourse. They are only pretending to be. Behind their appeals to postmodern attitudes toward language, truth, and otherness is their true belief in content: corporate, political, and religious beliefs that (I hope I'm not being paranoid here – or rather, I hope I *am*) they want to *prevail*, as Fish puts it. In short, they may be playing our postmodern game, but they're sure not playing by our rules, and they're playing for keeps.

So what, then, should be our response? Is it time to abandon the language games and just say what we mean? Worry less about discourse and more about content? That's what Jonathan Franzen argues:

> the time has come for form's dialectical counterparts, content and context, to return as the vectors of the new. . . . When the times get really, really awful, you retrench; you reexamine old content in new contexts; you try to preserve; you seem obsolete. Think of Mandelstam, Akhmatova, and Brodsky continuing, in the belly of the Soviet beast, to write of nature and the human heart. The day comes when the truly subversive literature is in some measure conservative. (38)

I wonder, though, if we can go back to a state of innocence about the transparency of language, discourse, and narrative, to pretend that we don't see the process of representation sitting there between word and object. Wallace takes a different approach. Rather than ignoring discourse, the cynical, self-aware irony that he finds so destructive, he uses it, creating narrators and characters who are hyperaware of language, in an attempt to break through the irony to something genuine and sincere. That his fiction continues to focus on the *attempt* suggests that he doesn't see himself as having succeeded yet. These responses seem at opposite ends of the spectrum, but what they are responding to – the bankruptcy of language that they see as the upshot of postmodernism – is the same.

Franzen's and Wallace's takes on postmodernism, like Fish's and some of the others I looked at earlier, make a distinction between discourse and content, a distinction I find problematic. It seems to me that discourse and content are interwoven and that discussions that try to separate them are choosing to emphasize one aspect of postmodernism – discourse, the language games – over others. Useful here is Hayden White's term, which he used as the title of one of his books, *the content of the form*. In looking at history, White argues that things in the past happened – there is a *reality* – but once they happen, we have access to them only through discourse: people's memories, letters, eyewitness accounts, other documents, the stories that can be told about them. And what we need to realize, White says, is that the forms we use to tell these stories have their own contents that interact with and affect the materials they treat. When narrative, for example, treats the events of the past, it brings to them the demands of its own form – i.e., a beginning, a causally related series of events, an end – that create the conditions by which the events will be known. Other treatments will create different conditions and different knowledge. White also makes the helpful point that historical narrative is possible only when a set of events can be explained by more than one story. Historical narrative, then, has built into it an element of persuasion, the desire to prove to an auditor that *one* narrative is truer, more likely, more useful than another.

All this is helpful in a couple of ways. First, in recognizing (as postmodernism has helped us to do) the discourse-based process of representation through which we know our world, we are not denying or abandoning content. As much as they self-referentially foreground discourse, writers from Gaddis to Barth to Pynchon to Reed to DeLillo to Acker to Wallace seem to care deeply about the word and things like justice, equality, and freedom and seem to want us to care about them too. Second, our recognition that multiple narratives about the same phenomena can simultaneously and contradictorily exist doesn't force us to admit that all narratives are equally valid. Speakers are obliged to offer the most persuasive narrative they can conjure, and if they don't or if other narratives are more persuasive, listeners are under no obligation to accept it. That we know our world through discourse does not deny facts. Gravity is a fact; it is explained and made knowable through discourse. Evolution is a fact; within the field of biology there are different narrative explanations seeking to be the most persuasive in explaining it. The Holocaust happened. There were no Weapons of Mass Destruction in Iraq.

Despite the deleterious fallout that Heller, Jameson, and Wallace posit, postmodernism, if we think about it as discourse interwoven with content and discourse with a responsibility to persuade, is still useful, maybe vital, in the current political scene. More than ever, listeners and readers need to be made aware of how discourse attempts to persuade them to accept a particular version of reality. With so many of the sources of discourse emanating from corporate-controlled sources, the official versions of reality can be quickly reified, and with the number and volume of the many distracting discourses, it can be hard for us to even notice it happening. The more we're unaware of the role of discourses in creating a version of reality, the more likely it is that we'll see not a *version* of reality, but reality, the *only* reality.

To negotiate the Right's version of reality, which seems depressingly all encompassing at the moment, we need two things that postmodernism – postmodern art – can do. First, we need a public of critical thinkers, and in the wake of postmodernism critical thinking is marked by being discourse-savvy. Engaging postmodernism forces one to become discourse-savvy. Second, postmodern art, in its unexpectedness, its refusal to give us what we expect, can shake us out of our dominant-discourse-induced complacency, the complacency that lets us pompously insist that we have a right not to hear anything we don't already agree with. One answer to Wallace's idea that postmodernism has trickled down into cheap, cynical irony can be found in Curtis White's story "Remember John Lennon":

> Everybody of my generation has the same memory. We were twelve or thirteen or we were twenty-one, for that matter, and we were going to be veterinarians or we were, like Ringo, going to own a hairdresser's parlor. We walked into the record store and saw the cover of *Sgt. Pepper's Lonely Hearts Club Band*. We
> thought together, "Life can be other than it has been." (156)

I love this passage because it speaks to my own experience. In my immediate postbaccalaureate years I worked in public relations and was settling comfortably into the Reagan-era weltanschauung. But then, my encounter with Thomas Pynchon's masterpiece, *Gravity's Rainbow*, shook me out of my burgeoning conservatism, reconnected me with my progressive ideology, and made me aware of the cultural processes I'd been caught up in, the ones that can make certain values seem natural and inevitable while others are dismissed as impractical and naive. Art can do that. Even in our linguistically fallen world, even in the land of Limbaugh, even in the age of distracting discourses, art can still surprise us and make us see that other realities are possible.

Anyway, that's what I believe. It's what keeps me reading; it's what keeps me writing; it's what keeps me teaching. It's what gives me hope in a very dark time. Postmodernism may be to a great extent responsible for the state of discourse I've described here, the age of distracting discourses, but it also offers a way of negotiating our way through it. Postmodernism isn't only the stuff that pointy-headed English professors embrace or only the dumbed-down pastiches of self-referentiality that infest television and movies. There's the stuff in between that surprises without being inaccessible, that reveals the interconnectedness of discourse and reality, and that challenges us to think, really think, about who we are and where we are. This is the stuff, whether we call it postmodernism or something else, that can help us find ways to define, claim, and enact freer and better versions of reality.

Notes

---

[1] See Rothschild's article about this event ("Enforced Conformity"), and Hedges's transcript of the speech, complete with audience reaction.

Works Cited

Bagdikian, Ben H. *The Media Monopoly*. Boston: Beacon Press, 1983.

Fish, Stanley. "Our Faith in Letting It All Hang Out." *New York Times* 12 Feb. 2006, sec. 4: 15.

Franzen, Jonathan. "I'll Be Doing More of the Same." *Review of Contemporary Fiction* 16.1 (1996): 34-38.

Hedges, Chris. "Heckled in Rockford." *Progressive* Jul. 2003: 24-26

Heller, Agnes. "Existentialism, Alienation, Postmodernism: Cultural Movements as Vehicles of Change in the Patterns of Everyday Life." *A Postmodern Reader*. Ed. Joseph Natoli and Linda Hutcheon. Albany: State U of New York P, 1993. 497-509.

Jameson, Fredric. *Postmodernism, or, The Cultural Logic of Late Capitalism*. Durham: Duke UP, 1991.

McCaffery, Larry. "An Interview with David Foster Wallace." *Review of Contemporary Fiction* 13.2 (1993): 127-50.

Pynchon, Thomas. *The Crying of Lot 49*. 1966. New York: Perennial, 1986.

—. *Vineland*. Boston: Little, Brown, 1990.

Riccardi, Nicholas. "School Busts Teacher for Bush-Bashing." *Chicago Tribune* 5 March 2006, sec. 1: 4.

"Rockford College in Brief." *Rockford College*. 2005. 22 Feb. 2006 <http://www. rockford.edu.>

Rothschild, Matthew. "Enforced Conformity." *Progressive* Jul. 2003: 19-23.

—. "A Seditious Nurse." *Progressive* April 2006: 14-15.

Thomas, Cal. "Al Gore Should Study Definition of 'Treason.'" *Bloomington-Normal Pantagraph* 17 Feb. 2006: A6.

White, Curtis. *The Idea of Home*. Los Angeles: Sun & Moon, 1992.

White, Hayden. *The Content of the Form: Narrative, Discourse, and Historical Representation*. Baltimore: Johns Hopkins UP, 1987.

~ 4 ~

Attending to Suffering in/at the Wake of Postmodernism[1]

Jennifer Geddes

A Moment in Postmodernism

In 1997, at a conference on "Religion and Postmodernism," Mark C. Taylor gave a multimedia presentation entitled "Betting on Vegas." Playing on the language of gambling –using phrases like "my deal," "your deal," "betting on Vegas," "the draw," "I'll put my cards on the table," "my wager" – he provocatively framed his presentation as a wager on the significance of Las Vegas to contemporary critical theory, arguing that "you cannot understand America today unless you understand Las Vegas; and if you cannot understand America, you cannot comprehend contemporary culture and the future it opens and/or closes" (Taylor 229). Recognizing that many would think of Las Vegas as a trivial topic – "Nothing seems more obvious, more straightforward, more superficial than Vegas" (229) – Taylor confronted head-on the scepticism that he knew awaited him in his audience: "Is the spectacle before you a put-on – yet another gesture of tiresome postmodern irony under the guise of exhausted academic respectability?" (230). By referring to his presentation as a spectacle, he drew a parallel between it and the religious spectacle about which he was speaking, Las Vegas, which he declared to be "perhaps one of the most religious phenomena in the United States…Las Vegas is where the death of God is staged as the spectacle of the Kingdom of God on earth" (230).

      The presentation was dazzling, carefully and artfully constructed. An interesting parallel existed between Taylor's discourse, way of framing the essay as a gamble, and playing with words, on the one hand, and the language, framing, and play of "Vegas" itself. It was as if Taylor's presentation emerged from Las Vegas culture. His presentation itself was a gamble, a "betting on Vegas." But just what did that mean? Taylor ended his presentation by declaring that

> To bet on Vegas is to bet on nothing. And to bet on nothing is to bet on betting. Betting on nothing expects nothing in return. Absolutely nothing. This is, of course, a gamble – a huge gamble. But when everything becomes dicey, we are forced to confess that we have always been gamblers. It's all (a) crap(shoot). There you have it; I've laid down *my* cards on the table. Now it's *your* deal; always *your* deal. (242-243)

Taylor was betting on the proposal that the virtual reality of Las Vegas was a crucial prism through which to view contemporary culture, specifically its functioning as a virtual reality: "recent developments in electronic and telematic technologies disclose all 'reality' to be virtual. Virtual reality is not merely a specific technology but it, more importantly, a trope for our current cultural condition" (242).

> Jacques Derrida responded with the following:
> My question takes the form of a fiction. Could we imagine the same presentation, with the same apparatus, about the same technological and economical structure, with a different example, something else in the United States which would be indicative of the same state of technology, of capital? For instance, jails. Could you imagine the same thing with respect to American jails? (243)

The question was an odd one. Derrida was not merely asking Taylor to give another example of what he had been talking about, as one might do either for clarification ("I'm not quite getting it – could you give me another example that might illustrate your point?") or for an expansion of the relevance of the point being made ("Do you see this same cultural logic at work in other arenas?"). He was asking Taylor if he could imagine the same presentation about something other than Las Vegas. It was a little like asking someone if he could imagine changing the topic of his presentation.

It was also an odd question because, as Derrida stated, it took the "form of a fiction." It was asking Taylor (and we who were present) about the capacities of his (and our) imagination – "Could we imagine... Could you imagine..." To answer, one would have to imagine one's presentation otherwise. One would have to take the form of the presentation, "the same apparatus," and imagine it with images, sounds, and spoken words related to jails rather than Las Vegas. Derrida was not only asking about the capacities of Taylor's imagination, he was also asking about the capacities of the presentation, the apparatus, to speak of, to present, a different topic. He was asking if the presentation made was one that could be made about a "real jail."

Three times Derrida tried to get Taylor to talk about jails. The first time, Taylor declared that "On the issues of prisons and light, Foucault only began to glimpse the scale of panopticism that is on display at Vegas. In a certain sense, part of what goes on in the prison is this kind of surveillance" (243). The answer seemed to suggest that surveillance is better understood on display in Vegas than in prisons. When Derrida persisted – "But I mean real jails" – Taylor again focused on the way in which surveillance in Vegas exceeds that of a prison, declaring that "Surveillance in Vegas is amazing. Those casinos are virtual jails. There is not one move that you make there that is not on display. Now I understand the difference between the casino as jail and real jails" (243). Again Derrida made his point: "But Vegas is not a real prison." But Taylor argued that "That way of putting it is too simple. The question we need to ask is, what is the difference between so-called real jails and the kind of society or culture constructed around Las Vegas?" (243).

Derrida and Taylor seemed to be talking past each other. Derrida kept asking about real jails, and Taylor kept talking about Las Vegas. They mirrored each other in their persistence and in their refusal of the other's terms of conversation. The strange notion of the "real" became a point of contention between them. Derrida persistently resisted the connections that Taylor made between jails and casinos, surveillance in Las Vegas and surveillance in prisons.

Why was Derrida so insistent on "real jails"? What was at stake in the distinction between Las Vegas and prison? One way to read Derrida's initial question is to see it as pushing towards the ethical limits of Taylor's presentation. Imagining Taylor's presentation as being about the injustices of the American jail system – as Derrida asked Taylor to imagine – was difficult to do because of its dramatic, provocative, and flashy style. The presentation style mirrored the very phenomenon Taylor was exploring: it took on the showiness of Las Vegas and dazzled us with images, sounds, word plays, and puns.

Such a presentation about "real" prison life would have been disturbing, suggesting that the author had not recognized the suffering of which he spoke, a suffering that elicited and demanded attention, of a different sort than the kind that Las Vegas elicited.

It seemed as if Derrida was asking Taylor to imagine how he might have spoken otherwise if his presentation had been about the suffering and injustices of the American prison system. (The connection between the prison, injustice, and suffering was clearer at the conference, where Derrida referred to chain gangs in the prisons of the American South, than they are in the printed version of their exchange.) Derrida's question offered a jarring juxtaposition to Taylor's presentation, and the image of prison chain gangs posed a jarring juxtaposition to the image of the casinos and luxury hotels. Derrida's question suggested that jails are sites of the same economic and technological structures as Las Vegas, but that in jails these structures have rather more destructive consequences. It is one thing to be under surveillance while gambling in a casino and quite another thing to be under surveillance while working chained to fellow prisoners. In other words, Taylor's presentation didn't explore these structures deeply enough – his fascination caused him to linger at the shiny surface.

How do we think about the virtual and the real when confronted with suffering? Do we need to speak differently, present otherwise, imagine otherwise, if we are confronted with suffering? What about the real suffering of the real prisoners chained together in a real prison gang? Is virtual reality a trope for their cultural condition? Who is the "we" here? Whereas Taylor argues that "In the world on display in Las Vegas, the real becomes virtual and the virtual becomes real" (242), this seems also to have been the case in his response to Derrida's question about prisons. When Taylor finds it too simple to distinguish between casinos and jails, something has been lost from sight. Perhaps Derrida remains "stuck in classical binaries and oppositions" (242) but perhaps Derrida's question enacts the ways in which suffering breaks into postmodern discourse, calling it to develop new ways of thinking, responding, and speaking.

Interestingly, Taylor's presentation was calling us to think and write differently, proposing:

> To think differently, we must write differently, and to write differently, we must think differently. While we have been learning to think differently for

> many years, writing practices and the technologies they presuppose have remained virtually unchanged – even when the authors claim otherwise. … Deconstructive strategies have become distressingly familiar and thus in all too many cases, we know the argument before we read the text. To overcome this critical impasse, if, indeed, it can be overcome, we must learn to write even more transgressively. (242)

Taylor then suggested that we write with bits and images and sounds, proposing that with these we would be writing more transgressively and thus less distressingly familiar prose.

But Derrida's questions pointed in another way that deconstructive strategies might become importantly unfamiliar. He was asking about the ways in which attending to suffering and injustice, rather than to the decadent surface of Las Vegas, might reshape Taylor's writing and presentation. He was asking how he might write and think differently if he were attending to the suffering of prison chain gangs under surveillance, rather than attending to the surveillance of Las Vegas casinos. What if instead of focusing on gambling, dealing, and betting, Taylor had focused on systemic injustice, inhumane prison practices, and sites of human suffering? How would the answer to Taylor's initial question, "what's at stake?," change? Behind Derrida's question was, I think, a frustration. He suggested that on display was Taylor's ability to see deeply into cultural phenomena, to bring to view things that were invisible to the rest of us, to creatively depict the sense of a place, with its tones, textures, and undercurrents; and yet the end to which these abilities were put was one of entertainment. Taylor's presentation performed the very aesthetics and ethics of the place it was seeking to reveal.

This short exchange crystallized something beyond mere speculation on the choice of a different topic: first, it revealed suffering as a source of critique and provocation to postmodernism, and, second, suggested possible resources in postmodernism – itself a source of cultural critique and provocation – for responding to suffering. It enacted the ways in which suffering both calls postmodernism into question and elicits resources from within postmodernism to respond to those questions.

The Turn to Ethics and Suffering

Since at least the early 1990s, an increasing number of books of literary and cultural theory have focused on questions of ethics and suffering – two topics that had been neglected (if not considered taboo) in the previous few decades. Scholars debate just when this turn to ethics in theory began, but Geoffrey Harpham gives us a satisfyingly concrete date: "On or about December 1, 1987, the nature of literary theory changed…one thing, and perhaps only one, was clear: ethics was on the agenda" (Harpham 20-21). The cause of this radical transformation was the discovery that literary theorist Paul DeMan had written several articles published in a Belgian collaborationist newspaper during the Holocaust. This discovery, Harpham argues, sent the world of theory into a tailspin, with the relationship between theory, ethics, and human suffering becoming a central topic of discussion. Before this time, he argues, ethics was considered a universalising and binary discourse of the Enlightenment. In fact, some saw ethics as "the particular way in which people preserved a good conscience while overriding or delegitimating the claims of others" (Harpham 18). With the discovery of DeMan's collaborationist writings, several theorists began to rethink the relation of theory to ethics. Among them was Jacques Derrida:

> Painful though it was, the controversy seems actually to have stimulated Derrida not only to expand and deepen a meditation on ethics that was, as we have seen, present in his work from the very beginning, but to move his general critique in a new direction, his formidable style becoming in the process much more flexible and accessible. (Harpham 21-22)

The days of ethics as something old fuddy-duddies, moralistic schoolteachers, or the pious concerned themselves with were over.

While many suggest a broader (or later) time span than the one Harpham provocatively puts forward for the turn to ethics, few scholars disagree that such a turn has taken place. It has become the concern of theory that leans to the left and of theory that leans to the right, crossing political, ideological, and methodological divides. In the debate about whether postmodernism is concerned with ethics, those on one side of the debate declare postmodernism to be a relativistic, narcissistic hermeticism written in elitist discourse that is blind or indifferent to suffering; those on another side retort that postmodernism began in ethical concerns, as a critique of oppressive power, and has proceeded by deconstructing and destabilizing the very structures that oppress, repress, and obscure.

The most interesting aspect of the debate is, to my mind, its point of agreement: both sides agree that a concern with ethics is a good thing, both argue for or against the value of postmodern thought using criteria that value ethics. Those who argue that postmodernism is not concerned with ethics do so to condemn it; those who argue that it is concerned with ethics do so to defend it. In other words, both sides argue that theory *should* have ethical concerns. Distance from engaging questions of ethics is seen as a failing. The fact that both sides agree that ethics is critically important is the surprising aspect of this debate.

Related to the rise of interest in ethics is the intensified interest in suffering and how we should respond to it. Today many scholars of ethics are focused on questions of suffering, but this has not always been the case. Ethics as a branch of philosophy (and theology) has most often focused on two constellations of concerns: (1) obligations, duties, laws; and (2) virtue and character. More and more, ethics has come to be understood, outside the specialized fields of philosophical and theological ethics, as less about universal laws or virtuous character and more about how to respond to those who suffer. Certainly these things cannot be separated – how one responds to one who suffers will depend on the laws one sees oneself as bound or committed to follow and to the kind of virtues that have been developed in one through one's family, community, and culture – but the point being made here is that responding to suffering has become a touchstone of what it means to be ethical.

Indeed, questions of ethics and suffering have marked the most interesting theoretical works in postmodernism. Richard Kearney and Mark Dooley have argued that "questioning ethics…is now a pivotal preoccupation for many of the leading figures working within contemporary European philosophy. In our post-Heideggerian, post-metaphysical, climate we are beginning to realize that to poetically dwell requires us also to ethically dwell. No amount of neo-Nietzschean aestheticizing can dispense with the need for moral and political vigilance" (Kearney and Dooley 1-2). Emmanuel Levinas's work, which focused on questions of ethics and suffering as early as the 1960s with the publication of his book *Totalité et Infini*, has had a profound influence on the growing interest in these questions, and the number of books on Levinas's work grows steadily. Books such as Simon Critchley's *The Ethics of Deconstruction* and Richard Kearney's *Strangers, Gods and Monsters: Ideas of Otherness* explored the constellation of ethics, the suffering other, and postmodernism.

An even more surprising turn has been the growing interest in religion and postmodernism, which is, I think, connected in significant ways to the growing interest in ethics and suffering, but this is a point that must be argued elsewhere. From the publication of Mark C. Taylor's *Erring: A Postmodern A/Theology* over twenty years ago to Jacques Derrida's move towards religious questions in his later works, such as *The Gift of Death, Adieu to Emmanuel Levinas*, and *On the Name*; John D. Caputo's *The Prayers and Tears of Jacques*; Jean-Luc Marion's *God without Being*; and Richard Kearney's *The God Who May Be* – the interest in religion shows no signs of abating. And world events only seem to make the questions raised in these studies more pressing.

Outside postmodern theory, ethical literary and cultural theory has been gathering steam with the works of Martha Nussbaum, Richard Rorty, Charles Taylor, Stanley Cavell, Wayne Booth, and others. Wayne Booth notes that in "the last fifteen years or so, there has been an explosion of interest in questions about the ethical effects of reading literature. Previous to that explosion there was a grotesque avoidance of such questions" (Booth xi). Daniel R. Schwartz suggests that we are "in the midst of a humanistic revival or at least a neohumanist burst of energy" (Schwartz 3). In the last few years, several anthologies and readers have focused on the relationship between ethics and literature, including *The Moral of the Story: An Anthology of Ethics Through Literature*, edited by Peter Singer and Renata Singer, and *Ethics, Literature, and Theory: An Introductory Reader*, edited by Stephen K. George.

Many scholars see the interest in ethics and suffering as a move away from postmodernism, but I think postmodernism was critical in turning scholars' attention to these topics. By exposing the cracks in seemingly comprehensive totalities and reading authoritative texts against themselves, postmodernism's critiques created space in which previously marginalized and silenced voices were able to speak.

What these voices had to say brought to scholars' attention a whole range of ethical issues, experiences of suffering, and aspects of human experience (including the religious) that had previously not garnered attention. Interestingly, these revelations called for ways of thinking, reading, and responding that exposed the limitations of postmodernism's approaches. In response, many scholars understood to be writing within the field of postmodernism began to consider different kinds of questions, ways of reading, and approaches. In other words, the very delegitimizing of grand narratives by postmodern thought opened up space that allowed and encouraged the particular narratives of those not in power to be told and heard, but that in doing so, this "delegitimizing" gesture has brought forth narratives that describe, express, and protest a range of suffering, injustice, and evil that postmodernism has been ill equipped to respond to – hence its turn to questions of ethics, suffering, and religion. John D. Caputo and Michael J. Scanlon suggest that postmodernism has "made some room" for religion:

> ...the contemporary moment which has loosened the grip of the old Enlightenment, questioned its intimidating authority, complained about the exclusionary force of its certainties and axioms (among which secularism has enjoyed pride of place), and thereby made some room for a religious discourse and restored the voice of a religious imagination.... Our wager was, the more enlightened we get about Enlightenment, the more likely religion is to get a word in edgewise. (Caputo and Scanlan 2)[2]

It has also made room for ethics and suffering. As more and more suffering gets a word in edgewise," the theory that is confronted by it changes, learns to read, present, speak, and write in the different ways to which the telling of suffering calls us.

Of course, whether one sees this shift as a significantly new stage in postmodernism or as the passing of postmodernism depends on what one thinks postmodernism is – and stating the difficulty of defining just what postmodernism is has become an almost necessary precursor to any work that uses the word, especially since just what is meant by "postmodernism" shifts from author to author. I propose that postmodernism be understood as a complex constellation of ideas, texts, scholars, and artists that have overlapping elements but no clear core that stands as a solid, unchanging referent. Some of these overlapping elements include ways of reading that seek to destabilize a text by a close reading of its own logic against itself, a rejection of grand narratives as forms of oppressive power, and a valorisation of the fragmentary, temporary, and particular over against notions of the whole, the permanent, and the universal. An ontologically rigid understanding of postmodernism will lean towards seeing the recent moves towards ethics, suffering, and religion as pointing towards the death or departure of postmodernism. A view of postmodernism that includes the notion of radical change as consistent with a continuation of identity over time might see these moves as awakenings within postmodernism. Either way something of significance has occurred in recent contemporary theory with this turn to ethics, suffering, and religion, and we would do well to explore it and to engage in the ongoing effort to learn ways of reading, responding to, and writing about the ethical issues, suffering, and aspects of human experience that have been brought to our attention by it.

"Attending the Wake of Postmodernism"

Where are we and what are we doing if we find ourselves "attending the wake of postmodernism"? The word "wake" conjures up at least three rather different scenarios. How we read it can radically alter how we understand the mourning and attending to which the title of this book refers. Most obviously we can think of a wake as a vigil over a corpse before burial. In this scenario, the focus is on our reverence for the dead one. If the wake of postmodernism is a vigil over its corpse, attending it involves being present to mourn, remember, and celebrate its life. Are we mourning the death of postmodernism, then, keeping watch over its corpse before its final burial and celebrating its life now that it has ended?

　　A wake can also be that which is left behind after a violent, turbulent, or hasty departure, such as the track left in the water by a boat speedily making its get away. Maybe postmodernism has left us in its wake, and we are standing in the space it has left behind, in its trace, attending to its after effects. In this scenario, the focus is on the violence done to we who are left behind, we who exist in the turbulence of absence, and the departure is experienced as a kind of betrayal. This is sometimes the way we experience the death of a loved one, as if the one who has died – the "dearly departed" – has purposefully left us. If the wake of postmodernism marks postmodernism's departure, its betrayal of us, the focus of our attending is on its absence and our loss.

But could it be that the "wake of postmodernism" refers not to its death but to its awakening from some slumber, whether dogmatic or otherwise? Perhaps we are witnesses to this event of its coming to a new consciousness, to being otherwise – in which case, mourning might be out of place. We may need to rethink what it means to attend (to) something. For the word "attending" can also refer to a mode of engagement with something or someone: paying attention to, listening to, caring for, watching over. With these meanings, our action moves beyond merely being present to becoming engaged through our attention to the words and needs of the other(s) before us. Postmodernism comes in complex and contrasting forms and configurations, but one trait that seems fairly consistent across the spectrum is a skilful attention to deciphering what lies hidden, to uncovering logics that are disguised and power plays that are clothed in hospitality within literary and philosophical texts. Postmodernism is skilled at critique, deconstruction, dismantling totalities, confusing binary oppositions. But it has sometimes, in some forms, been too entranced with its own rhetoric, too entertained by its own cleverness, too absorbed in its own fascinations. Might we be involved in mourning, not the death of postmodernism, but its narcissistic naïveté, in which case the "work of mourning" might better be cast as the "work of maturing"?

Drawing on these multiple valences of "attending the wake of postmodernism," we might creatively rethink "the mourning after" not as our mourning after the death (post-death) of postmodernism, but rather as postmodernism's awakening to the voices of those who were able to speak in its wake, that is, in the wake of its deconstructive efforts. The mourning after might be an ethical response to the suffering brought to our attention by those who now have space to speak.

Levinas and the Temptation of Temptation

To return to the exchange between Taylor and Derrida, what would a presentation on real jails request of us? What sort of presentation would be required to speak of the suffering of chain gangs? In one of his nine Talmudic readings, Emmanuel Levinas describes "the temptation of temptation," suggesting it characterizes the modern, Western individual. It might be an even more apt description of the situation of the postmodern individual. Someone tempted by temptation is characterized by an eagerness and impatience to experience everything, including the evil and suffering this everything involves, but without the risks associated with such experiences.

So how does one fulfil this desire to experience "everything" without suffering the destructive danger of evil and suffering? Through knowledge. Levinas connects the temptation of temptation to the temptation of knowledge; knowledge allows us to participate in a way that keeps us safe from the risks associated with other forms of engagement. The temptation of knowledge, or philosophy, subordinates action to knowledge of action, and in so doing prevents the spontaneity of response that might make generosity possible and prevents the encounter with the other that precedes knowledge. Like Odysseus, the tempted ego "can listen to the song of the sirens without compromising its return to its island. It can brush past evil, know it without succumbing to it, experience it without experiencing it, try it without living it, take risks in security" (Levinas 33). In the temptation of temptation, the individual can participate in everything yet remain outside everything. One might read Taylor's presentation as enacting this very temptation of temptation, where an academic presentation betting on Vegas remains outside, even while it participates in, the dangers of betting in Vegas. On another level, writing about surveillance in Las Vegas might also be seen as taking "risks in security"; for just as the surveillance of Las Vegas involves fewer risks than the surveillance one might experience in a prison chain gang, so, too, studying surveillance in Vegas involves fewer risks and places fewer ethical burdens on one than studying the surveillance of a prison.

The temptation of temptation has extreme ethical consequences: "It will no longer leave the other in its otherness but always include it in the whole... From this stems the inability to recognize the other person as other person, as outside all calculation, as neighbor, as first come" (Levinas 35). Scholars studying suffering must resist the temptation to enclose that suffering within their theoretical construct. Because "temptation makes nothing irreparable," it also makes nothing forbidden and everything safely permissible.

Mistakes can be erased, risks taken safely, and, hence, nothing is really at stake.

Levinas suggests that there is an "order prior to the one in which a thought tempted by temptation is to be found" (Levinas 36). The contemporary turn to ethics, suffering, and religion might be a move in the direction of that order, towards a kind of responsiveness to the other that is not reducible to a presumptuous or distanced knowing. And this move is one that postmodernism itself has helped to make possible. By displaying the oppressive power structures, whether textual or cultural, that silence the voices of those on the margins, postmodern thought creates space in which the voices of those who have been ignored, oppressed, and silenced are able to speak. Grand narratives and metanarrative are dismantled making room for particular narratives.

However, so focused have been postmodernism's reading and interpretive strategies on critique, exposure, and fragmentation, and on dismantling power structures, that it has lacked modes of engagement that can attend and respond to the suffering spoken by those for whom it has made way. In the exposure of postmodernism's limitations, some postmodern thinkers have begun to take up questions related to ethics, suffering, and religion. How does postmodernism, with its expertise in dismantling, respond to the utterance of that which has already been dismantled, that is, the dismantled narrative of the victim of evil, torture, and suffering? While some thinkers are so surprised by the "turn" to ethics, suffering, and religion that they announce postmodernism's demise, might this turn to ethics, to suffering, to justice, to religion, even to "humanism' (if we dare to use the word in the same sentence as "postmodernism"), be a move that brings together the best of postmodern thought with a working through of its most significant failings?

Notes

¹ I would like to thank Charles Mathewes and Neil Brooks for reading an earlier draft of this paper, and the Virginia Foundation for the Humanities and the Institute for Advanced Studies in Culture at the University of Virginia for financial and collegial support during the writing of this paper.

Works Cited

Booth, Wayne C. Foreword. *Ethics, Literature, & Theory: An Introductory Reader.* 2nd Ed. Ed. Stephen K. George. Lanham: Rowman & Littlefield, 2005. xi-xii.

Caputo, John D. *The Prayers and Tears of Jacques Derrida: Religion Without Religion.* Bloomington: Indiana University Press, 1997.

—. and Michael J. Scanlon. Introduction. *God, the Gift, and Postmodernism.* Eds. John D. Caputo and Michael J. Scanlon. Bloomington: Indiana UP, 1999. 1-19.

Critchley, Simon. *The Ethics of Deconstruction: Derrida and Levinas.* Oxford: Blackwell, 1992.

Derrida, Jacques. *The Gift of Death.* Trans. David Wills. Chicago: The U of Chicago P, 1995.

—. *Adieu to Emmanuel Levinas.* Trans. Pascale-Anne Brault and Michael Naas. Stanford: Stanford UP, 1999.

—. *On the Name.* Ed. Thomas Dutoit. Stanford: Stanford UP, 1995.

Harpham, Geoffrey Galt. *Shadows of Ethics: Criticism and the Just Society.* Durham: Duke U P, 1999.

George, Stephen K. *Ethics, Literature, and Theory: An Introductory Reader.* 2nd Ed. Lanham: Rowman & Littlefield, 2005.

Kearney, Richard. *Strangers, Gods and Monsters: Ideas of Otherness.* London: Routledge, 2002.

—. *The God Who May Be: A Hermeneutics of Religion.* Bloomington: Indiana UP, 2001.

—. and Mark Dooley. *Questioning Ethics: Contemporary Debates in Philosophy.* London: Routledge, 1999.

Levinas, Emmanuel. "The Temptation of Temptation." *Nine Talmudic Readings.* Trans. Annette Aronowicz. Bloomington: Indiana UP, 1990. 30-50.

—. *Totalité et Infini: Essai sur l'extériorité.* The Hague: Martinus Nijhoff, 1961.

Marion, Jean-Luc. *God without Being: Hors-Texte.* Trans. Thomas A. Carlson. Chicago: U of Chicago P, 1991.

Schwartz, Daniel R. "A Humanistic Ethics of Reading." *Mapping the Ethical Turn: A Reader in Ethics, Culture, and Literary Theory.* Ed. Todd F. Davis and Kenneth Womack. Charlottesville: UP of Virginia, 2001. 3-15.

Singer, Peter, and Renata Singer, eds. *The Moral of the Story: An Anthology of Ethics Through Literature.* Oxford: Blackwell 2005.

Taylor, Mark C. Taylor. "Betting on Vegas." *God, the Gift, and Postmodernism.* Eds. John D. Caputo and Michael J. Scanlon. Bloomington: Indiana University Press, 1999. 229-243.

—. and Jacques Derrida "Betting on Vegas: Discussion." *God, the Gift, and Postmodernism.* Eds. John D. Caputo and Michael J. Scanlon. Bloomington: Indiana University Press, 1999. 243.

—. *Erring: A Postmodern A/Theology.* Chicago: U of Chicago P, 1984.

~ 5 ~

Soul Service:
Foucault's "Care of the Self" as Politics and Ethics

Jane Flax

The apparently widespread belief that ethics and postmodernism are irreconcilable is puzzling to me. After all, postmodernisms, at least as articulated by writers categorized as postmodernists such as Lyotard, Derrida, or Foucault arose in part as deeply political and ethical responses to specific twentieth century horrors including the Holocaust, the gulag, the Algerian War and other bloody exits from overt colonialism, and the invention and use of the atomic bomb. In relation to such events, scepticism concerning grand narratives, the normative powers of reason, and the emancipatory potential of science is an appropriate ethical position. Considering the damage wrought in its name, a desire to chasten the hubris of an agentic subject for whom the world is material to exercise its mastery reflects concern for our species and its habitat. Nor have anti-foundationalism, decentred notions of subjectivity and discourse-dependent accounts of truth kept contemporary writers such as Judith Butler, Paul Gilroy, Wendy Brown or myself from engaging homophobia, gender domination, or racism in our intellectual and practical work.

This belief that ethics and postmodernism are irreconcilable rests upon several problematic assumptions: that ethics requires foundations; that without an objective, universalizable standard no ethical judgments are compelling; and that without an autonomous, agentic subject, no moral accountability or responsibility is possible. As I have elsewhere discussed why I find such assumptions problematic,[1] I will not offer an extensive analysis here. However, I would like to point out that critics of postmodernism often offer circular arguments. Rather than allowing for multiple ways to practice ethics, they posit a particular construction of it (often an Aristotelian, Kantian or Platonic one) as ethics tout court. Then by definition any approach that deviates from their preferred mode is either not ethics, amoral relativism or nihilism. Furthermore, as I will discuss below, those asserting such claims also erroneously place far too much importance on arriving at correct, usually quite abstract, principles and not nearly enough on imagining practices that could motivate and sustain ethical actions. A kind of magical thinking often ensues, as if deriving general normative principles is both a good in itself and a practice that necessarily initiates and sustains a just life world.

Perhaps this association of postmodernism and amorality also has something to do with its modes of transmission, primarily through academic literary criticism, into the United States. Somehow in the process discourses meant to analyze and disrupt murderous social practices were either depoliticised or overly politicized. Often in literary studies essays were abstracted from their historical and philosophic contexts and turned into rather arcane and absolutist techniques for analyzing texts. Paradoxically, and simultaneously, postmodernist ideas were demonized by some cultural conservatives and liberal theorists. A caricatured and wildly over-empowered postmodernism served as a convenient site for the culture wars and as a target for all sorts of rage about potential shifts in power and social practices. Often the actual work of writers such as Foucault were and remain more gestured at than read. I have lost count of the times academics judge, say, Foucault's ideas about power by citing a few pages from *Discipline and Punish* while completely ignoring his far more complex later ideas. People seem to arrive at their take on something and once they feel they have got it, apparently no further thought is required. The interpretation is now canonical. While understandable as a labour saving device, this approach is likely to miss a lot of what writers who frequently change their ideas, such as Foucault, have to offer.

Perhaps in a hundred years a historian of ideas will rediscover all this activity around "postmodernism" and find it an amusing artifact of our dysfunctional hothouse academic culture. However, in present time, the stubborn and misinformed assertions about the anti-ethical practices of postmodernism are unfortunate. The work of Foucault in particular offers many resources to recognize and work with central ethical dilemmas of contemporary (self-defined) democracies. These include, as Janara puts it, "the psychodynamics of envy, desire and materialism" that are "native to democracy" (792),[2] and a dominant mode of subjectivity organized around "identity" and its entitlements. These dynamics are a consequence of a paradox intrinsic to democracy. As Danielle Allen points out, "democratic citizens are by definition empowered only to be disempowered. As a result, democratic citizenship requires rituals to manage the psychological tension that arises from being a nearly powerless sovereign" (41).[3] Disempowerment is pervasive in democracies because despite the promises of sovereignty and self-rule, often the law or public action will not conform to an individual's will. No citizen can participate in all public matters that affect their lives, achieve all their ends or win every conflict about a policy or resource distribution. Despite its importance in the founding narratives of modern democracies, the juridical subject (discussed further below) is a myth.

In the United States, racism, patriarchy, slavery and their lingering effects have enabled democratic citizenship to elide this paradox. Allen argues that for much of our history, citizenship was structured through relationships of dominance and acquiescence, not equality.[4] One effect of race and gender domination is that the sacrifices and disappointments endemic to self-rule are distributed unequally. Domination systematically skews the distribution of social goods in favor of the privileged and hence enables them to manage status anxiety and envy. The acquiescence of the disadvantaged perpetuates the illusion that the system is fair and its principles are pure. Another tactic employed to avoid the paradox is attempting to banish the diversity of wills altogether by positing a unitary subjectivity that properly practiced will express a uniform desire. Deviations are explained through a variety of narratives, from sin or heresy to lack of reason, false consciousness, inadequate identification with one's true group or perhaps foreign ethnicity or blood. Deviants must be corrected, contained, disenfranchised, expelled or destroyed for the public good.

Only when the disadvantaged insist on a more equitable distribution of social goods (including political recognition and respect) and a redistribution of sacrifice, is the democratic paradox more evident. However, even at such times, American citizens lack the practices, of subjectivity and political action, that would enable us to develop and sustain more egalitarian democratic politics. The habits of and supporting domination and acquiescence are deeply ingrained in the citizenry. They will not simply wither away; instead we require new practices of subjectivity and political action. The lingering race/gender disparities in distributions of social goods and esteem,[5] the structuring of our current institutional politics by a desperate search for someone bad whom we may legitimately dominate – terrorists, gays who want to marry, foreigners who will take our jobs or resources, those who threaten the (Christian) values founding the state, etc. – are all evidence of our collective inability to forswear old subjective and political habits and reconsider our practices.

Foucault's "Care of the Self"

Foucault provides valuable resources for the project of analyzing our attachments to these dysfunctional habits and imagining less oppressive ones. Through his ideas about "care of self," he intends both to induce scepticism regarding dominant narratives and to suggest alternatives. Foucault's rethinking of subjectivity, particularly as articulated in his essays on "care of the self," suggests a "practice" approach congruent with an orientation to action and ethics. His account of freedom moves outside the narrative of the juridical subject, and his emphasis on habits and practices and the ones he recommends suggest some modes of containing the malignant psychodynamics of democratic citizenship. In the disciplines of care of self, subjectivity is constituted through an ongoing set of practices oriented toward enabling us to act, to meet our obligations to our ethical commitments and to others. The orienting point is the ethical commitment, and one must learn and acquire as habits what must be done to approximate it. Taking on ethical commitments is itself a practice that must be learned and sustained. Care of the self entails developing habits that sustain such practices, including an engaged detachment and sceptical attachment to all of them. Acquisition of habits is never permanent, hence these processes are more like disciplines requiring constant practice than self-formation.

His approach differs from much of contemporary psychology and ethics. Foundational assumptions of prevailing paradigms of subjectivity include that intrinsic to humans is a self and that this self is the locus and cause of our identity. Further, it is assumed that each self possesses and is constituted by an essence or substance and that this essence is best understood in terms of interiority, that is, something that occupies and **is** us deep inside. To the extent that we actualize this essence and that it then governs our actions, we are free. Foucault's approach to subjectivity is so outside this paradigm that it is difficult to fully appreciate and make use of its radical departures and rich possibilities. It is easy to misunderstand what Foucault means by subjectification. Modernist narratives of the autonomous self create a binary: subject/object. If we are not self-generating subjects, then we are mere objects, utterly determined by our circumstances. In constructing a different discourse, Foucault rejects this binary and instead tracks its genealogy ("Sexuality" 177).

Foucault occupies neither of two positions dominant within existing discourses concerning the self; he is neither an essentialist nor a social constructionist. His concern is not with nurturing or developing an innate essence to which we must be true. Nor does he posit a fixed human nature to which our social arrangements must conform. Rather, he claims that the subject "is not a substance. It is a form, and this form is not primarily or always identical to itself" ("Ethics" 290). Unpacking this statement is neither simple nor easy. In making this claim, Foucault does not offer an alternative account of the self. Rather, as he rejects the idea that it is a substance amenable to more or less adequate accounts, he abandons the entire framework in which the issue is intelligible. Discourse shifts from investigations into the self's true nature to subjectivity. He refers to subjects, not persons, of processes of subjectification, not identity. Subjectivities are effects of historically contingent and specific practices; hence, analyzing them requires genealogies of their constituting practices. Subject connotes the double sense of actor and acted upon, not as separate aspects of our being, but as mutually constituting and contemporaneous processes. These processes simultaneously enable and constrain, empower and subjectify.

While his emphasis on socially situated practices might overlap with social constructionist ideas, Foucault pursues a radically different trajectory. He does not assume a coherent, stable inside is eventually constructed from social relations. Inside/outside is not a relevant binary in his discourse. Rather, for him, no one thing is being constructed; subjectivity is a dynamic process, more a complex network of often conflicting forces, demands and resistance with multiple lines and forms of explanation. For him, no privileged sites of subjective formation can be assumed, and the subject is neither a dependent effect of determinant causes or social relations nor an undetermined autonomous actor.

Furthermore, the locus of his investigations is different; he focuses neither on macro levels of social structures nor micro levels of individual subjects. Rather, Foucault "wished to study those forms of understanding which the subject creates about himself" ("Sexuality" 177). Such understandings are simultaneously forms of action. To grasp his notion of practice, we must side step the binaries of thought/action and structure (objective)/experience (subjective). Practices are forms of activity inhabited by thought. Thought is broadly conceived as "every manner of speaking, doing, or behaving in which the individual appears as a knowing subject, as ethical or juridical subject, as subject conscious of himself and others...thought is understood as...action insofar as it implies the play of true and false, the acceptance or refusal of rules, the relation to oneself and others" ("Preface" 201).

The Technologies of the Self: Agency as Practice

Contrary to frequent claims, Foucault does not deny agency, but rather relocates its sites of production. The historical contingency of subjective constitution has important political consequences; it means that practices of subjectivity are not fixed or immutable. While bounded and historically specific, our practices are neither invariant nor deterministic structures. As subjects practice the practices that constitute them, both subjects and practices mutate. They change, and hence new relations and practices of subjectivity (within and between subjects) are invented and practiced. Furthermore, over time Foucault's ideas about subjectivity, power and political action change and become increasingly complex. He says that "I have been obligated to change my mind on several points" ("Sexuality" 177). Central to this rethinking is his elaboration of practices he calls "technologies of the self." Technologies of the self, while related to and potentially shaped by biopower, are not its derivative effects. In exploring them, new possibilities of exercising freedom and creativity emerge.[6] It is puzzling to me that more scholars do not attend to this turn in Foucault's thinking. Contrary to a frequent criticism – that the only politics congruent with postmodernism is "identity politics" or nihilism – Foucault's later essays are powerful critiques of the foundational assumptions of such practices. Furthermore, they are both exemplars of and provide tools for practicing postmodernist ethics and politics, particularly, as I will describe below, a normative, "object centred" politics. I certainly do not mean to suggest that his writings are or ought to be immune from criticism. The absence within them of any sustained consideration of practices of raceing, gendering and postcoloniality is particularly unacceptable.[7] Nonetheless, despite its many imperfections, in the current conditions of global politics, avoidance or simplistic dismissal of Foucault's work is particularly unfortunate. The intimate and apparently necessary relations between domination, identity politics and violence are viciously evident. The need to resist claims framed in terms of pure identities and teleological destiny is palpable.[8]

In pursuing his investigation into forms of understanding, Foucault discovered a type of technique of which he was previously unaware: "techniques that permit individuals to effect, by their own means, a certain number of operations on their own bodies, their own souls, their own thoughts, their own conduct, and this in a manner so as to transform themselves, modify themselves, and to attain a certain state of perfection, happiness, purity, supernatural power" ("Sexuality" 177). He calls these "technologies of the self." Foucault insists that while technologies of the self interact with those of domination, they are not themselves technologies of domination. On the contrary, technologies of the self can be practices of freedom, creativity, aesthetics and ethics. Such freedom is not absolute or unaffected by its social context. Any self technology does imply "a set of truth obligations: discovering the truth, being enlightened by truth, telling the truth. All these are considered important either for the constitution of, or the transformation of, the self" ("Sexuality" 177-178). Furthermore, the available technologies of the self are "not something invented by the individual himself. They are models that he finds in his culture and are proposed, suggested, imposed upon him by his culture, his society, and his social group" ("Ethics" 291).

Relations of power are intrinsic to technologies of self, as they are to other forms of subjective constitution. However, Foucault does not equate practices of power with those of domination ("Ethics" 299). Power relations require freedom. For Foucault, power is relational. These relations exist only among practicing subjects. Power relations are "possible only insofar as the subjects are free" ("Ethics" 292). It is because there is freedom that relations of power exist. Subjects practicing a relation of power may not be equally situated, but each must have some degree of freedom. In power relations, subjects try to control or alter other's behaviours, and they resist other's efforts to control them. Such attempts would be unnecessary or impossible if others in one's social field were mere objects. In engaging in a practice, however, subjects encounter others who are likewise engaged. Since no practice is uniform, differences produce friction and resistance; subjects tend to insist on their own practices. Furthermore, since these relations exist in different forms and at different levels, any subject's situation will vary depending on the relations in which it is located. I might be quite advantaged in one relation and disadvantaged in another. Thus, resistance is intrinsic to power relations ("Sex, Power" 167); power relations are "strategic games that subject the power relations they are supposed to guarantee to instability and reversal" ("Preface" 203). Power relations are also mobile and mutating, so positions within them (and the positions available) can shift. In contrast, a state of domination exists when an "individual or social group succeeds in blocking a field of power relations, immobilizing them and preventing any reversibility of movement by economic, political, or military means" ("Ethics" 283). In practices of domination, the strategic options available within a power relation never succeed in reversing the relations among its practitioners. The power relations are fixed and extremely asymmetrical. It is a game whose rules ensure that only one party can win ("Ethics" 292).

Care of the Self: Practicing Freedom Ethically

Subjectification is vulnerable to colonization by many technologies including those of government or governmentality. Through techniques of governmentality, relations of domination are often established and maintained. Governmentality for Foucault is a variegated set of policing type practices exercised through both formal technical-rational networks and non-state surveillance activities. A consequence of this colonization is the displacement of other possible self-technologies. Foucault wishes to resist such colonization through juxtaposing resistant practices of subjectivity such as "care of the self." To articulate such technologies, he investigates texts by classical Greek and Roman writers. In my view what matters about this investigation is not whether it uncovers the truth or deep meaning of the texts. Foucault does not claim to excavate a pristine point where philosophy went astray or forgot something or to rediscover a principle that should have been our foundation all along. Contact with a philosopher does not revive the old, but can produce something new ("Ethics" 295). Rather, what is important is how Foucault imagines other practices of subjectivity via his encounter with the texts (Nehamas 157-188).

Foucault argues that in worlds of classical Greece and Rome care of the self was conceived as a task that one must engage in throughout life. It is an activity, not only a form of contemplation. Care of the self is not a preparation for living; it is a form of living ("Hermeneutic" 96). It is a kind of work with its own methods and objectives. In the modern world there has been "an inversion in the two principles of antiquity, 'Take care of yourself' and 'Know yourself.' In Greco-Roman culture, knowledge of oneself appeared as the consequence of the care of the self. In the modern world, knowledge of oneself constitutes the fundamental principle" ("Technologies" 228). Care of the self "was considered both a duty and a technique, a basic obligation and a set of carefully worked out procedures" ("Ethics" 295). It is also a creative and aesthetic practice in which innovation and consideration of beauty and pleasure are central. The point of this technology was to attempt to "develop and transform oneself, and to attain a certain mode of being" (Foucault 1997e, 282).

Furthermore, in the classical world, knowing oneself did not necessarily mean discovering the deep truth lying within. In some practices truth and the subject are not linked through "uncovering a truth in the subject or ...making the soul the place where truth resides, through an essential kinship or an original law, the truth; nor is it a matter of making the soul the object of a true discourse" ("Hermeneutic" 101-102). Rather knowing oneself required internalizing texts concerning how to care for oneself so that the substance of these teaching is literally incorporated and assimilated as one's own practice ("Hermeneutic" 101-102). Philosophy provides "soul service;" it is a therapeutic practice, dedicated to the care of the soul ("Hermeneutic" 94). It is less concerned with the question of under what conditions can the subject produce reliable truth and more about how subjects should live. Certain kinds of knowledge are necessary for living well, but such knowledge has multiple sources, many of which do not depend for their production or truth upon a purified foundational subject.

Care for the self is not a narcissistic or solitary practice. Relations with others are intrinsic to this mode of being, for care of oneself is understood as necessary for the proper exercise of citizenship and interpersonal relations. One is obligated to care for the self partially out of our duty to others. Extensive work on the self is required if one's practice of freedom is to take place within a way of being that is beautiful, honourable and worthy of praise ("Ethics" 286). If one does not practice the correct power over oneself, one cannot rule others well or be a good friend, relative, parent or spouse. A tyrant is one who is a slave to his desires and forces others to satisfy them. Furthermore, it is understood that carrying out this task requires an assortment of activities and resources, including relations with other persons, especially friends and teachers ("Hermeneutic" 99). Indeed, Foucault argues that practicing care of the self enabled a rich variety of relations (and hence subjective practices), particularly ones between adult males, for which there is no modern equivalent ("Hermeneutic" 99).

Politics and Ethics: Beyond the Juridical Subject

The political correlative of deep subjectivity is the juridical subject. Just as the subject is the foundation of knowledge in Cartesian epistemology, in modern liberal political theory the juridical subject founds and grounds the state. Juridical subjects exist prior to the state; their modes of subjectivization are not effects of governmentality or historically contingent technologies. They temporarily surrender some of their innate powers; the congealing of these powers in institutions of the subject's creation originates the state. Freedom exists as long as the law conforms to their inner being. Conformity to such law is simply obedience to their own reason or will. This genre of political theorizing is thus an identity theory writ large. Modern liberal political theories reflect and depend upon assumptions about their founding subject to account for the state's existence and legitimacy. These assumptions also provide the standards for normatively evaluating the state's laws and policies.

This political discourse logically gives rise to correlative practices: interest group and contemporary identity politics. The logic of the discourse requires its practitioners to define themselves as split subjects; they possess both a universal and a particular will or desire. Their desire takes the form of unitary "interests."[9] There is a sovereign abstract "I" that can identify and put forth claims based on these bounded interests; for example, as a mother I am interested in child care; as a patient, I am interested in health care. A group is an aggregate of sovereign individuals who share an interest. However, the subject cannot be merely an aggregate of its interests, because then it would lack the neutral substance necessary to ground the universal or articulate universally binding principles. Hence it must also possess an undetermined essence, and its capacity for autonomy and the ability to choose freely among its desires without being determined by them is rooted in and enabled by this substance. Thus the capacity for autonomy requires a deep, undetermined subjectivity. As a desiring subject, it possesses its "interests," but in its universal being, the subject is not possessed by them. No desire or historically contingent practice constitutes the true subjectivity of the chooser. Furthermore, not only are the subject's desires conceived as extrinsic to its true self, but the existence of these "interests" is treated as unproblematic social facts. Neither the conflict and relations of domination that may produce a felt interest nor the fluid and contradictory aspects of subjects and their practices are acknowledged. Subjects are rational individuals who know what is in their interest; these subjects and their interests are not heterogeneous, mutually determined, uncertain in effect or internally contradictory.

Similarly, contemporary identity politics also adopts a logic of a unitary deep inside. This deep inside is not abstract or universal in the sense of constituting every subject. Instead, it is homogeneous and concretely universal. That is, it is a uniform essence constituting a specific class of subjects. This essence grounds a unique subjectivity and generates its difference from all other subjects. Identity politics requires its practitioners to constitute their being through a particular but definitive quality – sexuality, gender, or race, for example. There is a universal and discoverable truth of this being. Individual subjects speak its truth, and this truth warrants the legitimacy of their claims.

The truth also serves as the basis for normative evaluation and ethical practices. So, for example, one can be held accountable for not being "black enough" – that is, deviating from the prescriptive practices constituting black subjectivity. In discovering this truth and conforming to it, subjects liberate themselves and institute the possibility of freedom.

Object Centred Politics and Technologies of the Self

For me a crucial payoff of Foucault's approach to subjectivity is that it facilitates a parallel shift I have been attempting in the fields of politics and justice. While some are highly critical (for example, Nussbaum[10]), other writers, including Bauman, Brown, Coles, and Honig[11] are pursuing a similar trajectory. This shift entails reconceiving the problems and practices of democratic politics through an object rather than subject oriented focus. In other words, inquiry and activity center not around questions of identity (who are we and what do we require to be or remain us) but action (what has or could be done and what are their consequences). Arguments for and justification of actions require consideration of their qualities and effects as processes and accounts of their (always imperfectly known and unpredictable) outcomes. Criteria for evaluation might include aesthetic or hedonistic ones or whether actions potentially enlarge or constrain the range of available practices and practitioners, but ontological or teleological claims about fostering development of an individual or collective deep inside would be irrelevant. Shifting the practices of democratic politics in this way might generate new capacities for an engaged detachment among our citizens. In turn this could facilitate the work of mourning as we collectively consider our current practices and what we could do otherwise. My ideas are tentative and need a lot of work, but for both political and theoretical reasons, I think this approach is worth pursuing.

In my view subject centred politics – whether of abstract or concrete identities – are deeply flawed, and, as can all too readily be seen in the contemporary world, extremely dangerous. Resisting domination or inventing more just political practices cannot remain contingent on identity, that is, on the subject finding its Truth and seeking to bring itself and the world into conformity with it. This applies equally to subjects in subordinate or dominant positions. The virtue of the subject also cannot depend on its Truth, and its virtue cannot be the basis for stipulating equality of treatment or respect. Subject centred politics remain within the problematic genre of (auto-) biography; they rest on a nostalgia for a singular "subject of history." They articulate a yearning for a purposive history in which time is the unfolding of this subject's biography. A desire for a guaranteed happy ending motivates them; however variably it may be specified, whether it is to bring freedom into the world, unfold its innate capacities, serve God's will, die a martyr, etc., the subject's redemptive fate is preordained. However, I remain unconvinced such a subject or fate exists. Although advocates of various possibilities abound, no decisive argument has persuasively identified a single, unitary Truth of our being – reason, victimization, human capacities, religion, etc. – that can unproblematically ground claims to justice or engender ethical practices. I have not been dissuaded from reading these eschatological stories as expressing the fantasies and dreams of situated, complex subjectivities.

Furthermore, identity based practices lend themselves too readily to practices of domination/acquiescence, irresponsibility, violence, annihilation of the "other," and terrorism. They launch us into investigations of the worth and character of the subject as measured by preordained standard and a search for the commonalities of a subject position that is simultaneously a disciplining of its objects into conformity. Its subjects must be uniform, unworldly, and pure. As the bearer of the redemptive possibilities for humankind, they cannot simultaneously be generators of and invested in relations of domination or even strategic participants in power games. The resistant leakage of inter- and intrasubjective heterogeneity and imperfection provokes predictable responses – nihilism, terrorism and totalitarianism. The nihilist develops a protective cynicism and detachment. In contrast to purity all is corrupt, and thus we are responsible for nothing. The terrorist or totalitarian refuses to accept the impossibility of purity and assigns the sources of imperfection to others. For the greater good, vast force is justified to eradicate the polluting ones. Death, even random murder, is justified in the name of the good.

Developing "object centred" political strategies offers new political possibilities. Objects include modes of pleasure, ways of life, discrete political acts, new power relations, public spaces of all sorts, and ethical commitments as well as material resources. Complex attachments to particular objects and practices replace subject centred theories and practices. Instead of depending on a unitary or redemptive subject as the agent of change, we can develop practices of politics based on a mutual desire for particular objects or outcomes, for example, reducing or resisting domination in a specific social field. Diversity does not preclude a mutual attachment to particular objects. A powerful motivation for political activity is attachment by highly diverse constellations of subjectivities to a particular object. Their basis of attachment to a common object need not be uniform. However, an attachment to a particular object renders coalitions both possible and necessary. These attachments will unfold and gather force in ways we cannot predict, generating, perhaps, new desires and relations of solidarity and opposition.

Acknowledging that there is no place outside power relations and historical practices need not lead to nihilism or indifferent amorality. Since there is no guaranteed good or neutral outside available, we have to make the best of, resist, or reinvent the historical practices constituting us.[12] While such politics is not utopian, it is concerned with generating new practices within the worlds constituting subjects in present time. Its goal is not to reform the given, but to unmask its contingency thereby opening up spaces to imagine new power games or to play existing ones differently. Freedom exists not in a return to or reconciliation with our pure, undetermined essence, but in the capacity to participate in power relations and their accessibility to us. In its focus on action and responsibility, this approach overlaps with Hannah Arendt's[13] emphasis on action, but it rejects her contempt for "the social"[14] and her notion of action as heroic, natal performance. Action includes and requires practicing the mundane habits and nurturing the social relations that sustain our capacities and desire for acting. Since our desires and heterogeneous practices are us, we cannot escape them. Deploying our multiplicity is a requirement for, not an impediment to, acting justly. We cannot articulate any useful principles or practices of justice without or outside the practices heterogeneous networks generate. Only intense engagement, not a Rawlsian veil of ignorance or a disembodied Arendtian arete, can engender reflection upon or resistance to their effects.

How do we foster such politics? Technologies of the self, particularly in the form of care for the self, are an important element. The care of the self can engender an attachment to practicing subjectivity such that ways of life are multiplied and endlessly reinvented. Innovation and creativity requires more than tolerance or a commitment to diversity or inclusivity; for such practices can actually serve to simply validate the ways of life in which the subject is already engaged. For example, following Habermas (188-299), we could advocate protecting the efficacy of rational discourse and the autonomy of public space and ensuring a broader range of participants within them. However, this approach leaves undisturbed important assumptions including the privilege of reason and speech, rather than a multiplicity of practices including aesthetic ones, as the means of arriving at public goods.

Adherence to mere tolerance can permit subjects a passive attitude toward other ways of life; we can treat them as irrelevantly exotic though valid for others. Instead, no longer able to assume even a purely subjective truth lies accessible within, care of the self requires perpetual tutoring by and engagement with others. We must actively seek them out, imaginatively take up alternatives and consider our own from foreign viewpoints. Others might attain a kind of knowledge of us, engage in a generative self technology or be attached to a good to which we, immersed in our own practices are blind. Such experimental practices are self-reinforcing, for the more possibilities we actively engage, the more we unsettle the illusion of identity and recognize the consequences of routinely privileging a particular range of commitments.

Thus, contrary to many critics of postmodernism, its necessary ethical correlative is not an anything goes relativism.[15] While we lack recourse to any neutral trump to resolve conflict or a transcendental justification for our actions or chosen ways of life, it does not follow that we are no longer committed to them, obligated to their ethical stipulations or responsible for their consequences. Innocence is ruled out. Part of what each subject realizes in interacting with others is how we are differently affected by determining social relations. We discover that most subjects occupy several places at once – we resist, impose, enjoy and suffer from different kinds of power. While such unevenness is unlikely to disappear, a commitment to multiplying ways of life can also engender investment in playing games of power that minimize domination. Uniformity becomes suspect; it could be a symptom of domination, of a frozen power game that one is obligated to resist whatever one's position might be within it.

To foster a suspicion of uniformity and an appreciation of conflict does require a certain kind of subjective knowledge and a capacity for engaged detachment. In recommending a particular sort of detachment and recognizing the ongoing practices upon which it depends, Foucault and Freud[16] overlap. Rational thought is not a sufficient or unproblematic way to attain such knowledge and detachment. We can use our reason to rationalize, to obscure passions motivating a seemingly rational choice. The capacity for detachment rests on the subject's recognition of its own historical contingency, not a presumption of universality. Paradoxically, the more we acknowledge the contingency of our desires, the less we are determined by any one of them. Immersion, not abstraction, allows us to be more objective. We juxtapose one desire against another and realize our own internal instability. In acknowledging contingency, we also recognize that our desires and practices could be otherwise. If they could be otherwise, other practices are equally possible. Recognizing our will, we must take responsibility for such choices while acknowledging that other moves are plausible. While not vitiating our loyalty, our commitments will appear as choices whose continuance depends on our willingness to keep choosing them and their consequences and on our location within networks that generate and render them intelligible.

This engaged detachment is necessary for ethical behaviour. Foucault defines ethics as the "considered form that freedom takes when it is informed by reflection" ("Ethics" 284). Reflection, however, is a practice. It is neither an innate capacity nor the effect of an autonomous pure reason. Like any practice, it requires the appropriate technologies and power relations. Like any practice, it must be endlessly renewed and taken up. The capacity for reflection depends upon the continual confrontation among subjects and public spaces which both require and nurture such interaction. Instead of a search for consensus, such interaction intentionally seeks disjunctions. Agreement will not necessary result from such interaction, nor is it the governing purpose. When genuine understanding is reached, unresolvable conflict will result as frequently as empathy, reflective equilibrium, or an ideal speech community. Reflection and communication cannot dissolve the diversity of subjective practices and meaning systems. Hence power games are intrinsic to freedom. Ethical politics cannot promise transparent communication or Habermas's universal pragmatics. However, subjects attempting to practice them continually struggle with how "to acquire the rules of law, the management techniques, and also the morality, the ethos, the practice of the self, that will allow us to play these games of power with as little domination as possible" ("Ethics" 298).

However, practitioners of richer technologies of the self cannot serve as ground or guarantee of emancipatory action; such subjectivities are not simply replacements for unitary ones. Reflexivity cannot perfectly control the other practices of subjectivity and is itself pervaded by them. Subjects may act on hate as readily as empathy. Even concern for the other is not pure; it is animated in part by narcissistic fantasies, including those of one's own reparative powers and will to power, that inevitably encroach on that we wish to respect and preserve (Coles 497-498). Hopes for more fit modes of ruling rest in what democratic citizens might learn to desire or resist desiring, our mutual care for multiple public spaces (Honig 115-112), the openness of power games and the practices sustaining them. Contrary to Rousseau, what freedom we might enjoy does not depend on willing the general, but on taking responsibility for practices arising within very particular, context specific locations, including domination/acquiescence social relations, and ensuring the presence of other empowered subjects. We have to accept that ethical practices of democratic citizenship require and reflect the willing by unstable subjects in concert with others, equally tenuously situated, of imperfect and uncertain alternatives. This acceptance requires the availability of practices, public spaces, and subjective technologies Foucault anticipates but we must endlessly reinvent.

NOTES

[1] See Flax "Taking Multiplicity Seriously" and "On Encountering Incomensurability"; see also Bauman's *Life in Fragments* and Flathman's *Freedom and its Conditions.*

[2] See also de Tocqueville's *Democracy in America.*

[3] See also Honig's *Democracy and the Foreigner.*

---

⁴ See also Flax *The American Dream in Black and White* and "'Monster's Ball,'" Glenn's *Unequal Freedom,* Holland's *The Body Politic,* Mills's *The Racial Contract,* Olson's *The Abolition of White Democracy, and* Shklar's *American Citizenship.*

⁵ See Hero's "Social Capital and Racial Inequality in America," Loury's *The Anatomy of Racial Inequality,* and Williams's *The Constraint of Race.*

⁶ See Nehamas's *The Art of Living* and Veyne's "The Final Foucault and His Ethics."

⁷ See Stoler's *Race and the Education of Desire.*

⁸ See Gilroy's "Against Race."

⁹ See Hirschman's *The Passions and the Interests.*

¹⁰ See for example Nussbaum's "In Defense of Universal Values"

¹¹ See Brown's *Politics Out of History,* Bauman's *Life in Fragments,* Coles' "Traditio," and Honig's *Political Theory and the Displacement of Politics* and *Democracy and the Foreigner.*

¹² See Flathman's *Freedom and its Conditions.*

¹³ See Arendt's *The Human Condition, 2ⁿᵈ ed.*

¹⁴ See Pitkin's *The Attack of the Blob.*

¹⁵ See Retallack's *The Poethical Wager* for a wonderfully elegant illustration of this point, and also Bauman's *Life in Fragments.*

¹⁶ See Freud's "Analysis Terminable and Interminable."

Works Cited

Allen, Danielle S. *Talking to Strangers: Anxieties of Citizenship since Brown v. Board of Education*. Chicago: U of Chicago P, 2004.

Arendt, Hannah. *The Human Condition, 2ⁿᵈ ed*. Chicago: U of Chicago P, 1998.

Bauman, Zygmunt. *Life in Fragments: Essays in Postmodern Morality*. Cambridge, MA: Blackwell, 1995.

Brown, Wendy. *Politics Out of History*. Princeton: Princeton UP, 2001.

Coles, Roman. "Traditio: Feminists of Color and the Torn Virtues of Democratic Engagement." *Political Theory* 29.4 (2001): 488-516.

de Tocqueville, Alexis. *Democracy in America*. Ed. Harvey Mansfield and Delba Winthrop. Chicago: U of Chicago P, 2000.

Flathman, Richard E. *Freedom and its Conditions: Discipline, Autonomy and Resistance*. New York: Routledge, 2003.

Flax, Jane. "Taking Multiplicity Seriously: Some Consequences for Psychoanalytic Theorizing and Practice." *Contemporary Psychoanalysis* 32.4 (1996): 577-594.

—. *The American Dream in Black and White*. Ithaca, NY: Cornell University Press, 1998.

—. "On Encountering Incommensurability: Martha Nussbaum's Aristotelian Practice." *Controversies in Feminism*. Ed. James P. Sterba. Lanham, MD: Rowman & Littlefield, 2001. 25-45.

—. "'Monster's Ball': Representations of Race and Gender in the Contemporary United States." *Black Renaissance/Renaissance Noir* 5.1 (2003): 57-68.

Foucault, Michel. "Preface to *The History of Sexuality, Volume Two*." Rabinow 199-205.

—. "Sex, Power and the Politics of Identity." Rabinow 163-173.

—. "Sexuality and Solitude." Rabinow 175-184.

—. "Technologies of the Self." Rabinow 223-251.

—. "The Ethics of the Concern for the Self as a Practice of Freedom." Rabinow 281-301.

—. "The Hermeneutic of the Subject." Rabinow 93-106.

Freud, Sigmund. "Analysis Terminable and Interminable." 1937. *Sigmund Freud: Collected Papers v. 5*. Ed. James Strachey. New York: Basic Books, 1959. 316-357.

Gilroy, Paul. *Against Race: Imagining Political Color Beyond the Color Line*. Cambridge: Harvard UP, 2000.

Glenn, Evelyn Nakano. *Unequal Freedom: How Race and Gender Shaped American Citizenship and Labor*. Cambridge: Harvard UP, 2002.

Habermas, Jürgen. *Jürgen Habermas on Society and Politics: A Reader*. Ed. Steven Seidman. Boston: Beacon, 1989.

Hero, Rodney E. "Social Capital and Racial Inequality in America." *Perspectives on Politics* 1.1 (2003): 113-122.

Hirschman, Albert O. *The Passions and the Interests: Political Arguments for Capitalism before Its Triumph*. Princeton: Princeton UP, 1997.

Holland, Catherine A. *The Body Politic: Foundings, Citizenship and Difference in the American Political Imagination*. New York: Routledge, 2001.

Honig, Bonnie. *Political Theory and the Displacement of Politics*. Ithaca: Cornell UP, 1993.

—. *Democracy and the Foreigner*. Princeton: Princeton UP, 2001.

Janara, Laura. "Brothers and Others: Tocqueville and Beaumont, U.S. Genealogy, Democracy, and Racism. *Political Theory* 32.6 (2004): 773-800.

Loury, Glenn C. *The Anatomy of Racial Inequality*. Cambridge: Harvard UP, 2002.

Mills, Charles W. *The Racial Contract*. Ithaca: Cornell UP, 1997.

Nehamas, Alexander. *The Art of Living: Socratic Reflections from Plato to Foucault*. Berkeley: U of California P, 1998.

Nussbaum, Martha. "In Defense of Universal Values." *Controversies in Feminism*. Ed. James P. Sterba. Lanham, MD: Rowman & Littlefield, 2001. 3-23.

Olson, Joel. *The Abolition of White Democracy*. Minneapolis: U of Minnesota P, 2004.

Pitkin, Hanna Fenichel. *The Attack of the Blob: Hannah Arendt's Concept of the Social*. Chicago: U of Chicago P, 1998.

Rabinow, Paul, ed. *Michel Foucault: Ethics, Subjectivity and Truth*. New York: The New Press, 1997.

Retallack, Joan. *The Poethical Wager*. Berkeley: U of California P, 2003.

Shklar, Judith N. *American Citizenship: The Quest for Inclusion*. Cambridge: Harvard UP, 1991.

Stoler, Ann Laura. *Race and the Education of Desire*. Durham, NC: Duke UP, 1997.

Veyne, Paul. "The Final Foucault and His Ethics." *Foucault and His Interlocutors*. Ed. Arnold I. Davidson. Chicago: U of Chicago P, 1997. 225-33.

Williams, Linda Faye. *The Constraint of Race: Legacies of White Skin Privilege in America*. University Park: The Pennsylvania State UP, 2003.

Other References

Rawls, John. *A Theory of Justice*. Cambridge: Harvard UP, 1971.

—. *Political Liberalism*. New York: Columbia UP, 1993.

—. *Justice as Fairness: A Restatement*. Cambridge: Harvard UP, 2001.

Wolin, Sheldon. 'The Liberal/Democratic Divide: On Rawls's *Political Liberalism*." *Political Theory* 24.1 (1996): 97-119.

Žižek, Slavoj. "Fantasy as a Political Category: A Lacanian Approach." *The Zizek Reader*. Ed. Elizabeth Wright and Edmond Wright. Cambridge, MA: Blackwell, 1999. 87-101.

Žižek, Slavoj, "Enjoy Your Nation as Yourself." *Theories of Race and Racism: A Reader*. Ed. Les Back and John Solomos. New York: Routledge, 2000. 594-606.

6

Mood Swings:
The Aesthetics of Ambient Emergence

N. Katherine Hayles & Todd Gannon

On or about August 1995, postmodernism died. Or at least one version did – the one characterized by shock, disorientation, and hyperbole at the meteoric rise of the information age. The demise was heralded by the IPO of Netscape, the first commercial Web browser to be both robust and user-friendly. As the World Wide Web exploded at exponential rates, experiences of virtuality ceased to be confined to high-tech research laboratories funded by military grants and became part of everyday life in developed regions across the globe, including North America, Japan, Europe, and India, among others. Fredric Jameson's idea that space, mirroring the inconceivable complexities of the infosphere, had become fractally complex was not so much proved wrong as displaced by the increasingly banal activity of surfing the web;[1] Jean-François Lyotard's assertion that the contemporary period is marked by an "incredulity towards metanarratives" was absorbed into the cultural mainstream, only to come smack against a return to fundamentalism and simplistic global explanations emanating alike from evangelical Christians and Islamic extremists (xxiv); Jean Baudrillard's titillating suggestion that reality had "imploded" into hyperreality ceased to function as a transgressive theoretical conceit, displaced by the everydayness of navigating virtual spaces that somehow left no one in doubt reality was as "real" as ever.[2] With late capitalism showing no signs of giving way to a successor regime, the adjective began to appear less like a description and more like wishful thinking. As Bruno Latour already observed a couple of years ago, critique as it was practiced in the heyday of high theory, epitomized by the difficult productive obscurities of deconstructive rhetoric, has seemed to have run out of steam, with current practitioners sounding more nostalgic than cutting-edge.[3]

The shift from one period to another, or as Raymond Wiliams put it, one structure of feeling to another, is signalled less by successful solutions than by changing foci of attention. The problems the previous era found compelling have not so much been solved as they have ceased to be interesting. The new sensibility can aptly be characterized as a change of feeling, a shift in the mode of address, a new focus of attention. Let us call it a mood swing.[4] We are less interested in coining a clever new term to denote it than in describing its characteristics. Our target areas to assess its manifestations are literature and architecture, fields in which the two of us respectively have major investments. One of us is a literary critic with significant interdisciplinary interests, and the other a practicing architect and student of architectural and cultural theory. The two fields in which we count ourselves among the stakeholders have more in common than may at first appear. Literary studies was one of the major vectors through which postmodernism and deconstruction entered the North American scene, and architecture was foremost among the applied fields in which interpretations of deconstruction reached material instantiation.

Postmodernism in architecture was inaugurated when Charles Jencks declared the end of modern architecture to be July 15, 1972, 3:32pm, the moment Minoru Yamasaki's Pruitt-Igoe housing project (1952-55) was imploded. Standing for less than twenty years, the work symbolized for Jencks all that was wrong with the architecture of the modern period: sterile, inhumane, anonymous, and most importantly for Jencks, insufficiently equipped legibly to transmit information. Jencks brought the term postmodernism into architectural parlance and became its most enthusiastic proponent, with the many editions of his *Language of Post-Modern Architecture* functioning as a serialized chronicle of the movement. Borrowing from the semiotics of Umberto Eco, Jencks championed an architecture of legible, multivalent meaning. From this point on, the practice of "reading" buildings, shorthand for the rigorous interpretation of architectural configuration previously practiced in a few vanguard institutions, became commonplace in architectural schools around the globe. Following Jencks and borrowing heavily from critical theory in other disciplines, intellectual architects devised robust techniques for writing cultural critique in architectural form. During the same period, Peter Eisenman drove advanced architecture further into a linguistic frame of mind. Influenced by the writings of Saussure, Chomsky, and later Derrida, Eisenman introduced a difficult indexicality to the cutting edge of architecture that paralleled deconstructive rhetoric in literary studies. Simultaneously, architectural publications mushroomed in number and intensity, as practicing architects and critics alike produced project monographs, critical essays, and theoretical texts at an unprecedented rate. By 2000, however, the major vehicles of critical writing in architecture launched during the period – *Assemblage*, *Oppositions*, and *ANY* – were all defunct.

Like contemporary literary studies, architecture has turned away from postmodernism and ventured into new structures of feeling. A broad set of thematics, perhaps more readily apparent at the intersections of literature and architecture than in either field alone, characterizes the shift. In both disciplines, we see a renewed emphasis on the materiality of surfaces, an effect closely related, we will argue, to the deep penetration of digital technologies into the practices of architecture and the conditions of production for contemporary electronic and print literature. Entwined with this attention to the materiality of surfaces is intermediation, a term that implies both mediation and intervention. As we use the term, it refers to the complex dynamics between old and new media, specifically digital and print media. As computers penetrate and inform everyday practices in virtually all areas of society and culture, performance acquires a more active role in the production of texts as well as buildings than was previously the case with print media, creating possibilities for dynamic physical and textual environments that change in response to user intervention and real-time data flows. The increased flexibility that digital technologies allow in creating ambient effects has also led to experiments in the limits of legibility for literature, and for architecture, a turn away from the tendency to "read" structures to an emphasis on the changing environmental inflections of ambient surfaces, along with renewed interest in the relation of architecture and affect. Enhancing the power and flexibility of design practices in literature and architecture, digital media have also reinforced and extended the ways in which human intelligence is enfolded together with machine cognition. This entwining has been accompanied by a sharper, deeper realization that agency is distributed across an entire complex system that contains both human and nonhuman actors, so that compositional practices for both literature and architecture are now, more than ever, not simply the enactment of pre-existing ideas but rather fluid transformative processes influenced both by the capabilities of intelligent machines and the creative intuitions and rational plans of human participants.

In richly diverse ways, then, these emphases connect with the spread of networked and programmable media. To rehearse only a few of the factors at work, we note that in architecture, computers have all but replaced the drawing board; 3D modeling, digital fabrication, and cinematic pre-visualizations are commonplace.[5] As Michael Speaks has pointed out, significant design theorization now takes place through the processes of design as well as fabrication, so that computation pervades architectural thinking on preconscious as well as conscious levels.[6] In literary studies, the advent of electronic literature as a significant component of the twenty-first century canon has transformed reading and writing practices, introducing strong performative aspects and expanding the sensory range of texts not only into visual but also into kinesthetic, haptic, and proprioceptive realms. Moreover, even print texts have been transformed as contemporary printing technologies incorporate computers and digitally-driven machines into every aspect of the design, production, and marketing of books. As a result, the legacy systems of speech and writing now dynamically interact with code as a language system addressed both to humans and intelligent machines, a situation that manifests itself in transformations of linguistic surfaces in both print and digital literature.

Just as postmodernism as an aesthetic did not emerge in isolation but rather as part of a constellation of forces that converged as the economy shifted from an industrial Fordist regime to what David Harvey has called the postmodern "regime of accumulation," so the mood shift we trace has complex connections with the emergence of network culture and what Manuel Castells has called "informationalism."[7] After delineating the characteristics of the shift, we will return briefly to discuss this entanglement. Let us turn now to a detailed exposition of materiality and intermediation, with glances at the other factors involved. In the analysis that follows, our two voices will together weave the story of the mood swing toward what we call the aesthetics of ambient emergence.

Materiality in Architecture: "Light Construction"

In September 1995, swift on the heels of Netscape's launch, the Museum of Modern Art in New York opened "Light Construction," an international survey of projects that marked what curator Terence Riley dubbed a "shift in sensibility." [8] As he states in the exhibition catalogue, this new sensibility "not only reflects the distance of our culture from the machine aesthetic of the early twentieth century but marks a fundamental shift in emphasis after three decades when debate in architecture focused on issues of form. In projects notable for artistic and technical innovation, contemporary designers are investigating the nature and potential of architectural surfaces" (9).

An important ingredient in this new sensibility was a keen attention to material effects, chiefly to those produced by glass. Though a key material in the theoretical conceptions of Modernism, glass as "Light Construction" saw it had less to do with the idealized transparency espoused in the early 20th century than with an array of materially contingent reflections, obscurities, opacities, and translucencies.[9] These effects, difficult to discern in traditional architectural representations, are not a function of architecture's abstract configuration but rather emerge from the interplay of that configuration with its brute physicality. Turning the tables on half a century of formalist compositional criticism, "Light Construction" celebrated the visual noise produced by fleeting reflections on glass surfaces, that troublesome feedback disdained in the work of Walter Gropius and ignored in the work of Le Corbusier by Colin Rowe and Robert Slutzky in their famous analysis of the former's Bauhaus in Dessau and the latter's Villa Stein at Garches.[10] The exhibition's attention to materiality highlighted the shortcomings of formalist interpretations that bracket individual works as autonomous objects and pointed to the necessity of considering the complex dynamics between architectural form, its specific material instantiation, and the particularities of its environmental context.

"Light Construction" traced a shift in attention away from projects such as Peter Eisenman's DAAP in Cincinnati to projects like Herzog and deMeuron's Signal Box auf dem Wolf in Basel (figs. 1-4). From his early work in the 1970s to the present, Eisenman has drawn extensively on literary and linguistic theory, even collaborating with

Figure 1: Peter Eisenman, *Aronoff Center for Design and Art*, Cincinnati, Ohio, 1996. View at entry.

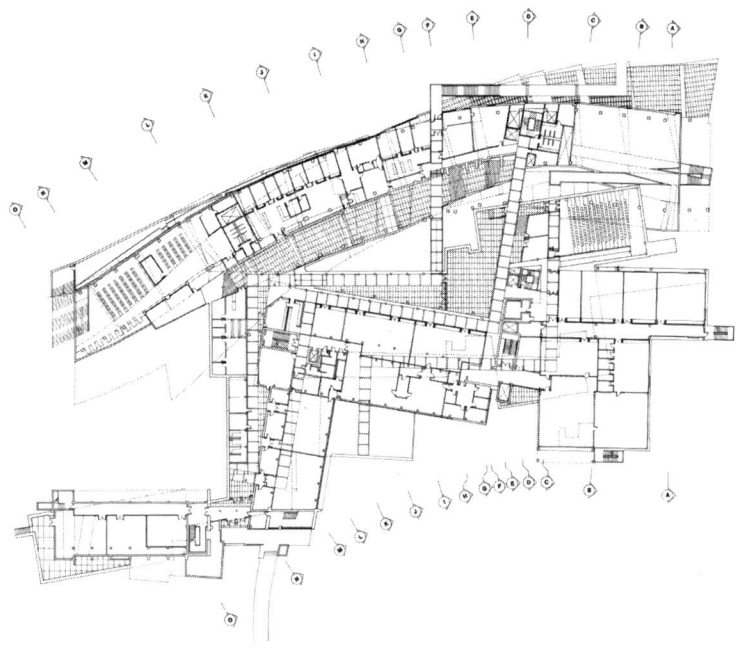

Figure 2: Peter Eisenman, *Aronoff Center for Design and Art*, Cincinnati, Ohio, 1996. Second level plan.

Figure 3: Herzog and deMeuron, *Signal Box Auf dem Wolf*, Basel, Switzerland, 1995. General view.

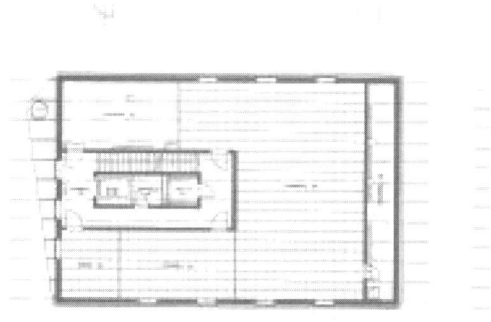

Figure 4: Herzog and deMeuron, *Signal Box Auf dem Wolf*, Basel, Switzerland, 1995. Second level plan.

Jacques Derrida on a design for the Parc de la Villette in Paris.[11] Throughout Eisenman's oeuvre, these theoretical influences are developed through relentless elaboration of architectural representations such as floor plans and sections as well as more abstract configurational diagrams. Like many practitioners through the 1970s, poor economic conditions offered Eisenman few opportunities to build his radical ideas, and the majority of his projects of the period remain unbuilt, their lasting influence a function of the extensive publication of his elaborate drawings and models. The few built projects of the 1970s, like the DAAP in Cincinnati and much of his later work, tend to be clad in cheap, neutral materials that primarily operate as notational signifiers. Of primary importance is the ability to read individual compositional components (signalled in Cincinnati by variously coloured EIFS, an inexpensive synthetic plaster[12]) as legible signs affiliated with one or another formal system. For Eisenman, drawings, texts, and completed buildings carried equal weight within the overall architectural project.

Herzog and deMeuron, on the other hand, eschewed overt theoretical references, complex plans, and fragmentary geometries, advancing instead simple cubic volumes clad in seductive skins of copper, patterned glass, natural stone, and other exquisite materials. HdM's floor plans, distilled to minimal, expedient solutions of functional needs, offer little formal interest. For the buildings' complexity, one must turn away from these abstract representations of the building form to the material instantiation of the building surface. In the Basel Signal Boxes, simple Cartesian volumes are uniformly clad in continuous copper bands. In certain areas, these bands are subtly twisted to reveal faint hints of mysterious windows beyond. Whereas Eisenman's complex assemblage of overlapping grids and layered geometries produce multivalent formal relationships, each compositional element is delineated as materially unequivocal and distinct. HdM in contrast treats the entire building as a single entity and employs material and lighting effects to modulate the illusion of depth across a continuous surface. In short, Eisenman suppressed materiality to underscore formal effects, while HdM suppressed form to foreground materiality.

This comparison of a programmatically complex architecture school and an effectively uninhabited container of electrical switching equipment is perhaps a bit unfair. Both practices represent extreme cases of their respective ambitions, and in the ten years since the exhibition, the work of Eisenman and HdM has approached each other in many ways, with the former experimenting much more aggressively with material effects and the latter producing increasingly complex formal configurations. But the contrast between these two seminal works of the 1990s, particularly the role of representational drawings and theoretical content in each, clearly illustrates some of the telltale symptoms of the mood swing that swept through the discipline in the 1990s.

Though "Light Construction" championed a formal pluralism and included an array of diversely configured projects, Riley's show at the Museum of Modern Art was often characterized as dismissing "blobs," projects that explored increasingly complex geometries, in favour of "boxes," projects in which formal configuration took a back seat to material and perceptual concerns (Riley 437). Structured as such, the debate was confined to purely formal terms and missed the broader implications of the exhibited works' renewed attention to materiality. The exhibition paralleled the rise of computers in the design studio; as programs became more robust and practitioners more facile, the formal debate between blobs and boxes was not so much decided as rendered irrelevant. To a computer, a blob and a box are fundamentally identical –each reducible to a distribution of a fixed number of pixels on a screen, and each described by equally complex program algorithms, binary codes, and fluctuating voltages.[13]

Whether aligned more closely to the configurationally complex "blobs" or to the geometrically restrained "boxes," practitioners of all stripes, spurred on by the computational horsepower of the computer, tended toward increased attention to material effects. Digital technologies allowed an expanded ability to measure and draw complex configurations, while structural forces in even maddeningly complex forms could be accurately calculated. With CAD/CAM technology,[14] these intricate shapes, at first confined to the virtual space of digital representation, have become increasingly cost effective to fabricate. In addition, powerful rendering packages allowed for the economical and realistic study of materials and lighting effects in the virtual space of the computer. These convincing simulations enabled increasingly subtle studies of material effects on even the simplest forms. Material conditions that previously could be represented only through painstaking and often prohibitively expensive analogue techniques were now easily produced and effortlessly manipulated. Combined with the robust economy of the dot com boom, these technologies produced the ability to move the paper experiments of the 70s and 80s into the physical world, and the profits these technologies generated launched a generation of clients and patrons eager to underwrite an avant-garde architecture of the information age.

Literary/Literal Materiality

For literature, the emphasis on materiality in the 1990s and beyond has been catalysed by the deep penetration of digital technologies into literary arenas. For electronic literature, materiality implies exploring the medium through which the works are created and performed; for print literature, a complex recursive dynamic has emerged in which the centuries-old print tradition becomes entwined with the new capabilities for print afforded by digital technologies in the composition, typesetting, and production of books. Moreover, since print and electronic texts are in continuous conversation with each other, second-order effects (i.e., effects in which the changes in one medium stimulate related changes in another) further complicate and enrich explorations of materiality in both print and electronic media.

Since literature is, unlike architecture, primarily a semiotic practice, a definition of materiality applicable to this context is in order. Materiality should not be confused with physicality. Whereas the physical aspects of any object are potentially infinite and neutral in themselves, materiality is intimately bound up with the quest for meaning. (As Jerome McGann has eloquently pointed out, meaning is not something that literary texts produce but rather the thing for which they search (111).) To emphasize the distinction between physicality and materiality, we have elsewhere defined materiality as those physical aspects mobilized by a work's signifying strategies to create meaning (Hayles, *My Mother* 103). The definition implies materiality is not pre-given and cannot be specified in advance; rather, it is an emergent property, subject to debates about whether a given physical characteristic is or is not important to a work's meaning. One of the distinctive characteristics that digital media have introduced into the production of literary texts is the use of code to generate the screen's flickering signifiers. Increasingly, writers who work in networked and programmable media insist that their work should be understood to consist not only of the screenic display but also the underlying code, and as Loss Pequeño Glazier among others has noted, writers in digital media are creating a wide variety of strategies to ensure their works cannot be fully understood without taking the code into account.[15] The strategies evident in print texts are more indirect, but there too interactions between the linguistic surface of the printed page and the code that produced it are mobilized to create a variety of material effects.

John Cayley's work exemplifies the mood swing in which information technology is engaged not for its shock value but for its penetration into cultural arenas, especially poetics and aesthetic theory. Cayley practices what he calls "literal art," a phrase that punningly invokes letters as well as the materiality of writing surfaces.[16] He creates works that explore the analogy between the discreteness of alphabetic language (where 26 elements can be combined into an infinitude of different words) and binary code. Because both letters and code are discrete rather than continuous, they share a pragmatics and aesthetics of fragmentation and recombination. Cayley's practice emphasizes the complexity of writing surfaces, particularly their construction as sites for negotiation between linguistic texts and the computer algorithms generating them. [17]

He points to this interpenetration with a key question: "Is the display really a monitor of the programmaton's symbolic processing, or is it a window on computing's attempts to match and then exceed... the illusionistic simulations of film and television?" (LENS 6). To pose the question is already to suggest the answer, for the query implies that the screen can function in both roles simultaneously (perhaps with a slight sneer at "illusionistic simulations"). In Cayley's work, the screen is used to create a legible textual surface that simultaneously functions as a dark window onto the code creating the display. Two related works illustrate the dynamic; both use an algorithmic substitution of letters that cycles between different languages and/or different states of legibility. In *Translation*, text on the right is complemented on the left by a visual display of glyphs the changes of which indicate how the algorithm is proceeding, a process also enacted by textual transformations as words cycle between different languages and states of legibility, as well as by the work's ambient music. Cayley suggests that if a user stares at the mutating glyphs long enough, she can gain an intuitive understanding of how the algorithm works (similarly, perhaps, to the video game player who through much practice can anticipate the computer's moves). In *Overboard*, the text (taken from an account of the Mayflower crossing in Governor Bradford's *Of Plymouth Plantation*) describes a man who fell overboard and, clinging to a rope, was dragged along under the water until he could finally be pulled on board again. The text presents various stages of legibility, figured by Cayley as surfacing, floating, and sinking (or drowning). [18] Here reading becomes unavoidably algorithmic, less a practice of re-creating an imaginative world than of participating in a rhythmic dance of letters and glyphs reflecting algorithmic transformations wrought by the computer.

The complexity of a writing surface created by code is further explored by Giselle Beiguelman in "Code Movie 1," a collaboration with Helga Stein who created the soundtrack. In this clever and amusing work, dancing symbols morph into various patterns in time with the music; the symbols are not words, however, but hexadecimal codes extracted from jpg images and reworked in Flash. Thus the surface reflexively references the codes that produce it, conceptually performing what Douglas Hofstader calls the "eternal golden braid," whereby the apparatus producing the representation becomes itself part of the representation. [19] Similar dynamics are enacted by writers identified with "codework," including MEZ (aka Mary-Anne Breeze) in such works as _][ad][Dressed In a Skin C.ode_, Talan Memmott in

Lexia to Perplexia, and Ted Warnell and collaborators in the collection *SyntacticalError.*[20]

Even when the writing surface is the print page, digitality leaves its mark on design and layout, especially the innovative graphics and increased visuality characteristic of many contemporary experimental novels. Frequently, digital code also appears in the represented worlds of these texts, creating the possibility for the kind of reflexive play noted above for digital works. Salvador Plascencia's *The People of Paper* is a good example of how the traditional dynamics of print novels are becoming entwined with digital representations.

The narrative's initiating act is the creation of a woman literally made of paper by Antonio, an "origami surgeon" gifted with the magical power to fashion living organs and entire organisms out of paper. Merced de Papel, as she is later christened, is the first instance of the novel's push toward literality in performances that entangle the represented world with the material surfaces on which the linguistic signifiers are inscribed. The literalization extends to encompass the conceptual hierarchy that distinguishes between author, narrator, and character in a descending scale of ontological dependence (that is, the author creates the narrator, the narrator creates the characters, etc.). The putative author enters the narrative as a character first called Saturn and then "Salvador Plascencia." Reflecting his ontological priority, he resides in a room whose floor is the sky of the characters. The central conflict revolves around the resentment that one of the characters, Federico de la Fe, feels toward Saturn's penetrating gaze, a surveillance he interprets as an intrusion of his privacy and limitation of his freedom as an autonomous subject.

This arrangement is exploited not so much for metafictional ends as for an exploration of the entangled materialities of the inscribed page and the represented world created by the inscriptions. For example, Merced de Papel's many abandoned lovers recognize one another by the paper cuts they sport on lips and tongues from having oral sex with her; one deliberately inflicts a fresh cut when he nostalgically licks the edges of the pages on which she appears as a character. In another instance of entangled materiality, Saturn, whose rejection by his lover is echoed in the sense of loss pervading the world he surveilles, cuts his rival's name from the narrative, an act within the represented world that leaves an actual die-cut hole in the page surface. This and other visual/material effects are economically feasible for a mass market book, of course, only because digital technologies offer unparalleled flexibility in the printing process.

Code explicitly enters the text as a linguistic signifier in the interior monologue of a mechanical tortoise, represented as a block of ones and zeros. The mechanical tortoises, who stand in for intelligent machines capable of cognition and agency, are hunted and killed so that Federico de la Fe and his colleagues can use the tortoises' lead shells to shield themselves from Saturn's gaze. Read as a metonymy for the code generating the textual surface, the tortoises's shells (and by implication, the tortoises themselves as intelligent machines) are used to disrupt the ontological hierarchy that positions the putative author above the characters, suggesting that the assumptions characteristic of a print novel are morphing as digital technologies reconfigure, literally and materially, the print page.

Intermediation and Sublime Banality

As a term, intermediation has a rich history. Used extensively in the financial world to indicate mediators for financial transactions, it has also been appropriated to describe various kinds of software and software applications and even used as the name of a German art group. Denoting both mediation and intervention, intermediation has elsewhere been parsed by us by means of three related but distinct analytical cuts through the complex dynamics characteristic of the contemporary entanglement of print and digital media: interactions between language and code, electronic textuality and print media, and analogue and digital modes of representation.[21]

One site where intermediation is at work is in algorithmic text generation. Although algorithmic text generation preceded digital computers by centuries, as Florian Cramer points out in his history of the topic,[22] computers greatly facilitated the process. They also created the possibility of mutable text that constantly changes, either in response to the user's actions or through random or timed sequences. There are several senses in which algorithmic text generation enacted by digital computers displays intermediation. Frequently the databases from which text generators draw consist of prescripted phrases taken from print media or alluding to printed works. Slicing and dicing phrases that in their "natural language" state were coherent, the text generators produce neologisms and nonsense phrases, as well as surprising juxtapositions that can be eerily insightful or hilarious. The disruption and strange familiarity characteristic of such works bespeak the interpenetration of language by code, as well as the interaction of electronic textuality with the print tradition. Moreover, such work manifests a hybrid ancestry of human intelligence and machine cognition, a point Brian Kim Stefans underscores when, in extensive annotations to his computer poem "Stops and Rebels" published in his print book *Fashionable Noise*, he refers to the program creating the poem as the "Demon."

In digital literature, algorithmic text generation has become a pervasive technique, used in works as diverse as Stuart Moulthrop's *Reagan Library*, Loss Pequeño Glazier's *white faced bromeliads on 20 hectares*, Jim Andrews and collaborators' *Stir Fry Texts*, John Cayley's *Overboard* and *Translation* (discussed earlier), and a host of others. Millie Ness's "Sundays in the Park," one of six components of the collection "Oulipoems" co-authored with Martha Deed, shows intermediation at work. Referencing the constraint-driven practices of the French OuLiPo writers, the "text machine" displays phrases that the user can cycle through by clicking on them, with two to six different permutations for each phrase group. The phrases in a group are related to one another through punning homophonic variations, relationships accentuated by two female voices reading in a gentle cacophony different versions of the text. For example, "start war in bag dead" becomes, when clicked, "is tart warren baghdad;" "know wee puns of master ruction" becomes "know weapons of mass destruction;" "know won reeds fill awe sophies" becomes "no one reeds philosophies" and so on. Sliding in and out of legibility, the phrases create a kind of verbal wallpaper against which patterns emerge, giving a sense of political content while at the same time suggesting the phenomenon of floating signifiers that are impossible to pin down to exact denotations.

The sense of patterns emerging from an ambient background and then dissolving back into noise is a pervasive trope in contemporary digital works. Although the L=A=N=G=U=A=G=E poets used similar techniques (a heritage acknowledged by many of the writers noted above), digital media allows the transformation of durable inscriptions into mobile text, activating in the process the complex dynamics of intermediation. For example, in William

Poundstone's *3 Proposals for Three Bottle Imps*, a Flash work that combines animated text with animation proper, extensive citation and intermediation allows idiosyncratic connections to emerge between the Cartesian devil and the Cartesian subject, a methodology modelled after Raymond Roussel's idiosyncratic connections in *Locus Solus*. The Cartesian devil, known since the Renaissance, refers to a toy device that consisted of a tube of water in which was placed a tiny folded figure made of special materials.[23] When the water was heated, the figure would rise, expand and unfold; when the water was cooled, the figure would shrink back to its original size and sink. In *Locus Solus*, Roussel's narrator imagines a further elaboration in which a "subtle mechanism" would generate a motto "written in fine bubbles of air laid out calligraphically;" this fictional account provides the inspiration for the calligraphic text Poundstone writes to accompany his animations. The Cartesian devil, connected to the Cartesian subject by a shared adjective as well as Poundstone's narrative, suggests a process whereby a mind whose existence provides the one surety in a world of doubt is transformed into a mutable subjectivity whose continuous morphing occurs in conjunction with the ambient conditions of an enveloping environment.

"An Allegory of Genius," one of the bottle imp proposals, performs as well as relates the kind of epistemology suited to this mutable subjectivity. The text, accompanied by a looping soundtrack that accentuates the theme of ambient emergence, is putatively taken from a story by Vasari that tells of an Italian Renaissance painter, Piero di Cosimo, who was fascinated by all manner of freaks and monsters. Piero was especially attracted to a wall on which the "sick of the city aimed their spittle," perceiving in the bubbling mucus dancing patterns that he used as inspirations for his paintings. One day he discerned on the wall a sea monster, the epitome of all that was "gross and appalling in nature." Capturing the form in a painting, he presented it to Giuliano de Medici, who found it so repulsive he promptly covered it with a green cloth and consigned it to a closet. When Catherine de Medici inherited it, she whimsically returned it to the wall, whereupon the rabble spat upon it, so that it gradually sank back into the randomness from which it emerged. The narrative then continues by providing examples of bottle imps, a linguistic construction that is also visually performed by the animations showing the imps expanding, rising, shrinking, and falling.

3 Proposals for Bottle Imps suggestively illuminates why the aesthetics of ambient emergence should be characteristic of the contemporary moment. As the Internet and World Wide Web are increasingly integrated into everyday routines in developed regions of the globe, they provide a vast and continuously changing landscape within which contemporary subject formation takes place. Moreover, this is a landscape defined by the dynamics of intermediation. Although most Web content remains text, increasingly graphics, images, animation and sound combine with it to create complex surfaces whose behaviours perform and enact the interpenetration of language and code, electronic textuality and print, analogue and digital representations. As digital effects cycle back into print, their aesthetic influences older media such as print novels as well, producing a range of second-order effects that in turn cycle back to digital media, thus creating feedback loops that provide ever-changing backgrounds against which mutable patterns emerge.

In Mark Z. Danielewski's *House of Leaves: A Novel*, the difference between the postmodern era and the contemporary emphasis on ambience manifests itself as successive layering, presenting a kind of textual archaeology in which various strata testify to different kinds of aesthetic concerns. The centrality of intermediation is immediately evident in this print novel's determination to include within its leaves an astonishing variety of media, including film, video, photography, telegraphy, painting, collage, and graphics, among others. The novel's implicit rivalry with the digital computer's ability to represent all other media with its binary code came close to the surface in Danielewski's long interview with Larry McCaffrey and Sinda Gregory. Asked if the computer was important for the composition of this unusually designed text, Danielewski replied:

> I didn't write *House of Leaves* on a word processor. In fact, I wrote out the entire thing in pencil! And what's most ironic, I'm still convinced that it's a great deal easier to write something out by hand than on a computer. You hear a lot of people talking about how computers make writing so much easier because they offer the writer so many choices, whereas in fact pencil and paper allow you a much greater freedom. You can do anything in pencil! (117)

When McCaffrey pressed him on the issue, however, Danielewski admitted the necessity of digital technologies for the book's production:

> There's no doubt computers, new software, and other technologies play a big role in getting any book ready for production these days. They also make it easier for a publisher to consider releasing a book like mine that previously would have been considered too complicated and expensive to typeset by hand. Yet despite all the technological advantages currently available, the latter stages of getting *House of Leaves* ready for production involved such a great deal of work that Pantheon began to wonder if they were going to be able to publish it the way I wanted. So I wound up having to do the typesetting myself. (118)

Digital technology functions here like the Derridean *supplement*; alleged to be outside and extraneous to the text proper, it is somehow also necessary. The construction suggests that at issue is the text's ability to posit its origin without digital technology; conversely, including digital technology would alter the text's fundamental view of its own ontology.

These suggestions become explicit in the text's consideration of how other media have been threatened, and implicitly transformed, by the interpenetration of digitality. Divided between Zampanò's critical commentary on the film *The Navidson Record* and Johnny Truant's footnotes on Zampanò's manuscript, the layers include footnotes on Johnny's footnotes as well as interjections by the Editors, not to mention some two hundred pages of Exhibits, Appendices and Index. Particularly revealing is Zampanò's discussion of digital photography. Distinguishing between documentaries and films representing fictional stories, Zampanò notes that documentaries "rely on interviews, inferior equipment, and virtually no effects to document real events. Audiences are not allowed the safety net of disbelief and so must turn to more challenging mechanisms of interpretation which, as is sometimes the case, may lead to denial and aversion" (139). The film at the book's centre, *The Navidson Record*, purports to be a documentary, but the main object of its representation, the house on Ash Tree Lane into which Will Navidson moves with his partner Karen Green and their two children in an attempt to shore up the couple's shaky relationship, turns out to be an impossible object whose inside is bigger than its outside. At first the surreal excess measures a mere quarter of an inch but then stretches into distances greater than the diameter of the earth and older than the solar system. With its shifting walls, ashen surfaces, and labyrinthine complexities, the house's interior is not only impossible to map but also impossible to inhabit, for it destroys any artefact left within it. Combining an unrepresentable topography with an uninhabitable space, the house confronts those who enter its mysterious interior with the threat of nothingness that, far from being mere absence, has a terrible ferocious agency, figured by the beast-like growls Will and others think they perceive issuing from its interior. Moreover, even the film that putatively records this impossible object has an indeterminate status, for as Johnny Truant informs us in his introduction, *The Navidson Record* probably does not exist – which does not, however, prevent Zampanò from writing some 500 pages interpreting it and the hundreds of critics (some fictional, some real) that he cites from putatively writing thousands of pages of exegesis about it.

Lurking at the centre of the text, as at the centre of the house, is a nothingness so intense and unrepresentable that it goes beyond nihilism and paradoxically becomes a catalyst for the graphomania that the text both performs and cites. We may see in this configuration the staging of a central insight of deconstruction, the inability of language to posit its own origin – an insight that, far from leading to silence, catalysed the production of thousands of books and articles, as prolific a stimulus in the real world as the house is in its fictional realm. For *House of Leaves*, the result of the graphomania is the creation of a structure in which nothingness, allegorised in the beast that may or may not inhabit the labyrinth at the house's centre, is surrounded by layer after layer of interpretation, exegesis, commentary, and analysis. Moreover, this material is punctured with so many holes and rife with so much ambiguity that the exegetical process could clearly go on forever, as critical articles are written about the critical articles contained in *House of Leaves*, functioning at once as a print novel and a material manifestation of the house it fictionalises (a conflation evident even before the book is open in the cover design of a black-on-black embossed labyrinth).

Read as an allegory for our contemporary situation (a reading that all novels directly or indirectly invite), *House of Leaves* suggests that postmodernism has not so much disappeared as been swallowed up – or better, engulfed – by the flood of data, associations, information, and cross-references unleashed by the World Wide Web. The effect of an information landscape so vast and unruly has been to shift the focus for interpretive analysis to discerning patterns among its chaotic and unpredictable juxtapositions. The aesthetics of ambient emergence is a function, then, not only of the Web's incorporation into daily life but also of the sheer incomprehensibility of its vastness, a combination producing a condition that might be called sublime banality.

As if competing with this flood of information, *House of Leaves* inundates its readers with a roaring cascade of data, narrations, connections and complexities. Although as a print book *House of Leaves* cannot literally animate the text to create ambient effects, Danielewski employs a number of techniques to intensify the complex materiality of the textual surfaces. Adapting the techniques of Concrete poetry, the author often treats the page as an omnidirectional writing plane on which text can go in many different directions. As if enacting what it names, Chapter IX (titled "The Labyrinth" in an appendix) displays text written upside down, backward, horizontal, and other unusual orientations. Footnotes are nested within other footnotes and appear not only at page bottoms but in the middle or upper portions as well. In addition, the text creates elaborate echoes between the represented world and the page's materiality. The notorious footnote 144 (119-145), for example, purports to list everything that is *not* in the house's mysterious interior, a quixotic endeavour since there is nothing in the house. Although the list begins by listing house-like objects – heating and cooling systems, vents, wiring – it soon expands to include items like Christmas trees, thus making clear that the list could potentially go on forever. And go on it does, for pages and pages. Even that involves a twist, however, for when the footnote continues onto the verso, the text appears not as a linear continuation of the recto but as the backward-reading version of preceding page. It thus vivifies, by performing the opposite, a property of print books we take so for granted we cease to see it, namely that pages are (normally) opaque rather than transparent. Acting as a window, the footnote reminds us through inversion that there are no windows through which one can look into or out of the house's interiority and thus no way to gain an objective perspective that would stabilize the house's (and the text's) changing shapes and fluctuating meanings.

The blue colour outlining the footnote's textual blocks also is significant, since in the so-called "blue" edition, the word "house" (and its equivalents in foreign languages) always appears in blue, suggesting either a hypertext link or the blue screen used in films as a replaceable backdrop that can later be filled in with whatever background is desired. The footnote's blue outline suggests that the list is less an objective catalogue than a representation reflecting the writer's and/or reader's desires, acting in this respect not as a window but a mirror. Moreover, even when the words end the footnote continues, for it appears as a black block surrounded by a blue outline, an image that could signify either the absence of words or words so densely overwritten they have become a solid block of black ink. The play between presence and absence continues on the next page, where the footnote has apparently disappeared but nevertheless lingers as a block of negative white space defined by the surrounding words. This entanglement of the page's material properties with the nothingness that haunts the house and text is typical of the ways in which the book's surfaces ceases to be neutral containers for words and spaces and instead become active agents capable of signifying practices.

Further intensifying the page surfaces are the ways in which the text re-defines itself as a collection of leaves, all of which are capable of signification. Rather than performing as a conventional narrative that begins with the story's first word and ends with the last word, this text insists that it consists of *every* surface the book contains as a material artefact, including the front and back covers, the author and title pages, the copyright pages, the spine and colophon, the index, and the final acknowledgements. For example, at the bottom of the copyright page that conventionally follows the title page there appears "A Note on This Edition," which tells us that in the "Full Colour" edition, "The only struck line in Chapter XXI appears in purple." This seemingly innocuous note, which most readers would normally skip in their eagerness to begin the narrative, becomes crucially important to the interpretation of the final chapter of Johnny Truant's narration and thus to the story as a whole. The struck phrase, which comes immediately before the story of the deformed child that ends Chapter XXI, is a narrative interpolation: "~~what I'm remembering now~~" (518). In all the first editions the phrase appears in black, and only those readers who recall the note on the copyright page (now some 500 pages distant) will make the connection and imagine the line in purple.[24] Throughout purple is associated with Pelafina, Johnny's mad mother who was confined to a mental institution and committed suicide several years before the manuscript was putatively compiled. Her presence is directly manifested in the text only through the appendix that contains her letters. Readers who follow the editors' advice (72) and skip ahead to Pelafina's letters will recognize, however, that many details from those letters eerily echo through the main narrative about Will and Karen Navidson. The echoes suggest that in addition to Zampanò and Johnny Truant, either of whom might have made up the other, another contender for the one who is "actually" writing the text is Pelafina. Although this idea defies conventional logic, the struck phrase reinforces her claim to be the narrator telling the entire story, including those texts supposedly written by Johnny Truant and Zampanò. Reading the text from this perspective obviously forces a reinterpretation of all that has come before, so that precisely when the narrative should be winding down, it instead opens up in a way that throws everything up for grabs. That this startling reversal was set up by prefatory material most readers ignore indicates the intensity that the text imparts to even its most humble surfaces.

Other examples are the 98 index entries followed by the letters "DNE," evidently an acronym for "Does Not Exist." The strangeness of listings words that do *not* appear in the text carries the play between presence and absence into the index. Further enhancing this weirdness is a strategy that slowly reveals itself as a self-reflexive ploy. The DNE entries do indeed appear but in ways that separate them from the text proper, often in the textual apparatuses that Gérard Genette has called paratexts.[25] The paratextual index thus references not only the text but also its fellow paratexts, whose shadowy presences are both acknowledged and erased in the DNE appellation. Some of the DNE entries, for example, appear in bits of texts incorporated into the collages collected in "Appendix III: Contrary Evidence." Perhaps the most insidious is the entry "house (black) . . . DNE." The phrase functions as a visual oxymoron, for here as elsewhere in the text (of the blue edition), "house" is in blue. The astute reader, however, can find the elusive black "house" in the acknowledgements that appear on the book's penultimate page, where the reprint notice references "Vintage Books, a division of Random **House**, Inc." As a result of these kinds of strategies, readers are reconditioned to regard the text as the *entire* material object – an object, moreover, that constantly subverts its status as an object by performing as an active agent capable of affecting the world around it.

Within the text, the house's agency occupies an indeterminate status figured by the beast whose presence (and absence) seems to haunt the house's interior. Never actually seen, the beast can be inferred from the deep claw marks that Johnny Truant finds beside Zampanò's body, the seeming growls recorded on *The Navidson Record*, and the "fingers of darkness [that] slash cross the lighted wall and consume Holloway" (338). Everywhere the beast is mentioned, the text wavers between representing it as an actually existing creature and a consensual hallucination created by the characters. Typical is the passage where Johnny reproduces in the edited manuscript the unexplained burn holes that pepper Zampanò's notes, creating a play between the letters actually inscribed on the page and the absences signified by square brackets. "It seems erroneous to assert," Zampanò argues, " . . . that this creat[ ]e had actual teeth and claws of b[ ]e (which myth for some reason [   ] requires). [ ]t d[]d have claws, they were made of shadow and if it did have te[]th, they were made of darkness. Yet even as such the [

]still stalked Holl[ ]way at every corner until at last it did strike, devouring him, even roaring, the last thing heard, the sound []f Holloway ripped out of existence" (338). Even as we reconstruct the noisy message for ourselves by supplying the missing letters, the brackets puncturing the text evoke the nothingness that the beast paradoxically signifies in its very presence.

This play between the absence of presence and the presence of absence is intimately related to the house's ambiguous agency. Perhaps it acts on its own, or perhaps, as the fictional critic Ruby Dahl cited by Zampanò claims, the house merely reflects the personalities of those who venture inside it (165). Significantly, immediately after the beast consumes Holloway's body, the house goes crazy and eats Will's brother Tom, as if infected by the psychosis that drove Holloway to hunt his comrades, murder one and wound another, and then commit suicide.

Following Mark B. N. Hansen's key insight that there is a deep connection between the house and digital technologies, we arrive at a somewhat different explanation for its operation.[26] Increasingly human attention occupies only the tiny top of a huge pyramid of machine-to-machine communication, including cell phones, networked computers, ATMs, and RFID (Radio Frequency Identification) tags that give every indication of spreading faster than mould in New Orleans. Often these digital machines, ranging from the obvious to the nano-scaled, are coupled with sensors and actuators that carry out actions, from something as mundane as raising a garage door to the world-shaking launch of a nuclear missile. In the field of artificial life, for example, programs have been constructed that produce species capable of mutating and evolving in unpredictable ways. Genetic algorithms go further in evolving not just the output of the programs but the programs themselves. Programmable gate arrays go further yet in evolving the hardware, changing the patterns of the logic gates to arrive at the most efficient way to solve certain problems.[27] We would perhaps like to think that actions require humans to initiate them, but human agency is increasingly dependent on intelligent machines to carry out actions and, more alarmingly, to provide the data on which the human decisions are based in the first place. *House of Leaves* reflects these ambiguities in attributing the house's actions both to the humans who enter it and the beast that can seemingly act on its own, a non-human creature whose agency is completely enmeshed with that of the characters, the author, and the reader.

For digital technologies, the initiation of action ultimately translates into binary code. From the brute simplicity of ones and zeros, the successive layers of code build up constructions of enormous complexity, from genetic algorithms that produce advanced circuit designs[28] to the digital typesetting programs that produced *House of Leaves* as a material artefact. Although humans originally created the computer code, the complexity of many contemporary programs is such that no single person understands them in their entirety. In this sense our understanding of how computers can get from simple binary code to sophisticated acts of cognition is approaching the gap that yawns between our understanding of the mechanics of human consciousness – the neural structures, chemical transmitters, networked cells and molecular interactions from which consciousness must emerge – and the apparent autonomy and freedom of human thought. The parallel with computers is striking. As Brian Cantwell Smith observes, the emergence of complexity within computers may provide crucial clues to "how a structured lump of clay can sit up and think" (76).

Yet human cognition is unlike machine cognition in being mediated through emotions and the complexities of bodily processing. Despite similarities in the layered architectures of neural nets and coding languages, huge differences remain between human thought and machine processing. In particular, humans seek meaning while computers execute commands. Although research in such fields as artificial life, emotional computing and artificial intelligence is on-going to create computers that can achieve some sense of meaning, it remains to be seen whether an intelligent machine capable of sentience can ever be built. The nothingness with which the house – and the beast – are consistently associated in *House of Leaves* functions to provide a figure for the absence at the core of the text's multiple layers and acts of inscription – an absence that draws into the question the very possibility of meaning and, at the same time, paradoxically provokes a riotous excess of meaning-making.

As the litmus test separating human and machine cognition, meaning in *House of Leaves* may be recovered through the multiple layers of remediation that this print novel creates (as we have argued elsewhere),[29] and linked to embodied human reading (as Mark Hansen argues). Yet another implication lurks in the layered complexities of this print novel. An ambiguous agent, the beast both threatens and mimics the agency of the human characters. Above all else, the characters in the text, like the humans who read the text, are meaning-seeking animals. Nevertheless, they (and we) cannot determine the meaning of the beast's actions, or even if it exists. Its elusive presence that takes only a slight shift in perspective to transform into absence stands in for the digital technologies that, ignorant of meaning, nevertheless initiate actions that often have consequences for humans across the globe.

Like the nothingness infecting the text's signifiers, a similar nothingness would confront us if we could take an impossible journey and zoom into a computer's interior while it is running code. We would find that there is no there there, only alternating voltages that nevertheless produce meaning through a layered architecture correlating ones and zeros with human language. From the nothingness of alternating voltages emerges the complexities of digital culture, including effects that shift us away from postmodernism and toward ambient emergence. In this sense *House of Leaves* performs within its fictional world the banal miracle that produced it as a material artefact and that also produces us as readers of the complex surfaces of contemporary literature.

Paper to Pixels to Plastic: Intermediation through Analog Representation, Digital Fabrication, and Virtual Integration

Architects do not usually make buildings. Architects make instruction manuals that guide the construction of buildings by others. Configured as such, the discipline has always been pervaded by techniques of intermediation, and for much of its history, architects have developed ideas through representations on paper and in scale models and only later translated these concepts to wood, stone, and steel. But this disciplinary structure is of relatively recent vintage. In the Middle Ages, architectural innovation took place primarily in the field. The great cathedrals of the period were made possible in large part through tectonic advances in masonry construction. But as vaulting grew increasingly complex, complicated intersections were solved less by trial-and-error stonecutting and more through the use of projective drawings. The development of stereotomy in sixteenth century France, an arcane method for accurately delineating geometrically complex three-dimensional stone shapes, opened the way for a boom of innovative structural solutions in stone vaults.[30] During the Renaissance, linear perspective was developed by practitioners invested heavily in both painting and architecture; advances made in one field quickly came to bear on the other. In the intervening centuries, the increasing availability of paper and architecture's slow migration from the craft guilds to the academy widened architects' remove from the physical instantiation of their projects and intensified their dependence on techniques of intermediation.

Through the 1970s and 80s, architectural drawing remained the primary vehicle of advanced research in the field. Influential practitioners of the period, Eisenman, Bernard Tschumi, Daniel Libeskind, and others, resistant to capitulation with the machinations of advanced capitalism, produced dizzyingly complex drawings and collages, painstakingly hand-crafted and often accompanied by dense theoretical texts, giving rise to the phenomenon known as 'paper architecture'[31] (figs. 5-6). Some of the most important work in the field was being produced with no intention of being physically constructed.[32] As the computer entered into the design studio through the late 1980s and early 90s, its initial effects were felt in advancing the geometrical complexities of these theoretical investigations. But as the decade progressed, a constellation of conditions converged to radically transform the opportunities and ambitions of the paper generation.

The formidable graphic techniques developed through the 1970s by these architects helped them win prestigious competitions for built work as world economies rebounded, as evidenced by Eisenman's Wexner Center for the Arts in Columbus, Ohio (competition 1983, project completed 1989), Tschumi's Parc de la Villette in Paris (competition 1983, project completed 1993), and Libeskind's Jewish Museum in Berlin (competition 1989, project completed 1999). As they were awarded additional commissions through the 1990s, these firms integrated digital technologies into their studios to assist in the conceptualisation and documentation of their complex designs. Soon a younger generation, many of whom had worked as project assistants on these commissions, emerged from the shadow of their analogue mentors. Armed with a first-hand knowledge of computer technologies, close affiliations with computer-savvy fabricators and consultants, and unencumbered by the hallmark suspicions of capitalism that haunted the previous generation, practices such as Greg Lynn Form, UN Studio, servo, and others radically transformed the state of advanced architectural research as well as the organization of the practices conducting it.[33]

Servo, an international design collaborative with its four principals based in different cities throughout the world, stands as a new kind of networked practice made possible by digital technologies.[34] Founded in 1999, the firm focuses on the transformations of both architectural space and the practice of design these technologies have brought about. As is now commonplace in even the most conservative architectural practices, servo employs the latest modeling and animation software throughout the design process, but rather than employ these technologies simply to streamline traditional practice, servo aims to exploit unforeseen potential at all stages of design, practice, and construction. Depending on the internet to collapse the distance between its four principals, servo exhibits a

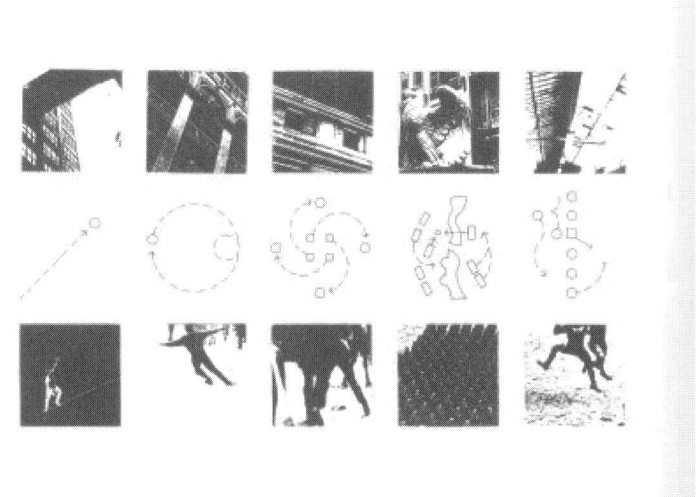

Figure 5: Bernard Tschumi, detail from *The Manhattan Transcripts, Episode 4: The Block*, 1980-81. Ink and cut-and-pasted gelatin silver photographs on tracing paper, 19" x 31."

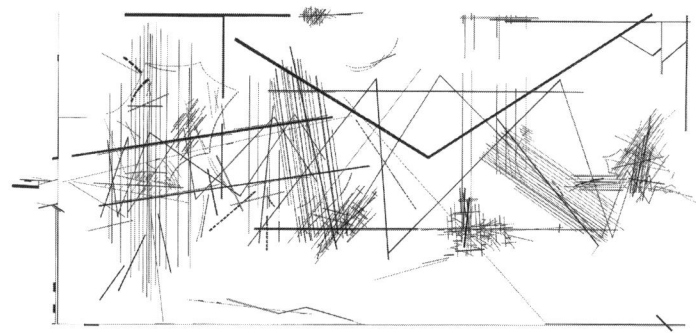

Figure 6: Daniel Libeskind, detail from *Chamber Works: Architectural Meditations on Themes from Heraclitus, Horizontal 14*, 1983. Originals lost, 22 1/4" x 30 1/8."

nimble flexibility difficult to achieve in larger, less technologically advanced firms. With their capabilities distributed across geographical borders and time zones, the firm has the ability to work normal hours around the clock, to draw on a vast pool of collaborators and fabricators around the globe, and to easily shift resources from one location to another as opportunities and interests dictate. In contrast to the stereotypical figure of the lone architect hunched over a drafting table, servo exists as a constantly fluctuating constellation of collaborators and consultants, a loose band of affiliated practitioners working in an array of production media and made to cohere not through physical proximity but rather through technological immersion.

Unlike the paper practitioners of the 1970s, servo's ambitions were from the start resolutely directed at translating their designs into physical space with the aid of computer-controlled fabrication technologies. Further, the firm incorporates an array of digital projections, real-time data sensors, and interactive control terminals within their built [35] projects, greatly expanding their work's repertoire of effects. Intermediation pervades their design process and designed projects with equal intensity, producing architectural interventions that inhabit an ambiguous zone between physical instantiation and virtual simulation.

Many of servo's projects have been commissioned by galleries and other cultural institutions, the relatively small scale of these commissions affording them the opportunity to maintain a central role in project fabrication as well as design. Rather than provide paper construction documents to a contractor, servo seamlessly integrates physical production with their design process, producing preliminary studies and final building components on the same machine. As pointed out by Michael Speaks, such rapid prototyping constitutes a new form of "design intelligence" in which digital technologies, dramatically increasing the rate at which iterations and alternatives can be produced, ushers in a wholesale re-conception of the design process (16). With advanced modeling and rendering software, the effects of even the most subtle adjustments to configuration, lighting, materiality, and other variables within project that once required time-intensive analogue labour can be instantly assessed in virtual simulations and alternative versions quickly produced with computer-controlled fabrication devices such as CNC milling machines, laser cutters, and 3-D printers. These machines are much more than expedient tools used to translate a preconceived idea from the mind of the designer to the material world. Instead, unexpected solutions emerge from the complex feedback loops between human designers and increasingly intelligent machines. The design process is no longer one of representational speculation, but rather of materially-specific iteration, and agency in the system is no longer lodged in the individual designer but rather distributed through a dynamic network of human actors and digital devices.

All of these technologies were employed in the completion of "Dark Places" (2006), servo's design for a digitised survey of contemporary art and architecture curated by Joshua Decter at the Santa Monica Museum of Art (figs. 7-8). From conception to completion, digital technologies and intermediation deeply pervade the project. Decter solicited submissions from 76 artists and architects from the United States and abroad. Some completed original work specifically for the exhibition, while others submitted previously existing materials. With the ambition to "reanimate relationships among art, architecture, media, and technological design," Decter re-presented each work, regardless of its initial medium, as a digitised video clip emanating from eight video projectors mounted within a glowing, sculptural armature designed by servo and suspended in the gallery.[36]

Servo's armature, like the practice itself, embodies many of the symptoms of the contemporary mood swing this essay elucidates. Constructed in translucent vacuum-formed plastic, the project's material effects are amplified by internal fiber-optic lighting that imparts an otherworldly glow. These lights are connected to real-time data sensors that cause light intensities and patterns to fluctuate based on the presence and ambulation of museum visitors. Decter's video clips are displayed using both front- and rear-projection systems, causing the featured artworks to inhabit the surfaces of the armature itself as well as the adjacent gallery walls. Interactive computer terminals mounted within servo's construct allow visitors to browse the collected works in any combination. The work is not a fixed object designed by a single creator but instead a set of complex feedback loops between content and context. These feedback loops shift attention from the specific properties of individual works to an immersive atmospheric ensemble that promiscuously mingles the real

Figure 7: Servo, *Dark Places*, installation at the Santa Monica Museum of Art, Santa Monica, California, 2006. General view of gallery.

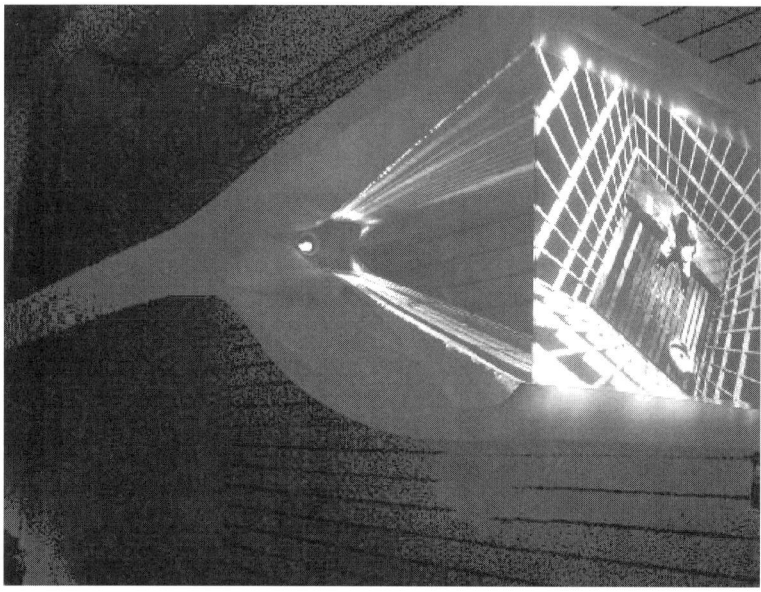

Figure 8: Servo, *Dark Places*, installation at the Santa Monica Museum of Art, Santa Monica, California, 2006. Projector detail.

with the virtual.

These shifts in focus – from element to ensemble, from close attention to distracted immersion, from autonomous objects and stable subjects to a complex dance between physical and virtual instantiations of each – signal the significant distance between today's most advanced practitioners and their postmodern predecessors. Rather than resist physical construction in order to develop theoretical arguments in abstract representations, servo, like many of their contemporaries,[37] aggressively employs digital technologies directly to engage the physical. Their ambitions are not critique and resistance, those postmodern aims that direct attention backward, either suspiciously to an object of critique or nostalgically to some (often imagined) lost past. Rather, these architects reject the cynical "impossibility of architecture"[38] and instead strive to innovate and project alternatives. Equipped with a formidable kit of new digital tools and techniques, today's most innovative designers exude a forward-looking optimism unthinkable under the sceptical regime of postmodernism. Though the discipline still maintains internal debates that parse the relative criticality of various camps within the field,[39] the marked transformations that have taken place over the last fifteen years have rendered these arguments increasingly irrelevant. Spurred by the increasing contamination of architecture by dynamic intermediations rather than critical theory, today's most innovative practitioners are moving the field away from the legible representation and negative critique. Unlike the deeply referential drawing projects produced by their counterparts in the 1970s, works like Dark Places do not solicit sustained close attention either to their representational content or to the formal specificities of the container. Instead, both content and construction are combined into a single entity that gives rise to powerful and dynamic atmospheric and performative effects. Though the appellation of this new condition is still up for grabs,[40] its effects, products of a renewed attention to materials and to the dynamic intermediations made possible by digital technologies, have insinuated themselves throughout contemporary architecture and literature to usher in a new, optimistic, and distinctly contemporary mood.

The Aesthetics of Ambient Emergence

We conclude with a few remarks about ambient emergence, our suggested name for the new aesthetic, and its connections with network culture and informationalism. Both words in the phrase have multiple connotations in this context. "Ambient," usually understood to mean "surrounding" or "encircling," refers first to the play of surfaces characteristic of the attention to materiality in architecture and to the play of shifting letters and words in digital literary works. For example, servo's construction of an architectural setting responsive to the location and number of viewers in the gallery creates transforming patterns as environmental conditions change; John Cayley's *Overboard* and *Translation,* which allow limited user interaction to shift the screen display between various modes of legibility, provide examples from electronic literature. Although print novels obviously have durable inscriptions and so cannot participate in changing environmental conditions, they too show the influence of the shift. Immersive fiction is often said to create a "world," but in fact the evocation of an atmosphere typically occupies only a small portion of the text; most of the focus is on the characters' perceptions and actions as they engage in the conflicts and resolutions that give plots their characteristic Aristotelian shape. Many contemporary novels are turning away from this traditional mode of discourse and instead attempting to create something like an ambient environment that does not so much serve as background for plot development as displace plot altogether. Examples include (among others) Joseph McElroy's *Plus*, William Gaddis's *The Recognitions*, David Markson's *Wittgenstein's Mistress*, and Kazuo Ishiguro's *Never Let Me Go.* Falling somewhere between conventional plot and evocation of ambience, Salvador Plascencia's *The People of Paper* shows the dynamics of intermediation at work The traditional narrative structure is satirized as Federico de la Fe and his colleague realize they are being forced into an escalating series of plot developments. They rebel against the formula first by attempting to think nothing at all while under Saturn's surveillance, and then, when that doesn't work, by everyone thinking different thoughts. The chapters follow various formatting schemes, one of which is a series of parallel vertical columns, with each column representing the thoughts of a character. As the characters rebel, the ordered columns break into a visual cacophony, overrunning the usual margins and breaking the rigid symmetry that previously defined the page space. The breakup can be read as an allegory about the shift from focused world to enveloping environment, from plot to ambience.

The shift in contemporary architectural and literary productions is deeply related, as we have shown, to the changed conditions that digital media have brought about, especially the advent of the World Wide Web. As computers move out of the desktop and into the environment through such technologies as RFID tags, sensors linked with real-time data flows, and "smart" devices in which nanodevices are embedded in everything from clothing to surfactants, the reach of digital technologies both expands and sinks into obscurity, increasingly becoming part of the environment we take for granted. Thomas Whalen has called this expanding sphere of networked and programmable media the "cognisphere," a term that emphasizes its ability to carry out independent cognitions and initiate actions beyond the awareness (and sometimes even the control) of humans.[41] In this larger context, "ambient" denotes not only the environmental emphasis evident in contemporary architecture and literature but also the sense that we are surrounding ourselves with new kinds of environments in which human and machine cognitions are deeply entwined.

"Emergence," the other term in play here, typically denotes the appearance of unpredictable complex patterns at a global level that result from interactions between local elements governed by relatively simple rule sets. Emergence has a rich scientific and philosophical history, linked with important research in a wide variety of fields, including neurophysiology, artificial life, scientific simulations, game theory, biology, and cognitive science, among others. One of the key ideas in theories of emergence is dynamical hierarchies, in which sites at many different interlinked levels interact with one another via feedback loops that operate between and among levels, creating continuously circulating interactions up and down the hierarchical chains. These kinds of structures are found everywhere complex systems operate, from the emergence of life from proteins and amino acids, to the emergence of consciousness from individual neurons.

Nicholas Gessler, a researcher in human complex systems, has used the term "intermediation" to analyse how emergent structures arise, arguing that a key move in building a dynamical hierarchy is capturing an emergent pattern at a low level and re-representing it in a different medium as a primitive (or elemental component) at a higher level of organization, which in turn results in a different emergent pattern at that level.[42] For example, atoms interact to form molecules, which create new patterns that are the emergent result of atomic interactions. Molecules in turn create proteins, the emergent result of molecular interactions, which in turn create cells, and so forth. In this way, each higher level piggybacks on a lower level by incorporating its results in a transformative process that makes what was an emergent pattern at the lower level into a component that, interacting with other components in a different context, leads to yet more emergences, which in turn are used by higher levels as they build contexts out of which new emergent structures will arise.[43] In Gessler's view, the shift in medium is crucial, since it is the re-representation of a lower level pattern in a new medium that allows its re-contextualisation as a primitive rather than a global result. In understanding how dynamical hierarchies work, we should keep in mind that such structures are never static, and that the patterns at each level are always in dynamic interaction with all the other levels. Atoms do not cease to move when they are incorporated into molecules, and molecules continually transform as they become proteins, just as proteins change and morph when they participate in the process of DNA replication. This framework, in recursive fashion, gives us a way now to re-contextualise our own argument. The complex dynamics of intermediation between print and digital media create feedback cycles in which the re-representation of emergent patterns leads to yet more emergences at different levels in the hierarchy, each interacting with and contributing to the overall emergences of the cognisphere, which in turn participates in interactions all the way up and down the dynamic hierarchies that produce it.

Perhaps the most typical way to understand these multi-causal, multi-agent interactions is through networks, the formal properties of which are analysed using graph theory. Graph theory, a form of mathematical analysis that considers networks to be comprised of nodes and edges, has been applied in a wide variety of contexts, including biological, technological, and sociological systems. As Eugene Thacker and Alexander Galloway point out in *The Exploit*, the disadvantage of graph theory is that it does not sufficiently account for the dynamical transformative aspect of networks; this deficiency is mitigated if we keep in mind the close connection between networks and dynamical hierarchies. While network models yield ways to understand complex interconnections between multiple components and linking patterns, dynamical hierarchies explore the circumstances in which these connections can lead to emergent phenomenon and transformative dynamics.

In *The Exploit*, Galloway and Thacker ambitiously attempt to show that network modelling provides new perspectives on everything from transnational economics to contemporary subjectivity. In a political context, the importance of networks arises not only from network culture as such; more generally, it derives from a shift away from centralized power centres toward networks as a means of political control and resistance. Galloway and Thacker argue that "in recent decades the processes of globalization have mutated from a system of control housed in a relatively small number of power hubs to a system of control infused in the material fabric of distributed networks." [44] Networks in themselves, they point out, are neither repressive nor liberatory; rather, they represent new ways to exercise and resist power. For example, as terrorist organizations have shifted toward semi-autonomous cells loosely connected together in a global network, the National Security Agency has adopted a mirroring strategy of using the immense telecommunication networks to identify potential terrorist plots. Regardless whether one sees the terrorists as freedom fighters or nefarious agents of evil, and NSA surveillance as protecting or eroding the freedom of American citizens, the point is that both groups seek to implement and disrupt power through a network model. The applicable domains for this kind of analysis have dramatically increased in scope and range, including not only the usual references to the Internet and World Wide Web but also such diverse phenomena as epidemiological vectors of contagious diseases, artificial intelligence implemented through neural networks, and the U.S. Army's plans to move from warfare strategies based on such traditional platforms as tanks, ships and planes to "swarms" that flexibly respond and reconfigure themselves using high-bandwidth communication networks. In brief, networks have become the new playing field for the exercise of power and the analysis of its dynamics.

Going along with this emphasis on networks is an increased attention to topology, mediation, materiality, and nonhuman agency, all of which are necessary, as Galloway and Thacker point out, to understand fully how networks function. Although the complexities of how these factors contribute to network functioning are beyond the scope of this essay to explore, they suggest the expanded contexts in which the aesthetics of ambient emergence, with its emphasis on surface, materiality, intermediation, and nonhuman agency should be understood not as an isolated effect but part of the world-wide transformations that information technologies and globalisation are co-producing.[45] To position the mood swing as an aesthetic is to point specifically to the cultural and artistic manifestations of the complex dynamics of networks and dynamical hierarchies. The larger contexts, however, remain inextricably involved in these interactions, as both cause and result of the inconceivably vast number of feedback loops dynamically operating throughout the entire complex system of the networked cognisphere.

What stands out in the mood swing as we have delineated it is the sense of expanded possibilities for artistic and aesthetic creation and expression. While none of the practitioners we have discussed are ignorant of the dangers of network culture and the inimical effects of globalisation, they are generally more interested in building than in critique, more oriented to discovery and innovation than to paranoia and suspicion. For them and others like them, the mood swing is not so much a change of attitude for its own sake as it is an attempt to embrace the constantly transforming sphere of interlinked networks and dynamical hierarchies, which are at once immeasurably beyond human ken and part of our everyday ordinary experience. Like consciousness and life itself, these interactions are the banal miracles that we take for granted even as they awesomely exceed what we can understand.

Notes

---

[1] Fredric Jameson in *Postmodernism, or the Cultural Logic of Late Capitalism* calls for "an aesthetic of cognitive mapping: a pedagogical political culture which seeks to endow the individual subject with some new heightened sense of its place in the global system" (54).
[2] See Baudrillard 1-3.

[3] See Latour's "Why Has Critique Run Out of Steam."

[4] In recent years, the term 'mood' has been appearing in architectural discourse with increasing frequency, due in large part to the writings of Jeffrey Kipnis – who used the term as a curatorial device in "Mood River," his 2002 exhibition at the Wexner Center of the Arts – and Sylvia Lavin. See Kipnis's "On those who Step in the Same River," and Lavin's "The Three Faces of Tel Aviv" (especially pages 88-113).

[5] For a cogent treatment on the transformative potential of architectural pre-visualization films, see Krakowsky's "Algorithmic Anthologies."

[6] See Speaks's "Design Intelligence, Part 1: Introduction."

[7] See David Harvey, 121-129 as well as Manuel Castells, 77, 100, 162, 164.

[8] Significantly, Riley did not attempt to elucidate the features of a distinct style, as had been the habit of MoMA curators since its inception. In particular, the specific determination of style manifest in Philip Johnson and Henry-Russell Hitchcock's influential 1932 exhibition "Modern Architecture: International Exhibition" stands as an important foil to Riley's "Light Construction." See the exhibition catalogue, *Modern Architecture: International Exhibition* as well as Johnson and Hitchcock's influential work, *The International Style: Architecture Since 1922*, which expanded upon the themes of the exhibition and effectively defined the terms of Modern Architecture as practiced through the remainder of the twentieth century.

[9] For an expansion of the theoretical underpinnings of the exhibition, see Gannon's *The Light Construction Reader*.

[10] See Rowe and Slutzky's "Transparency: Literal and Phenomenal." See also the sequel, "Transparency: Literal and Phenomenal, Part II," in which formal effects are further elaborated as emerging from complex two-dimensional patterns. Both essays are reprinted in Gannon, *The Light Construction Reader*.

[11] For a particularly lucid treatment of Eisenman's literary affiliations, see Krauss's "Death of the Hermeneutic Phantom." For more on Eisenman's collaboration with Derrida, see Derrida and Eisenman, *Chora L Works*.

[12] Critic Jeffrey Kipnis has described this notoriously inexpressive material as "the equivalent of architectural gruel." See his "P-Tr's Progress," in which he further elaborates on the suppression of material effects in Eisenman's work.

[13] The influences of computer code on the conceptualisation of work inflect architecture and literature with equal intensity. See Hayles's *My Mother Was a Computer*.

[14] The acronym stands for computer-aided design/computer-aided manufacturing, a process that seamlessly integrates digital design software with computer-controlled fabrication equipment.

[15] See Pequeño Glazier's *Digital Poetics*.

[16] See Cayley's "Literal Art."

[17] See Cayley's "Writing on Complex Surfaces."

[18] The piece is available for download on John Cayley's website, <www.shadoof.net/in>. He describes it in his "Overboard."

[19] See Hofstader's *Gödel, Escher, Bach: An Eternal Golden Braid*.

[20] Though produced through analogue means, certain strains of postmodern architecture strangely prefigure this conflation or process and product. In particular Peter Eisenman's extensive elaboration of design process in his early houses should be noted. See his "Cardboard Architecture: House I" and "Cardboard Architecture: House II."

[21] See Hayles's *My Mother*, 15-38.

[22] See Cramer's *Words Made Flesh*.

[23] Raffaelo Maggioti mentions the device in a 1648 pamphlet, *L'invention mia non consiste nel caldo, a ned freddo; ma nella Renitenza all Compressione*.

[24] Prior to the "remastered" edition, which appeared only very recently in May 2006, the blue edition showed "house" in blue but the struck Minotaur passages in black. The red edition showed "house" in grey and the struck Minotaur passages in red. The black-and-white edition, most commonly sold in Europe, had neither the blue "house" nor the red Minotaur passages. The "remastered" full colour edition has "house" in blue and the Minotaur passages in red, along with the struck line in Chapter XXI in purple. We surmise that the full colour edition was what the author wanted all along, but economic considerations limited the main text to only one additional colour until sales justified the "remastered" version.

[25] Genette says this about paratexts: "The paratext is what enables a text to become a book and to be offered as such to its readers and, more generally, to the public. More than a boundary or a sealed border, the paratext is, rather, a threshold, or . . . a 'vestibule' that offers the world at large the possibility of either steeping inside or turning back. It is an 'undefined zone' between the inside and the outside, a zone without any hard and fast boundary on either the inward side (turned toward the text) or the outward side (turned toward the world's discourse about the text), an edge, or as Phillippe Lejeune put it, 'a fringe of the printed text which in reality controls one's whole reading of the text'" (1-2).

[26] See Hansen's "The Digital Topography of Mark Z. Danielewski's *House of Leaves*."

[27] For an account of these fields, see Hayles's *How We Became Posthuman*, 222-246.

[28] The process of creating genetic programs that can design circuits is described in Koza et al., *Genetic Programming IV*.

[29] See Hayles's "Saving the Subject."

[30] For extended discussions of stereotomy and the innovations it made possible both in stone and on paper, see Pérez-Gómez's *Architecture and the Crisis of Modern Science*, 203-236, and Evans's *The Projective Cast*, 179-239.

[31] Some of the more influential drawings of this period were exhibited at the Wexner Center for the Arts in the 2001 exhibition, "Perfect Acts of Architecture." See Kipnis's *Perfect Acts of Architecture*.

[32] Throughout history, from Piranesi and Boullée to Finsterlin and Taut, architecture's vanguard has periodically turned its attention to theoretical speculations through the elaboration of unbuildable projects.

[33] For a discussion of Lynn and other of Peter Eisenman's well-known protégés, see Gannon's "The Shape of Things to Come."

[34] The four partners, David Erdman, Marcelyn Gow, Ulrika Karlsson, and Chris Perry, are based in Los Angeles, Zurich, Stockholm, and New York respectively.

[35] See www.s-e-r-v-o.com for general information on the firm and a presentation of its projects.

[36] See the exhibition catalogue, Decter's *Dark Places*.

[37] Similar tendencies can be seen across architecture's younger generation. Emergent (led by Tom Wiscombe), Gnuform (Heather Roberge and Jason Payne), and Xefirotarch (Hernan Diaz Alonso) are just a few of the firms led by designers in their thirties that share servo's digitally-driven material and atmospheric ambitions.

[38] Cf. Manfredo Tafuri: "...there can never be an aesthetics, art or architecture of class, but only a class critique of aesthetics, art, architecture and the city." See his influential "Towards a Critique of Architectural Ideology." Tafuri later revised and elaborated this text as *Architecture and Utopia: Design and Capitalist Development*.

[39] These conversations were succinctly traced over three issues of *Harvard Design Magazine* in 2004 and 2005. See Allen et al, "Stocktaking 2004: Nine Questions About the Present and Future of Design"; George Baird, ""Criticality" and its Discontents"; and Reinhold Martin, "Critical of What?"

[40] In architecture, R.E. Somol and Sarah Whiting have advanced "the projective," while in other fields, the terms "post-critical" and "posthuman" have both been appearing with increasing frequency. See Somol and Whiting's "Notes Around the Doppler Effect and Other Moods of Modernism," and N. Katherine Hayles's *How We Became Posthuman*.

[41] See Whalen's "Data Navigation, Architectures of Knowledge."

[42] See Gessler's "Evolving Artificial Cultural Things-That-Think and Work by Dynamical Hierarchical Synthesis."

[43] For a wide-ranging analysis of how the process works on a cosmic and global scale in the natural world, see Morowitz's *The Emergence of Everything: How the World Become Complex*.

[44] *The Exploit* is still forthcoming, so page numbers are currently unknown.

[45] We are grateful to Alan Liu for thoughtful comments that were helpful in re-thinking the larger contexts for our argument and for other insights.

WORKS CITED

Allen, Stan et al. "Stocktaking 2004: Nine Questions About the Present and Future of Design." *Harvard Design Magazine* 20 (2004): 4-52.

Andrews, Jim and friends. *Stir Fry Texts.* <http://www.vispo.com/StirFryTexts/ >.

Baird, George. "'Criticality' and its Discontents." *Harvard Design Magazine* 21 (2005): 16-21.

Baudrillard, Jean. *Simulacra and Simulations.* Trans. Sheila Fraria Glazer. Ann Arbor: U of Michigan P, 1995.

Beiguelman, Giselle. "Code Movie 1." *Electronic Literature Collection Vol. I.* Ed. N. Katherine Hayles, Nick Montfort, Scott Rettberg, and Stephanie Strickland. Forthcoming. Available for download at the Electronic Literature Organization site, <http: //www.eliterature.org>.

Cantwell Smith, Brian. *On the Origin of Objects.* Cambridge: Bradford, 1996.

Castells, Manuel. *The Rise of the Network Society.* 2nd ed. London: Blackwell, 2000.

Cayley, John. "LENS: The Practice and Poetics of Writing in Immersive VR: a Case Study with Maquette." *Leonardo Electronic Almanac.* <http://mitpress2.mit. edu/e-journals/LEA/forthcoming>.

—. "Literal Art." *Electronic Book Review* (2004). <http://www.electronicbookreview. com/thread/firstperson/programmatology>.

—. "Overboard: an example of ambient time-based poetics in digital art," *dichtung-digital* 32 (2004). <http://www.dichtung-digital.com/04/2-Cayley.htm>.

—. "Writing on Complex Surfaces." *dichtung-digital* 35.2 (2005). <http://www. dichtung-digital.com/2005/2-Cayley.htm>.

Cramer, Florian. *Words Made Flesh: Culture, Codes, Imagination.* <http://pzwart. wdka.hro.nl/mdr/research/fcramer/wordsmadeflesh/>.

Danielewski, Mark Z. *House of Leaves: A Novel.* New York: Pantheon, 2000.

Decter, Joshua. *Dark Places.* Santa Monica: Santa Monica Museum of Art, 2006.

Derrida, Jacques and Peter Eisenman. *Chora L Works.* New York: Monacelli, 1997.

Eisenman, Peter. "Cardboard Architecture: House I" and "Cardboard Architecture: House II." *Five Architects: Eisenman, Graves, Gwathmey, Hejduk, Meier.* Ed. Arthur Drexler. New York: Oxford UP, 1972. 15-24.

Evans, Robin. *The Projective Cast: Architecture and Its Three Geometries.* Cambridge: MIT, 2000.

Gaddis, William. *The Recognitions.* New York: Peter Smith, 1995.

Galloway, Alexander and Eugene Thacker. *The Exploit.* Minneapolis: University of Minnesota Press (forthcoming).

Gessler, Nicholas. "Evolving Artificial Cultural Things-That-Think and Work by Dynamical Hierarchical Synthesis." <http://www.sscnet.ucla.edu/geog/ gessler/cv-pubs/03naacsos.pdf>.

Gannon, Todd. "The Shape of Things to Come." *Log* 2 (2004): 7-13.

—, ed. *The Light Construction Reader.* New York: Monacelli, 2001.

Genette, Gerard. *Paratexts: Thresholds of Interpretation.* Cambridge: Cambridge UP, 1997.

—. *white faced bromediads on 20 hectares,* <http://epc.buffalo.edu/authors/glazier/ java/costa1/00.html>.

Hansen, Mark B.N. "The Digital Topography of Mark Z. Danielewski's *House of Leaves.*" *Contemporary Literature* 45.4 (2004): 597-636.

Harvey, David. *The Postmodern Condition: An Enquiry into the Origins of Cultural Change.* London: Blackwell, 1991.

Hayles, N. Katherine. *How We Became Posthuman: Virtual Bodies in Cybernetics, Literature, and Informatics.* Chicago: U of Chicago P, 1999.

—. *My Mother Was a Computer.* Chicago: U of Chicago P, 2005.

—. "Saving the Subject: Remediation in House of Leaves." *American Literature* 74 (2002): 77-806.

Hofstader, Douglas R. *Gödel, Escher, Bach: An Eternal Golden Braid.* New York: Basic Books, 1999.

Ishiguro, Kazua. *Never Let Me Go.* New York: Knopf, 2005.

Jameson, Fredric. *Postmodernism, or the Cultural Logic of Late Capitalism.* Durham: Duke UP, 1991.

Jencks, Charles. *The Language of Post-Modern Architecture, 6th ed.* London: Academy Editions, 1991.

Johnson, Philip and Henry Russell-Hitchcock. *The International Style: Architecture Since 1922.* New York: W. W. Norton, 1932.

—. *Modern Architecture: International Exhibition.* New York: The Museum of Modern Art, 1932.

Kipnis, Jeffrey. "P-Tr's Progress." *Eleven Authors in Search of a Building.* Ed. Cynthia Davis. New York: Monacelli, 1996.

Kipnis, Jeffrey, ed. *Perfect Acts of Architecture.* New York: Museum of Modern Art, 2001.

Koza, John R. et al. *Genetic Programming IV: Routine Human-Computer Machine Intelligence* New York: Spring, 2005.

Krakowsky, Tali. "Algorithmic Anthologies." *34 Magazine* 8 (2006): 207-215.

Krauss, Rosalind. "Death of the Hermeneutic Phantom: Materialization of the Sign in the Work of Peter Eisenman." *Houses of Cards.* Ed. P. Eisenman, R. Krauss and M. Tafuri. New York: Oxford UP, 1987. 166-84.

Lyotard, Jean-François. *The Postmodern Condition: A Report on Knowledge, Theory and History of Literature, Vol. 10.* Trans. Geoff Bennington and Brian Massumi. Minneapolis: U of Minnesota P, 1984.

Markson, David. *Wittgenstein's Mistress.* New York: Dalkey Archive, 1999.

Martin, Reinhold. "Critical of What?" *Harvard Design Magazine* 22 (2005): 104-109.

McCaffrey, Larry and Sinda Gregory. "Haunted House: An Interview with Mark Z. Danielewski," *Critique: Studies in Contemporary Fiction* 44.2 (2003): 99-135.

McElroy, Joseph. *Plus.* New York: Carroll and Graf, 1987.

McGann, Jerome. *Radiant Textuality: Literature After the World Wide Web.* New York:

Palgrave McMillan, 2004 Memmott, Talan, *Lexia to Perplexia.* <http://www.uiowa.edu/~Iareview/tirweb/hypermedia/talan_memmott/plex/indo.html>.

MEZ, _][ad][Dressed In a Skin C.ode_, <http://www.cddc.vt.edu/host/netwurker/>.

Morowitz, Harold J. *The Emergence of Everything: How the World Become Complex.* New York: Oxford UP, 2004.

Moulthrop, Stuart. *Reagan Library*.1999. <http://iat.ubalt.edu/moulthrop/hypertexts/rl/pages/intro.htm>.

Ness, Millie with Martha Deed. *Oulipoems.* <http://www.uiowa.edu/%7Eiareview/tirweb/feature/sept04/oulipoems/index.html>.

Pequeño Glazier, Loss. *Digital Poetics: Hypertext, Visual-Kinetic Text and Writing in Programmable Media.* Tuscaloosa: U of Alabama P, 2001.

Pérez-Gómez, Alberto. *Architecture and the Crisis of Modern Science.* Cambridge: MIT, 1985.

Plascencia, Salvador. *The People of Paper.* San Francisco: McSweeney's, 2005.

Poundstone, William. *3 Proposals for Bottle Imps.* <http://www.uiowa.edu/~iareview/tirweb/feature/poundstone03/Bottle.html>.

Riley, Terence. *Light Construction.* New York: Museum of Modern Art, 1995.

Rowe, Colin and Robert Slutzky. "Transparency: Literal and Phenomenal." *Perspecta 8: The Yale Architectural Journal* (1964): 45-54.

—. "Transparency: Literal and Phenomenal, Part II." *Perspecta 13/14: The Yale Architectural Journal* (1971): 287-301.

servo. <http://www.s-e-r-v-o.com>.

Somol, R.E. and Sarah Whiting. "Notes Around the Doppler Effect and Other Moods of Modernism." *Perspecta 33: The Yale Architectural Journal* (2002): 72-77.

Speaks, Michael. "Design Intelligence, Part 1: Introduction" *A+U: Architecture + Urbanism* no. 12.387 (2002): 10-18.

Stefans, Brian Kim. *Fashionable Noise: On Digital Poetics.* Berkeley: Atelos, 2003.

Tafuri, Manfredo. *Architecture and Utopia: Design and Capitalist Development.* Trans. Barbara Luigi La Penta. Cambridge: MIT, 1979.

—. "Towards a Critique of Architectural Ideology." Trans. Stephen Sartarelli. Rpt. in K. Michael Hays, *Architecture Theory since 1968.* Cambridge: MIT, 2000, 32-33

Whalen, Thomas. "Data Navigation, Architectures of Knowledge." Banff Summit on Living Architectures: Designing for Immersion and Interaction. Banff New Media Institute. Banff, September 23, 2000.

Warnell, Ted et al. *SyntacticalError.* <http://warnell.com/syntac/index.htm>.

7

New York, Los Angeles, and Other Toxicities: Revisiting Postmodernism in Rushdie's *Fury* and *Shalimar the Clown*

Gavin Keulks

Scholars of Rushdie's work generally conclude that his last great novel was *The Moor's Last Sigh* (1995); that novel was followed by two uneven and decidedly postmodern works: *The Ground Beneath Her Feet* (1999) and *Fury* (2001). Rushdie's 2005 effort *Shalimar the Clown* fared much better, securing a spot on the Man Booker Prize long-list, but some reviewers still noted that it "lacks the fecund narrative magic, ebullient language and intimate historical emotion" (Kakutani, "Kashmir" 1) of *The Moor* and, of course, *Midnight's Children* (1981), Rushdie's consensus masterpiece.[1] The purpose of this essay is not to quarrel with reviewers, as their relation to scholarship is tenuous at best. Rather, I seek to contextualize *Fury* and *Shalimar* as authorial self-appraisals, necessary revaluations of the inherent tensions within Rushdie's trademark blend of postmodernism and postcolonialism, textuality and politics. Despite their thematic disequilibrium, their tendency towards soliloquy or proselytizing, their possibly derivative characters and biographical subtexts, these novels should be seen as meditations upon—or necessary reassessments of – postmodern aesthetics. In both time-frame and mood, they probe postmodernism's achievements, icons, symbols, and limitations. Similar to the recent work of other celebrated postmodern stylists – Don DeLillo, Martin Amis, and Jeanette Winterson chief among them – Rushdie's latest novels are definitional and revaluative: they reappraise his achievements during the 1980s and 1990s, isolating themes and techniques that no longer seem valid, or effective, in the somberly realistic post-9/11 world. Vital to this artistic reappraisal is a swerve away from "radical postmodernism"[2] – although the qualifier "first-phase," "vulgar," or "classic" would suffice equally as well – an artistic winnowing that rejects relativist and dehistoricisized versions of postmodernism while seeking to reinvigorate humanist concepts such as of agency, subjectivity, and love amid an Americanized backdrop that remains precipitously postmodernist. In brief, these novels attempt to reconcile postmodernism and historicism, textuality and humanism, and although their attempts largely fail, the effort remains imperative for Rushdie – not only to avoid becoming self-derivative or predictable but, more importantly, to illumine a literary future *beyond* postmodernism – one that is more viable than a half-hearted, populist retreat to realism.

9/11 and the "Post-Postmodern"

Rushdie's career has been founded upon his ability to depict duelling realities, rejecting easy synthesis or simplification. Stylistically, his sentences thrive with hyperbole or high rhetoric, whether political, playful, or intertextual. In earlier decades such combinations helped inspire debate about the inherently unsatisfying term *magical realism*, critically tainted by its implied moral neutrality and its over-emphasis upon fantasticality: history masquerading as conjurer's trick. In recent years, similar debates have flourished around a host of rival, variant, and often duplicitous reconfigurations of the realist moniker. These include "critical realism," "dirty realism," "postmodern realism," "neorealism," "deep realism," "spectacle realism," "fiduciary realism," "hyper-realism," and, most famously, "hysterical realism."[3] However, none of these examples improves upon their common target – the increasingly vulnerable term *postmodernism* – and that is where I believe *Fury* and *Shalimar the Clown* can be most instructive.

Both novels thwart categorization in any such mutated realisms, many of which lack the definitional precision for which postmodernism itself was loudly criticized. Instead, their plots, characters, and themes continue to depend upon postmodern aesthetics. These novels oppose fabulation and mimesis, postmodernism and positivism, magic and realism, even going so far as to stage battles between the virtual and real worlds. Moreover, these battles take place in unmistakably postmodern sites: the internet in *Fury*; television in *Shalimar the Clown*. The time periods of both novels are also decidedly postmodernist: *Fury* is set in the late-1990s, as the movement wound down; *Shalimar* traverses nearly the same historical moment, shifting focus to what many people consider the apex of the postmodern period – the late-1980s through mid-1990s. Two American cities – New York and Los Angeles – are also central to an understanding of these novels' postmodernist critiques. Unlike Rushdie's more famous treatments of place – India, Kashmir, Pakistan, and London, especially – America seems to elude him. An author with residences in both London and New York, he has struggled to depict his adopted American homeland, even though he has used it before in *The Ground Beneath Her Feet*. In this regard *Fury* might be seen as both a mediating *and* a culminating text, an artistic terminus whose unsatisfying execution arguably inspired Rushdie's literary revisitation to Kashmir in *Shalimar the Clown*. Kashmir, however, suffers a far different fate, or artistic verdict, in *Shalimar* than does India in *The Moor's Last Sigh*, India and Kashmir both in *Midnight's Children*, or London in *The Satanic Verses*. In *Shalimar* its political realism becomes diluted – some would say "trivialized" – by the sheen of spectacle and superficiality that signifies Rushdie's Los Angeles, mirroring similar representational problems that suffused New York in *Fury*. A difficult relation to place therefore haunts both of these novels, and such theatricality stands at the core of their postmodern weakness and reconsideration.

Finally, and perhaps most important, both novels seem saturated by the furious emotions leading up to and following the 9/11 terrorist attacks, even though *Fury* was published exactly one week before that date. As Sabina and Simona Sawhney suggest, that novel's sense of limitless rage, thwarted transcendence, and unqualifed paranoia certainly anticipate that event.[4] Similarly, *Shalimar* – Rushdie's first post-9/11 novel – is his loudest denunciation of fundamentalism to date. From the vantage-point of 2005, it now seems ludicrous that following these attacks, postmodernism itself had been blamed for establishing a climate in which moral and ethical relativism could thrive.[5] "What was deliberately overlooked," Victoria Lipina-Berezkina counters,

> is the complexity of postmodernist art: its relativism and ambiguity is an artistic strategy but not the conviction of an artist that there are no human values worth defending. This art has its specific artistic strategies and

unconventional ways for serious thoughts about the crisis of humanity in the world. (278)

To varying degrees of success, and through altering states of conviction, *Fury* and *Shalimar the Clown* investigate the problems of politics, media, textuality, and postmodernism in the post-9/11 world. They reject the extremist, end-of-history ideologies that marked theoretical discussions during the late-1980s and mid-1990s and embrace instead a more centrist construction. However, such a reconstruction struggles to recuperate two conventional meta-narratives: 1) the concept of an autonomous self (or integrated subjectivity), which attempts to resolve the perennial quandary of postmodern agency; and 2) the trope of sentimentalized love, which is more often subverted than confirmed in Rushdie's earlier work. Of course, these issues face a complicated future in these works, striving for definition against an Americanized backdrop that remains toxically depthless and over-mediated. Saturated by information technologies that threaten to override their renewed humanist appeals, *Fury* and *Shalimar* seem ultimately to confirm a cinematic or televisual aesthetic. This is neither artistic misstep nor failure, I contend, but rather a necessary artistic revaluation. Despite stentorian pronouncements about its symbolic "death," postmodernism remains central to this revaluation, and these novels can be seen as Rushdie's contributions to post-9/11 debates concerning the "post-postmodern period" or what others, preferring conciseness, simply have called the "post-ironic" age.[6] As Klaus Stierstorfer explains, such "stock-taking" works tend to be written when the "age they describe is felt to be drawing to a close" (221), and indeed Rushdie's novels are especially concerned with the acts of depicting, diagnosing, and winnowing a postmodern "age." The "age of pulse was giving way to the age of tone," Rushdie writes early in *Fury* (8). Confirming the persistence of postmodernist spectacle, the protagonist then contemplates "the parallel and sometimes contradictory idea of the sovereign self" before plunging "into, yes, television" (14). Taking a backward glance at *Fury* while anticipating the insistence of the emergent "post-postmodern" era, the narrator of *Shalimar* remarks that "An age of fury was dawning and only the enraged could shape it" (272). In this "glistening new zero-tolerance world" (290), however, there are "no longer protagonists, only agonists" (295).

The Sound of *Fury*

"The noise was inside him now ... the sheer goddamn unbearable head-bursting volume of the third millennium" (47). So states the narrator of *Fury*, whose chief character is a 53-year-old Malik Solanka, an Indian professor of philosophy turned high-concept doll-maker and, eventually, web-designer. He has inexplicable feelings of rage for his wife and son, suffers from blackouts and memory losses, and has recently fled his comfortable London home to seek refuge and redefinition in New York City. As in all of Rushdie's novels, there is a mythic component to this tale, one involving the classical avenging goddesses, the Furies or Eumenides/Erinyes. In Greek and Roman mythology, these were the daughters of Mother Earth, formed from the blood that fell after Uranus was mutilated by his son. They seek justice for un-avenged crimes, especially those involving patricide, and pursue their victims until they descend into madness or suffer excruciating deaths. They are personified in Rushdie's novel through the characters of Solanka's middle-aged wife, Eleanor, and his two lovers in New York, the Serbian woman Mila and the Indian beauty Neela.

As befits a novel about New York, *Fury* is a congested and boisterous book. Lists proliferate, ranging across street-beatings, the nightly news, and America's fascination with media celebrities, the singing-masters of the postmodern age. And postmodernism is certainly a language that Malik Solanka understands. Numerous times, summoning Jean Baudrillard, he condemns the fury of this "retro age" (142), "this age of simulacra and counterfeits" (232). Elsewhere, he inveighs against the superficiality of contemporary life in words that crystallize the conflict between postmodernism and classical mimesis: "In a Woody Allen movie, the scene would have been shot in black-and-white, that *most unreal of processes*, which had come to *stand in for realism*, integrity, and art," Solanka propounds, reflecting on the coarse speech of a native New Yorker; "But the world is in color and is less well scripted than the movies" (40; emphasis added). Infuriating some readers, most notably James Wood, Rushdie employs cinematic analogues as thematic scaffolding. These references underscore the novel's intertextual matrix and buttress its postmodern erasure of hierarchical value, especially between high and low art, elitism and populism. A later passage articulates the Baudrillardian quandary precisely:

> There were posters everywhere for *The Cell*, the new Jennifer Lopez movie. In it, Lopez was miniaturized and injected into the brain of a serial killer. It sounded like a remake of *Fantastic Voyage*, starring Raquel Welch, but so what? *Nobody remembered the original. Everything's a copy, an echo of the past*, thought Professor Solanka. A song for Jennifer: We're living in a retro world and I am a retrograde girl. (142; emphasis added)[7]

Passages such as these testify to the novel's frenetic, often mannered stylistics, which Wood berated as grotesque: this "cartoonishness, which has been Rushdie's weakness throughout his career…[,] has been lucky enough over the years to be flattered by the term 'magical realism' and which really deserves the term 'hysterical realism,'[8] only proves that he is incapable of writing realistically – and thus oddly confirms the prestige of realism, confirms its difficulty, its hard challenge, its true rigor" (226-27).

In closely related ways, the novel charts a crisis of signification, a symbolic *katabasis* or underworld descent that has been traditionally defined by liminal crossings, disintegration, and reflective backward glances. This structure, of course, previously served Rushdie well in *The Ground Beneath Her Feet*, and indeed Solanka's problem, as he eventually comes to diagnose it, remains one of autonomy and self-integration. Despite his repeated laments about the contemporary world's refusal to provide any space for "messy humanity" (74),[9] what most disturbs Solanka is not metaphysical contingency but rather his *personal* decay. When one of his friends – who functions in the novel as Solanka's doppleganger – attempts suicide, that character (doubled even in nickname as "Dubdub") articulates Solanka's deepest fears, claiming that there's "No direct or proximate cause. You just wake up one day and you aren't a part of your life" (27). This scene also features Rushdie's strongest indictment of celebrity, which achieves its fullest expression only when coupled with postmodern ideology: "The attention he'd been getting, the celebrity status, had greatly aggravated Dubdub's existential crisis. The more he became a Personality, the less like a person he felt" (27). The scene ends on a declaratively postmodern note when the narrator demands, "No more of all that globe-trotting *Magic Christian* Derridada! No more *performance*" (27). Eventually,

Rushdie attempts to unify the divisions of consciousness that beset his postmodern Everyman, striving to bind, as he writes, Solanka's "breaking selves together" (86). But reconciling these "contradictions and impoverishments of the Western human individual" (86) mandates that Rushdie synthesize such schisms within postmodernism itself, and that proves far more difficult. To this end, he stages a battle in virtual space between the mechanized and the human – a quintessential "fight to the death between the counterfeit and the real" (177) – which accelerates the novel's interrogation of realism and postmodernism.

Predictably, perhaps, this is where the novel begins to teeter, doubling back upon itself in an act of thematic enfolding. Whereas it had earlier begun by establishing the primacy of symbolic exile and amnesia, loss of home and self, the novel concludes with thunderous sentimentality, adopting tones of moral righteousness that leverage definition against chaos, love against fury. These are manifested chiefly through the themes of integrated subjectivity and autonomy and – secondarily – through relationship and love. "Everything in him fought against the mechanization of the human" (182), Solanka muses, signalling his retreat from postmodern hyperreality in both its Lyotardian and Jamesonian forms: "For the real problem was damage not to the machine but to the desirous heart, and the language of the heart was being lost … This was the Jitter Bug that made people mad: excess not of commodities but of their dashed and thwarted hopes" (183). Central to this notion of emotional excess are Solanka's relationships with his two New York lovers – Mila and Neela – and this romantic triangle accentuates his problems of representation. As befits the novel's structure, Mila is aligned with postmodern superficiality, Neela with materialist depth.

In her role as postmodern seductress, or temptress, Mila confirms the shadowy margins between art and life: she is the leader of the "vampires" (a group of computer wizards) and has modelled her life upon "Little Brain," the figurehead of Solanka's BBC-series of animated dolls, which are widely marketed and reproduced. For many readers, Little Brain and her cohorts – plus their symbolic descendents, the internet-incarnate Puppet Kings – beg credulity. Yet Mila functions successfully in her programmatic role: she is the quintessential simulacra of radical postmodernism, a human manifestation of media-spectacle and vacuous centres. Modelling her life on an animated doll, she is consumed by her allegorical opacity. Her self-realization remains slightly better than a puppet, lacking autonomy, self-determination, and agency. In a radical postmodern framework, she can be seen as the ultimate terminus of the dual crises of identity and signification, as she epitomizes self-consumption *through* media; she personifies the iconography of erasure. Even her full name – Mila Milo (abbreviated from Milosevic) – invokes historical and subjectivist cancellation, compressing Serbian history (and humanist horror)[10] into cheap alliteration, childish assertions of *me*, *my*, and *lo(w)*.

Unsurprisingly, Solanka rejects Mila in favour of Neela, but the change is far more than aural. A freedom-fighter who involves Solanka with revolutionaries in her home-country, Neela seeks to return Solanka to history, retracing his postmodern *katabasis*. Yet that return (and its presumptive renewal) ultimately fails to reinvigorate "realism" – conceptualized either as an artistic category (such as Wood's "hysterical" form) or as psychological depth, which Solanka ultimately seeks. It fails equally to confirm political conviction or righteousness: the revolutionaries wear Puppet King masks, mocking Solanka's (and the novel's) quest for authenticity. This opposition between, and Solanka's altered relationships with, Mila and Neela function as a core-sample of Rushdie's literary revisionism in *Fury*: he renegotiates the borders of postmodernism, realism, humanism, and historicism in his own quest to render fantastical realities without resorting to essentialism or relativism. The problem remains a lack of synthesis, both artistic and political, and that is the core of the novel's failure and of Rushdie's artistic undertaking.

For all his manic, confused confessionalism, Malik Solanka remains no less than a tourist in New York – a figurative flâneur – and unlike in Rushdie's more successful novels, this exilic disorientation diminishes the book's desire to prophesize an age. Confirming Jameson's controversial analysis of postcolonial literature that is either "libidinal" and "private" or functions as "national allegory" (see "Third-World"), the novel enacts an incomplete artistic restructuring of radical postmodernism: a descent into the symbolic underworld of Baudrillardian/Fukayamian a-historicism, spectacle, and exhibitionism that culminates in an cancelled return to the real, distinguished by humanist ideals, moral/materialist conviction, and, pre-eminently, love. Like Rushdie himself, Solanka endeavours to "attempt the first phase of such a restructuring" (79). The "first day" of this "new phase" (91) seeks to re-stabilize subjectivity through both narration and love. After beginning with a series of classical postmodern criteria – absent centres, proliferating surfaces, fractured selves, ontological uncertainty – the novel stages an unsuccessful attempt to assimilate realist and humanist criteria (psychological depth, love, agency, and autonomy) within a series of persistent – and persistently toxic – postmodern settings. As Solanka laments near the novel's end: "The speed of contemporary life … outstripped the heart's ability to respond" (228). Probing those "Galileo moments" (188) that define human existence, Solanka discovers a truth that crosses postmodernist and realist lines: "The fullness of a living self is inexpressible, obscure" (165). Hence the novel's final sentence – "The earth moves, the earth moves round the sun" – simultaneously confirms Neela's love as well as the impossibility of ever articulating (much less acting upon) that love, especially in the novel's accelerated, over-determined, and hyper-mediated time-period – the 1990s – fictionalized as a period of dehumanizing consumerism and textuality, of televisual and net aesthetics, of triumphant spectacle and simulacra.

Solanka's 1990s remain heavily stylized, of course, but within his age of televised Little Brains and internet-incarnate Puppet Kings, redemption remains hopeless – as does artistic rehabilitation. Staging his war between "the counterfeit and the real" (177), Solanka endeavours to bestow upon his creations not only representation but also a "value system" – an act he hopes will permit the "possibility of idealism" (164). A parallel tale of two creators, Solanka's decision thereby mirrors Rushdie's own: both try to broker an impossible truce between realism and postmodernism, culminating only in rejection. "New York faded into the background," Solanka explains:

> everything that happened to him in the city … fed his imagination, as though prefabricated to fit into the structure he had already devised. Real life had started obeying the dictates of fiction, providing precisely the raw material he needed to transmute through the alchemy of his *reborn art*. (170; emphasis added)

For both Solanka and Rushdie, such "reborn art" or artistic reconstruction ranges across three levels of furious, toxic emotions, as Daniela Rogobete explains: one suffuses New York; one surrounds Solanka's puppet-show; and one saturates physical violence (66-67).

Significantly, Solanka finds contentment *only* on the second level – the puppet show – which happens to be the sole postmodern stage. "In flight from his own life's ugly reality," the narrator explains, Solanka "found in the fantastic … a ceaselessly metamorphosing alternative world in which he felt instinctively at home" (*Fury* 169). For Rogobete, this "imaginary world of [Solanka's] cyborgs" reflects our own anxieties about losing control over our own humanism as well as our creations. The novel flounders when it aspires to positivism or progressiveness; it thrives, by contrast, only within spectacle.

In this regard, Patrick Colm Hogan's critical model (from his analysis of *Midnight's Children*) is helpful in theorizing Rushdie's struggle to define a post-postmodern aesthetics. Solanka stumbles in similar ways as Saleem Sinai, who fails to control his Midnight's Children Conference, and *Fury* extends Rushdie's tradition of promoting "the localism of practical identity" (524) over "reflective" or "categorical identity" (517, 526).[11] But Hogan's model – like Jameson's between "libidinal" literature and "national allegory" – fatally discounts the ideological functions of Rushdie's allegorization.[12] In *Fury*, the subject of that ideology is not sociopolitical but literary genre and form, best seen as an artistic judgment upon the postmodern period and its most problematic forces. Rejecting relativist extremism and a-historicism *as well as* conventionalized or sentimental realist and humanist ideals, *Fury* comes to rest, finally, in an under-defined middleground between – but not *beyond* – each of these labels. It cannot be labelled a traditional postmodernist text because it reconstructs mimetic categories of character, subjectivity, love, and redemption. However, it certainly resists labelling as a realist text – in any of its contemporary, mutated configurations – because its portraits of contemporary reality orient not toward any positivist or empirical reality but rather to the hallmark sites and technologies of the postmodernist age: television, popular culture, and the internet. Paradoxically, emotional honesty thrives more successfully in these false, spectacle-driven, duplicitous worlds than in the presumptively "real" environments of the characters.

In brief, the novel is an illuminating, instructive failure, a book that struggles to define its rhetorical and emotional bases and in so doing clarifies the complexity of Rushdie's artistic manoeuvres. Such evolutions lie at the heart not only of the late-postmodern period which the novel depicts (the 1990s) but also foreshadow the post-postmodern, post-9/11, post-ironic tensions that *Shalimar the Clown* revisits. As Solanka himself concludes, in words that can easily apply to Rushdie's own efforts in *Fury*:

> When he had attempted to retreat ..., hoping to overcome his faults by a process of renunciation, of *giving up*, he had merely fallen into new, more grievous error. Seeking his redemption in creation, offering up an imagined world, he had seen its denizens move out into the world and grow monstrous; and the greatest monster of them all wore his own guilty face. (246)

The Trial of the Century: Prosecuting Postmodernism

To far greater depth and success, *Shalimar the Clown* extrapolates *Fury*'s rumination upon the status and future of postmodernism and realism, humanism and historicity. Whereas the earlier novel probed the millennial end of postmodernism, *Shalimar* retreats to its most celebrated ten-year span – the late-1980s through mid-1990s – casting a retrospective eye on postmodernist legacies from a decidedly more sombre, fundamentalist, post-9/11 perspective. Despite these world-altering events, two constants remain: as in *Fury*, topographical realism is rendered grotesque in *Shalimar* by the spectacle and iconography of information technologies; in addition, *Shalimar*'s emphases on popular culture and intertextuality threaten to obscure its political seriousness. Whereas *Fury* invokes the internet as the locus amoenus for its battle between the virtual and real worlds, *Shalimar* stages its competition first within a courtroom, then within the confines of an electronic security system, and these scenes confirm Rushdie's reconsideration of postmodern hyperreality, his artistic quest to counterbalance spectacle, autonomy, and vengeance.

As the characters of *Shalimar* migrate between Los Angeles and Kashmir, so too does the novel teeter between textuality and totalization, postmodernism and politics. Contemplating Los Angeles, one character muses that "there were no mysteries here or depths; only surfaces and revelations" (5); in Kashmir, however, a notable shift in perspective occurs: "this time the magic didn't work, the real world refused to be banished" (369). These two quotations – and their respective locales – relate differently to categories of representation, reality, and truth. In the first, surfaces invite revelation yet summon no mysteries or depths; in the second, the real which refuses to be banished – even in Kashmir – remains tainted by magic, no less present though residual. Indeed, over the course of the novel, these real and magical worlds openly oppose one another; in the less tolerant post-9/11 age, however, the term *magical realism* has never seemed more vacuous. The "real" threatens to concretize "magic" into didacticism; by contrast, "surfaces and revelations" threaten to crystallize reality into conflicting images and rhetoric, a discursive shimmer. Both categories seek figurative justice, which is the overriding theme of *Shalimar the Clown*. This justice, however, never emerges cleansed of didacticism, and whether such dogma is postmodernist or realist in nature, it assumes two, appropriately disconcerting, forms in the novel – fundamentalism and television.

One effective way of theorizing *Shalimar* is to note that it seems divided between two divergent forms of radicalism: radical Islam (or Islamism) and radical postmodernism. Significantly, these modes animate the allegorical opposition between the novel's two chief characters or nemeses: Shalimar the clown and India/Kashmira. Kashmira navigates between realms that are alternately representational and real, magical and mundane, fabulist and authentic. By contrast, Shalimar's character is intentionally less rounded. Although he is initially characterized by magical performance – he possesses the ability to fly and realizes with "growing concern" that "there were times … when the laws of theater might not precisely apply to real life" (93) – he is primarily depicted in binary terms: He is a Muslim from Kashmir whose rage over losing his Hindu wife, Boonyi, to "America's best-loved, and then most scandalous, ambassador to India" (5) prompts his embrace of fundamentalist Islam. As Jason Cowley remarked in review, although Rushdie endeavours to imagine a world in which *Hindu* and *Muslim* can be seen as pure labels, or harmless descriptors, this pluralism ultimately succumbs to didacticism (17). During a sequence of crucial scenes in the novel – within the courtroom and Kashmira's home – Kashmira emerges victorious over Shalimar; however her victory does not resolve the novel's dialectic between radical postmodernism and radical Islam. Rather, it reconfirms Rushdie's continued engagement with, and struggle to define, a literary mode *beyond* postmodernism that can reconcile humanist ideals and political determination with postmodernist referentiality and exhibitionism.

In this context Shalimar may be helpfully viewed as an extrapolation of Malik Solanka, redirecting fury now outward through fundamentalism, having unleashed it from solipsism, where Solanka had previously contained it. Rushdie also tethers Shalimar to the world, even despite his character's ability to fly; in so doing, he tempers Solanka's postmodernist characterization. Shalimar's motivation – one of the chief targets of postmodernist attacks[13] – is also never in question, unlike Solanka's. "Don't you leave me now, or I'll never forgive you, and I'll have my revenge" Shalimar prophesizes early in the novel, crystallizing his motivation and hamartia; "I'll kill you and if you have any children by another man I'll kill the children also" (*Shalimar* 61). Finally, love plays a central role in both Solanka and Shalimar's quests for redemption: both wager their identities in separate battles with world-historical forces – symbolized in *Fury* by Neela's revolutionaries and in *Shalimar* by the fundamentalist paramilitary sect that Shalimar joins. In both characterization and theme, therefore, the two books can be seen as companion novels, interrogating fury and revenge, postmodernism and historicity, textuality and politics.

These forces coalesce when Shalimar is tried on television for the murders of Maximilian Ophuls (the ambassador) and Boonyi Kaul, his lover and Shalimar's wife. Similar to the courtroom scenes in the Coen brothers film *The Man Who Wasn't There* (2001), this trial acts as an indictment of radical postmodernism, questioning positivist categories of truth and justice.[14] As in the film, fantasy proliferates in Shalimar's trial, threatening to subsume reality within spectacle. As in *Fury*, cinematic analogues play important intertextual roles too: Shalimar's lawyer frequently alludes to movies and even offers to arrange a viewing of *The Manchurian Candidate* for the jury, which the judge – exuding particularly playful syntactic zeugma – denies by "lowering his spectacles" (383). Modelling his defence on that film as well as *The Man Who Wasn't There*, Shalimar's lawyer proposes to invoke a "sorcerer's defense," stipulating that the letters Shalimar received in prison toxified him through black magic. Nor is the character of Kasmira herself – the author of the letters – exempt from cinematic intertextuality: she is a documentary filmmaker by profession and resides in Los Angeles. Kashmira's letters perfectly epitomize the novel's divided rhetoric between postmodernism and realism. They represent an assault upon Shalimar's conscience that, on one level, reasserts realist motivation and vengeance and, on another level, reconfirms the exact opposite: depthlessness and ubiquitous textuality. "It all made the new, senseless kind of sense," the narrator summarizes for the reader. Immediately afterward, the lawyers squabble in the televised courtroom, and one eventually quips, "Trust in the law and do your job.... This isn't *Perry Mason*. We're not on TV." "Oh yes we are," the other rejoins (384). Immediately thereafter, Shalimar's "Manchurian bubble burst[s]" (385) when Kashmira takes the stand and banishes – for the time being – postmodern spectacle and relativism.

     In her role as chief witness for the prosecution, Kashmira becomes the mouthpiece for Rushdie's indictment of radical postmodernism. Demanding truth and justice, speaking of crime and punishment, Kashmira invokes the stabilizing structures of realism: empiricism, positivism, progressive motivation, psychological depth, integrated subjectivity, and moral self-determination. "Here I stand. I am my mother and my father," she declares, stabilizing signification, identity, and lineage even in the face of Rushdie's playfully implied polysemy (punning on witness *stand*): "You achieved nothing. They are not dead not gone not forgotten. They live on in me" (379). This moment functions as one of the clearest affirmations of realism in the novel, concluding a trajectory that commences early in her portraiture and culminates only when she visits Kashmir, seeking answers to the past.[15] Significantly, however – even in the midst of her passionate indictment – Kashmira never escapes entrapment within representational technologies as well as postmodernist techniques. Shalimar's trial is condensed to television ratings and ultimately subordinated to more marketable and more entertaining (i.e. more performative) television-trials, including the Menendez brothers, O.J. Simpson, and Rodney King. In this light, Kashmira's "stand" on the stand becomes little more than a cameo or live performance – a reiterative act, subservient to genre. In more successful novels like *The Moor's Last Sigh*, Alexandra W. Schultheis explains, such strategies invite readers to consider the role of popular culture in social unification, pondering "its importance as an image of national identity" (582).[16] In *Shalimar*, however, such references fail to uphold their promise as the source (or "site") of "aesthetic and national renewal" (593). Instead, they function as cheapened simulacra, superficial expressions of America's obsession with media distraction and social scandal. As Frederic Jameson comments, traversing postmodern television and film: "memory seems to play no role in television, commercial or otherwise (or, I am tempted to say, in postmodernism generally): nothing here haunts the mind or leaves its afterimages in the manner of the great moments of film" (*Postmodernism* 71). Or, as Rushdie writes, coupling classical allusions with televisual aesthetics and identifying the novel's divided rhetoric: "But now the wheel had turned and it was that woman's name which was never spoken [... which now] was traveling the world's airwaves on, for example, CNN" (*Shalimar* 338).

During the trial, Kashmira assimilates postmodernism and realism, fantasy and fact, superstition and truth. She collapses the polarities between these representational spectra and attempts to navigate *not between* but rather *beyond* their opposition. Building upon similar manoeuvres in *Fury*, her failure to triumph over relativism and spectacle further reflects Rushdie's artistic struggles to depict the conflicting realities of contemporary Kashmir and America – realities in which rhetoric too easily metamorphoses into didacticism and remains hopelessly bound by postmodern transmission and reception: discursive, simulacral, and manipulated. Through Shalimar and Kashmira's court-room conflicts, the novel places radical postmodernism itself on trial, yet ultimately confirms that a verdict is elusive, precipitate, uninformed. Postmodernist ideals undoubtedly suffer under the conflicted rhetoric of the novel, yet conventional, over-determined meta-narratives of reality, truth, history, justice, love, and redemption arguably suffer more. Rushdie's refusal to reconstitute these values verifies his reluctance to reject postmodernism *in toto* in favour of any facile realist reconfiguration. Indeed this discomfort is epitomized by his polysemous refusal to "execute" – both stylistically and thematically – his refusal, that is, to execute Shalimar for the crime of murdering Kashmira's parents.

Jason Cowley has proposed that whereas *Fury* is teleological in nature, concerned with terminal points, stoppages, and endings (the end of a marriage, of dot-com mania, possibly of sanity itself), *Shalimar the Clown* is concerned, chiefly, with the possibility of renewal (17). New beginnings come under relentless attack in the novel, however, regardless of whether they are theorized as an end to political conflict in Kashmir, the waning of fundamentalist rhetoric, or Kashmira's independence from Shalimar the clown. Instead, it seems more legitimate to claim that the novel dramatizes the challenge, if not the *impossibility*, of renewal in the post-9/11 age. That is arguably why, in the novel's final scenes, Shalimar pursues Kashmira to her apartment and why Kashmira's love affair with Yuvraj also fails to succeed, having commenced in Kashmir but succumbed to the toxicities of America, to which Yuvraj relocates in false hopes of winning her love. In this regard, the novel confirms the death not only of toleration but also of love: "The age of reason was over," Rushdie writes, "as was the age of love. The irrational was coming into its own" (226). In *Shalimar* far more than in *Fury*, Patrick Colm Hogan's comments about restrictive "categorical identity" seem relevant – especially to Kashmira, who rejects her "vacuous" affiliation with her westernized name "India" in one of the novel's earliest descriptions:

> "India" still felt wrong to her, it felt exoticist, colonial, suggesting the
> appropriation of a reality that was not hers to own, and she insisted to
> herself that it didn't fit her anyway, she didn't feel like an India, even if her
> color was rich and high and her long hair lustrous and black. She didn't
> want to be vast or subcontinental or excessive or vulgar or explosive or
> crowded or ancient or noisy or mystical or in any way Third World. Quite
> the reverse (5-6).

Negotiating the difficulties of preserving dynamic identity in the midst of post-9/11 mindsets that homogenize conflict into sectarian opposition, the novel seems to depict what Rushdie, editorializing about Islamism in 2001, termed "westoxification" ("A war" 12). This contamination by the west[17] is rendered by Max's seduction of Boonyi and by the corresponding actions of Max's wife, who banishes Boonyi to her homeland while confiscating Boonyi's child, India/Kashmira.

Although the lost utopia of Kashmir gleans as the nostalgic centre of the novel, and although *Shalimar* could be read as a "paean of love to a destroyed homeland" (Walter 21), this realist and historicist depth is diluted and – for some readers – hopelessly trivialized by the Los Angeles sections. Emblematic of the increasingly sombre evaluative criteria of the post-9/11 years, at least two reviewers argued that the novel is "hobbled by Mr. Rushdie's determination to graft huge political and cultural issues onto a flimsy soap opera plot," something that appeared "weirdly impertinent given the complex and bloody phenomenon of terrorism in the real world" (Kakutani, "Kashmir" 1; see also Miller). Indeed, the Kashmir material appears improbably impressionistic, undermining realism and historicism as well as any presumed political commentary. By contrast to the description of Kashmir in *Midnight's Children*, or the larger analyses of India in that novel or in *The Moor's Last Sigh*, *Shalimar*'s Kashmir seems incurably psychological, memorial. This is epitomized in the novel's most criticized line: "Everywhere was a mirror of everywhere else" (355). In other words, despite the novel's desire to depict worldly events, it more clearly seems indebted to Rushdie's own relocations and crises – both artistic and biographical. Such relocations have included, of course, his third divorce and remarriage, the removal of the *fatwa* (although bounties remain), and resettlement in America. In an interview with Emma Brockes, Rushdie also confessed that he doesn't perceive the novel to be primarily about terrorism: the love story came to him first during composition (6). I contend that *Fury* and *Shalimar* represent his artistic attempts to reconcile these personal and political events, and – more importantly – such subjects are never exempt from Rushdie's artistic reconsiderations of realism and postmodernism, fabulation and historicity. These issues receive one final treatment in *Shalimar the Clown*, as Rushdie arranges them in a parting tableau which dramatizes his refusal to "execute" and depicts the difficulties of defining a post-9/11, post-postmodern, or post-ironic aesthetics.

In San Quentin prison – awaiting execution – Shalimar seizes the opportunity to escape then proceeds to Kashmira's home, where the novel's dialectic between realism and postmodernism concludes. Passing the threshold of her sheltered, gated compound, Shalimar and Kashmira are reclaimed by information technologies and postmodernist spectacle: he breaches her security system while she observes him on a television screen, contemplating whether to safeguard herself in her Panic Room, an unmistakably intertextual space. Crystallizing what Rushdie himself is doing on a modal or generic level – and paralleling the reconstructive "phases" that Malik Solanka invokes in *Fury* – Kashmira watches Shalimar on her "zone monitor" (396). Eventually, she too succumbs to textuality and dons night-vision goggles, reversing the pattern of victimization in, among other analogues, *The Silence of the Lambs* (1991), in which Jody Foster's character is similarly hunted. Preparing to pierce Shalimar's heart with an arrow – her weapon of choice – Kashmira becomes subsumed by her allegorical significance, assuming her destiny as the ambassador of altered states and mythological power, both romantic and martial (Cupid/Eros; Artemis/Diana). In a particularly significant passage, Shalimar breeches Kashmira's final "zonal alarm," enters her room, and "switch[es] modes" (398), sensing her advantage in the dark.

At this moment, Shalimar has symbolically introduced linear fundamentalist rhetoric and binary orthodox motivation into Kashmira's realm of representation, liminality, and informatic transmission. It is here that Shalimar will be judged, and ironically he will be judged according to the criteria he has ushered across this threshold: by the mandates of vengeance and fury, singlemindedness of purpose. This is precisely where Rushdie could have settled the novel's debate between realism and postmodernism, fundamentalism and textuality. The death of either Kashmira or Shalimar would resolve their dialectical opposition, asserting through closure and finality what the earlier court-room scenes failed to achieve: the rehabilitation of categories of "truth" and "justice" untainted by postmodernist spectacle or relativism. Instead, the novel's final sentence remains paradoxically firm yet ambivalent, implying Shalimar's demise yet refusing to enact it – refusing, that is, to execute Shalimar the clown, whether theorized as the novel or the specific character. The novel's final words affirm nothing other than the characters' allegorical and therefore textual value: "There was no possibility that she would miss. There was no second chance. There was no India. There was only Kashmira, and Shalimar the clown" (396). This ending asserts neither tolerance nor pluralism, neither realism nor postmodernism; it problematizes redemption or renewal and isolates a memorial image of its twined programmatic nemeses. Although the novel is unquestionably more historicist than its companion text *Fury*, ultimately no "salvational historicity" (Jameson, *Political* 148) perseveres in *Shalimar*. In short, the novel weighs the competing claims of postmodernism and realism and concludes with a tableau of thwarted closure, indicative *not* of Rushdie's diminishing talent or derivative techniques but rather artistic complexities of resolving such dialects in a contemporary age that – to Rushdie at least – seems persistently discursive, mediated, and textualized by information technologies.

Recapitulation and Conclusion

Regardless of one's beliefs – and there are passionate opponents on both sides of the aisle – it seems safe to say that postmodernism was not some critical chimera or mass illusion – not for writers such as Rushdie, nor for scholars. It was not a haphazard cultural accident that somehow bamboozled otherwise rational artists and theorists throughout the Western world.   Nor does it necessitate some exculpatory apologia or collective mea culpa, although its chief theorists – Ihab Hassan and Linda Hutcheon most notably – have already issued such proclamations.   Instead, it requires redefinition and refinement, a process in which Rushdie, among others, continues to remain engaged. There are unmistakable political components to postmodern literature and levels of moral seriousness in postmodern theory, both of which strive to evolve a "humanism without metaphysics" (Thalhofer 173) that could still culminate in a recuperative, perhaps nourishing, reconstruction – a postmodernism that is no longer radical or vulgar but moderate – and moderating. Whether theorized as a descriptive label or a historical period, postmodernism has exhibited its share of strengths and limitations, often in extreme grotesques. As Marxism failed, for all progressive purposes, during the 1980s and 1990s – the unmistakable time-frames of *Fury* and *Shalimar the Clown* – so too do politics struggle to transmute or redeem in these novels. And as feminism was granted the critical leeway to evolve a second and even a third-phase, so too might it be wise to withhold a final verdict on postmodernism, at least until writers such as Rushdie has thoroughly dispensed with its trademark themes and techniques. He has yet to do so, although artistic deviations are clearly apparent.

In attempting to winnow the debate over postmodern aesthetics, *Fury* and *Shalimar the Clown* dramatize the perennial problems between postmodern simulacra, indeterminacy, and referentiality and classical configurations of agency, autonomy, romance, and redemption. By embedding battles between relativism and historicity in their plots, these novels dramatize an artistic disequilibrium between engagement and despair, prophecy and textuality. That both novels falter – or fail – to resolve this quandary is beside the point. Their struggle between style and subjectivity, hyperbole and humanism, portrays the complex aesthetics that writers must face in mapping a literature *after* or *beyond* postmodernism. In Rushdie's hands, this has become a contradictory, sometimes unbalanced poetics that rejects opportunistic retreats to realism while striving to reconstitute select humanist ideals, primarily love, agency, and autonomy. His "approach, while eying towards an exhausted, solitary peace 'far beyond,'" Klaus Stierstorfer explains, "remains a frenetic and grandiose celebration of postmodernist culture" (233) that seeks to retrieve idealism from postmodernist cancellation: "an attempt to live with loss and uncertainty as a permanent condition, ... a move beyond the harsh individualism of utilitarian modernity, and towards a different way of accounting for and valuing human needs" (232). In pursuit of these ends, *Fury* revisits New York through the eyes of Malik Solanka, a fractured individual whose motivation is indeterminate and whose greatest achievements take place in the virtual worlds of television and the internet. He seeks integration and renewal yet fails to triumph over the depthless simulacra that define his world. Similarly, *Shalimar* returns to Kashmir and Los Angeles, dividing its focus between the characters Shalimar the clown and Kashmira Ophuls. Their motivation is far more determined than Solanka's – over-determined in Shalimar's case – and although they struggle to remain tethered to the world, their crises also become tainted, primarily by television and fundamentalism, variations upon the themes of textuality and performance.

Rushdie has always been an iconic writer, frequently invoked to totemize subjects such as postcolonialism, postmodernism, and magical realism – as well as obvious extra-literary, socio-political edicts. As he revisits these artistic modes, having been so invested in their development, he has two primary options: outright rejection, which becomes difficult so late in one's career; and immanent reconfiguration, reshaping the boundaries and values of analysis from within. I believe *Fury* and *Shalimar the Clown* attempt the latter, building upon (yet by no means concluding) earlier efforts in *The Moor's Last Sigh* and *The Ground Beneath Her Feet*. They grapple with radical constructions of self and community in an attempt to redefine a contemporary age that thwarts integration and remains dangerously mediated, divisive, and discursive. These irresolvable conflicts permeate the novels' divided rhetoric and modal ambiguities, and this equivocation continues to confirm the difficulties of wedding postmodernism's intensified rhetoric with reconstituted, mimetic constructions of reality, subjectivity, and renewal – the difficulties, in other words, of charting a course *beyond* postmodernism.

Notes

[1]   See also Miller as well as Boyogada.

[2]   Although the phrase is used by many scholars, Hans Bertens defines it well in *The Idea of the Postmodern* (1995): "Radical postmodern theory must be regarded as a transitional phenomenon ... After an overlong period in which Enlightenment universalist representationalism dominated the scene, and a brief, but turbulent period in which its opposite, radical self-representationalism, captured the imagination, we now find ourselves in the difficult position of trying to honor the claims of both, of seeing the values of both representation and anti-representation, of both consensus and dissensus. Postmodern or radicalized modern – this is our fate: to reconcile the demands of rationality and those of the sublime, to negotiate a permanent crisis in the name of precarious stabilities" (3). Günter Leypoldt also uses the term in his essay "Recent Realist Fiction and the Idea of Writing 'After Postmodernism'" (26), which strongly influenced my reading, as did Klaus Stierstorpher's collection *Beyond Postmodernism* and his excellent essay within it.

[3]   James Wood coined the term "hysterical realism," and it seems the most likely to persist. It is itself derivative, however, building most clearly upon Jean Baudrillard's "hysteria of the hyperreal." "Critical Realism" was spearheaded by Roy Bhaskar and Rom Harré; Joseph Dewey introduced "spectacle realism" in 1999; Ihab Hassan speaks of "fiduciary realism"; "Dirty realism" is attributed to Bill Buford, in *Granta*; and "deep realism" is used by John Somer and John Daly in their introduction to the *Anchor Book of New Irish Writing*. "Postmodern Realism" and "neorealism" are far more ubiquitous.

[4]   See also Rogobete 65: "Rushdie's warning about the insecurity lying beneath the American self-possessiveness turned right on September 11: [as *Fury* states,] 'unsecurity is at the heart of what we are, uncertainty per se, in and of itself, the sense that nothing is written in stone, everything crushes' (115)"

[5]   Cf. especially Stanley's Fish's editorial in defense, "Condemnation Without Absolutes" (*New York Times*, 15 October 2001).

[6]   David Foster Wallace's critique "E Unibus Pluram: Television and U.S. Fiction" (1990) makes one of the best pleas for a post-Rorty-esque, post-ironic age, soliciting a new generation of consumers who will "have the childish gall actually to endorse and instantiate single-entendre principles." See *Review of Contemporary Fiction* (23 June 1993).

[7]   A similar motif saturates the "forgeries" that Max Ophuls completes in *Shalimar the Clown*: "These aren't forgeries," he claims, "because there are no originals" (139).

[8]   In the original review, Wood's awkward interjection about "hysterical realism" does not appear. For more on this term see Wood's essay "hysterical realism" in *The Irresponsible Self*.

[9] The quotation begs fuller reproduction: "But now living women wanted to be doll-like, to cross the frontier and look like toys. *Now the doll was the original, the woman the representation*. ... Behind their high-style exteriors, beneath that perfectly lucent skin, they were so stuffed full of behavioral chips, so thoroughly programmed for action, so perfectly groomed and wardrobed, that there was no room left in them for messy humanity" (74; emphasis added).

[10] The allusion is of course to Slobodan Milosevic, President of Serbia from 1989-97 and thereafter of the Federal Republic of Yugoslavia until 2000 – the novel's appropriate time-frame.   In 2001 Milosevic was arrested and charged with international war crimes for his genocidal policies in Kosovo, Croatia, and Bosnia.

[11] Hogan equates categorical identities with "self-concept" – metaphysical structures of sex, ethnicity, race, religion, etc. Practical identity is more dynamic and aligned with tradition; it is "almost invariably mixed up with hierarchies of status, economy, and gender" and "almost always involves cruelty, hypocrisy, deprivation, pain" (531). Similarly, Lipina-Berezkina attempts to probe "beyond individual personality" to a "level of *mentality* – a complex integrity of mental and spiritual orientations of literary character, of author and of reader" in her essay on the death and return of the subject (270).

[12] In his otherwise impressive essay, Hogan remarks, "In general I believe that allegory is simply a technique Rushdie uses, with no necessary thematic consequences" (525). Rushdie's "deepest political commitments," he argues, "set him against... the antagonistic and discriminatory distinctions that go along with categorical identities" (526).

[13] The most famous exposition of this critique comes not from Rushdie but from Martin Amis: see *Money: A Suicide Note* (1984): "I sometimes think that, as a controlling force in human affairs, motivation is pretty well shagged out by now" (331). A particularly relevant variation – given the significance of television to Rushdie's novels under discussion, occurs in Amis's *Night Train* (1997): "Motive might have been worth considering,...might have been in okay shape half a century ago. But now it's all up in the fucking air. With the TV" (127).

[14] Günter Leypoldt's essay "Recent Realist Fiction and the Idea of Writing 'After Postmodernism'" (2004) opens with an extended critique of this film in this light. See especially pages 19-20.

[15] See page 11 – "She was not ridiculous, would never permit herself to sink into fantasy. The world was real. The world was as it was. She closed her eyes and opened them again and there was the proof of it. Normalcy was victorious" – and 12: "She wanted to inhabit facts, not dreams. ... She wanted to see below the surface, the meniscus of the blinding brightness, to push through the hymen of the brightness, into the bloody hidden truth. What was not hidden, what was overt, was not true." At the end of her Kashmir journey, she is driven past a gate/threshold, and "this time the magic didn't work, the real world refused to be banished" (369).

[16] Writing about *The Ground Beneath Her Feet*, Klaus Stierstorfer similarly argues that "multimedia overkill" functions in that novel to evoke a Baconian "post-orphic phase." He then annotates the aspects of this emergent phase, relating them to three characters who separately symbolize reactions to postmodern "playfulness and apparent lack of ethical commitment" (220).

---

[17] Two other editorials are significant to this reading of the novel: Rushdie's "Kashmir, the Imperiled Paradise" (*New York Times*, 3 June 1999) and "The Most Dangerous Place in the World" (*New York Times*, 30 May 2002), both of which make impassioned pleas for Kashmiri autonomy and indict India and Pakistan for betraying the Kashmiri people. The latter essay is controversial, of course, in that it proposes a Western peacekeeping force as solution and condones the "war on terror." For a cogent discussion of Rushdie's divergent attitudes in his nonfiction and fiction, see Sawhney and Sawhney 434-39.

Works Cited

Boyogada, Randy. "Does Rushdie Matter?: Celebrity is the Enemy of the Artist." Rev. of *Shalimar the Clown. Weekly Standard* 31 October 2005.

Brockes, Emma. "'I have the hatred in a trunk in storage.'" [Interview with Salman Rushdie.] *Guardian* 29 August 2005: 6.

Cowley, Jason. "From Here to Kashmir." Rev. of *Shalimar the Clown. Observer Review* 11 September 2005: 17.

Hogan, Patrick Colm. "'Midnight's Children': Kashmir and the Politics of Identity." *Twentieth Century Literature* 47.4 (Winter 2001): 510-44.

Jameson, Fredric. *The Political Unconscious.* Ithaca: Cornel UP, 1981.

—. *Postmodernism, or, The Cultural Logic of Late Capitalism.* Durham, N.C.: Duke UP, 1991

—. "Third-World Literature in the Era of Multinational Capitalism," *Social Text* 15 (fall 1986): 65-88.

Kakutani, Michiko. "A Dollmaker and His Demons in the Big City." Rev. of *Fury. New York Times Book Review* 31 August 2001: 31.

—. "In Kashmir, Toxic Love Breeds Terrorism." Rev. of *Shalimar the Clown. New York Times Book Review* 6 September 2005: 1.

Leypoldt, Günter. "Recent Realist Fiction and the Idea of Writing 'After Postmodernism.'" *Amerikastudien* 49.1 (2004): 19-34.

Lipina-Berezkina, Victoria. "American Postmodernist Literature at the Turn of the Millenium: the Death and Return of the Subject." Stierstorfer, ed. 269-90.

Miller, Laura. "*Shalimar the Clown*: An Assassin Prepares." Rev. of *Shalimar the Clown. New York Times Book Review* 23 October 2005: 16.

Rogobete, Daniela. "Diaes Irae: Faces of Wrath in Salman Rushdie's *Fury.*" *B.A.S.: British and American Studies* ix (2003): 61-8.

Rushdie, Salman. *Fury.* New York: Random House, 2001.

—. *Shalimar the Clown.* New York: Random House, 2005.

—. "A war that presents us all with a crisis of faith." *Guardian* 3 November 2001, *SaturdayReview*: 12.

Schultheis, Alexandra W. "Postcolonial Lack and Aesthetic Promise in *The Moors Last Sigh.*" *Twentieth Century Literature* 47.4 (Winter 2001): 569-95.

Sawhney, Sabina, and Simona Sawhney. "Introduction: Reading Rushdie after September 11, 2001." *Twentieth Century Literature* 47.4 (Winter 2001): 431-43.

Stierstorfer, Klaus. "Wobbly Grounds: Postmodernism's Precarious Footholds in Novels by Malcolm Bradbury, David Parker, Salman Rushdie, Graham Swift." Stierstorpher, ed. 213-34.

—. ed. *Beyond Postmodernism: Reassessments in Literature, Theory, and Culture.* Berlin and New York: Walter de Gruyter, 2003.

Thalhofer, Helga. "Paradox vs. Analogy: De Man and Foucault." Stierstorpher, ed. 157-76.

Walter, Natasha. "The children of paradise." Rev. of *Shalimar the Clown. Guardian Saturday Review* 3 September 2005: 21.

Wood, James. "The Nobu Novel." *The New Republic* 27 September 2001: 32-36. Rpt. "Salman Rushdie's Nobu Novel." *The Irresponsible Self: On Laughter and the Novel.* New York: Farrar, Straus, Giroux, 2004. 221-33.

8

Nothing to Write Home About:
Impossible Reception in Mark Z. Danielewski's *House of Leaves*

William G. Little

A funeral wake is an expression of hospitality, an event in which one who has died is taken in and honoured as a guest. While it makes room for the dead, a wake also aims to bring the host a measure of security. At one level, it re-creates, in ritualized fashion, the bereaved's psychic incorporation of the dead other, that preliminary part of the mourning process in which the self keeps the other alive in itself. At another level, it attempts to formalize a hope that the living's responsibility to the dead can come to an end. Specifically, it seeks to safeguard against the possibility that, in the future, the dead might show up unannounced to haunt the living. In this regard, the wake serves to show the dead how to be a proper guest.

In this context, the phrase "The Wake of Postmodernism" might be taken to suggest that, culturally speaking, postmodernism is a dead phenomenon destined to rest in peace. I wish to argue that such a destination is made wonderfully problematic by Mark Z. Danielewski's novel *House of Leaves* (2000), a text that one might be tempted to classify, too quickly, as a metafictional haunted-house tale. Along with its encyclopaedic range and formal experimentation, its metafictional quality gives the novel the look and feel of high postmodernist literature, with the result that, if such work's time has passed, *House of Leaves* threatens to appear dead on arrival. Not coincidentally, a figure in the novel named Johnny Truant takes possession of a trunk containing documents which, with his introduction and notes, are reproduced in *House of Leaves* and which he likens to the dead body of their recently deceased author, a blind man named Zampanò: "I just glanced over at the trunk. The first time I saw it, I mean when I discovered what was inside, it appalled me. Like I was staring at the old guy's corpse" (21)[1].

However, just as Zampanò's textual leaves haunt Truant as he labours to sort and edit them, *House of Leaves* might be said to rise from a grave containing a postmodern corpus characterized by intense self-reflexivity, the use of pastiche and/or parody, and, in some instances, the narrative structure of a funhouse. Danielewski performs this ghostly writing through complex consideration of the ethico-religious problem of responsibility, a consideration that appears vital at a time when fundamentalist ideologies are pressing the concept of responsibility into service for terrifying purposes. Drawing on Jacques Derrida's late work on hospitality and the gift, I wish to argue that the novel may be read as a religiously-minded meditation on the crucial, yet impossible, task of responding to an other that, marked by death, resists proper understanding, housing, burial. *House of Leaves* may be a death-bound postmodern text, but it throws into crisis the very concept of a wake. This crisis is apparent in the matter of classifying the novel. An effort to situate *House of Leaves* as a postmodern novel or as something clearly other than a postmodern novel (a post-postmodern novel?) is a placement project that leads, it seems to me, to a dead end. Indeed, the novel tells the story of cryptic spaces that appear within a private home and unsettle the concept of assuming residence, a dramatization of architectural displacement which suggests, among other things, Danielewski's determination to question the possibility that his literary leaves might be housed securely within a particular genre and, more broadly, to question the possibility of constructing firm walls between cultural periods.

I

The novel opens with a curious dedication, one that seems simultaneously to address and dismiss the reader: "This is not for you." For the newly arrived guest expecting to enter Danielewski's literary house without getting held up at the threshold, the dedication, posted at the doorstep, reads like a welcome note inscribed, paradoxically, by a hostile host. Insofar as its message is destined for the reader, it appears designed to leave the reader out of the picture. It might be kindly warning "you" off (i.e., you – reader – do not want to read this book; leave it alone). It might be sending a belittling message (i.e., the project of entering the house/reading the book is not one you – reader – are up for; leave it to those who can handle it). It might be casting a pre-emptive value judgment (i.e., this book is not going to be to your taste; it is not the kind of thing you – reader – go for; leave it for those who will appreciate it). It might be making a disclaimer about responsibility (i.e., this book does not work for your benefit; it does not give itself over to you; it does not appear for you, testify for you, speak on your behalf; it is not dedicated to you; it leaves you to your own devices). Read along these lines, the dedication lacks the features of ordinary hospitality. Its rhetoric of gift giving, of house warming – "This is [   ] for you" – seems hollow at the centre. If nothing else, it is the sign of a strange disposition.

Once these interpretive lines are cast, there is a danger in abandoning too quickly this matter of the dedication's strangeness. It seems important to remain, insofar as possible, dedicated to strangeness. For what is most strange about the dedication is that repeated explorations of its ambiguous grammatical construction reveal shifts of meaning that suggest *House of Leaves* is, in complicated ways, dedicated to the subject of hospitality. These shifts open up the possibility that "This is not for you" signifies something other than the withdrawal of a hand or an outright refusal to usher "you" into the house. Specifically, they suggest that the strange term that haunts the dedication – the "not" – might actually be offered to the reader as a gift of sorts: "Here, this book is 'not,' and it is for you." But what does it mean for "this" book to be described as (a) "not"? And how is it possible for "not" to be a gift? Can "not" be given? Can "not" be received? Can "not" speak for "you," work for "you," be dedicated to "you"? If this is hospitality, it would seem to violate every expectation of how hospitality is supposed to work.

In a piece titled "Hostipitality" comprised of extensive notes for seminar sessions he conducted, Jacques Derrida explores a number of interrelated concepts (death, God, forgiveness), each of which haunts the concept of hospitality. According to Derrida, conventional hospitality involves what might be called techniques of reception. Hospitality is at work when a host receives a guest with open arms: "If, while saying to the other, 'Come in,' I show him that I am sad or furious, that I would prefer, in short, that he not come in, then, then it is assuredly not hospitality. The welcome must be laughing or smiling, happy or joyous" (358-59). Playing off of the French verb *tenir* (to hold), he explains that the host employs a "welcoming apparatus" (361) which involves ex*tension* (of an invitation, of a hand, of a greeting, of a stay) to the guest and at*tend*ance on the guest. In sociological terms, the host is dedicated to holding itself out to the other. In philosophical terms, the host is dedicated to getting a cognitive hold of the other's difference. By arrangement, there is nothing unexpected. This sort of hospitality confirms the other's arrival on the self's property and, ultimately, confirms the self's appropriation of the other. The stranger is made familiar. The host puts the guest *at home* by making the guest legible. Consider, for example, the practice of signing a guest book. Consider also the important role now played by the camera: the passport photo that grants the guest an official identity abroad; the postcards and picture-friendly tourist sites that frame the guest's experience; the host's snapshots that prove the guests visited.

While these traditional techniques of reception require that the host perform a certain kind of giving (of time, attention, space) to the guest, the giving is qualified by the fact that the host receives something in return. Host and guest enter into a system of exchange. The guest responds to the host's invitation – the "This is for you" – in a reciprocal fashion that draws them into an economic relationship. By accepting the offer, the guest is placed in debt. This bind requires, among other things, that the guest leave on reasonable terms: leave the place as it was found; leave in good spirits; leave a token of appreciation; leave with a promise of return. These "leaves" represent dividends on an investment. Among other things, they insure that the guest will behave hospitably toward the host. The host can leave home with the expectation of being at home elsewhere. Customary hospitality turns a dwelling into a house of calculable leaves.

For Derrida, it is precisely because these techniques of reception are inseparable from calculation that they do not make for true hospitality:

> When one says "I invite you," it means: I pay and we are inscribed in the circular commerce of the most inhospitable exchange possible, the least giving. When one invites, not only mustn't one send invitation cards and say 'I invite you,' it is me who invites. Not only must one not say this, but

one must also not think it or believe it, nor make it appear – to oneself or to the other. (398)

To invite is to engage in accounting work, which means that whatever is given is not, ultimately, freely given. The host who, in a conscious spirit of giving, thinks or believes "I invite you" is always, in some fashion, looking out for self-interest. Derrida suggests that, beyond the scope of this credit-minded outlook, there is another hospitality which involves the giving of what he elsewhere terms "a gift." This sort of giving does not operate according to the logic of speculation. A gift is not related to proprietary interests. A gift is not a proper gift. It cannot be awaited, delivered, accepted, or even remembered as a "gift." A gift is given, but, paradoxically, not in such way that "you" and "I" would ever know it. A true gift is always a not-gift for you, a "this is not for you":

> *At the limit, the gift as gift* ought *not appear as gift: either to the donee or the donor.* It cannot be gift as gift except by not being present as gift. Neither to the "one" nor to the "other." If the other perceives or receives it, if he or she keeps it as a gift, the gift is annulled. But the one who gives it must not see it or know it either; otherwise he begins, at the threshold, as soon as he intends to give, to pay himself with a symbolic recognition, to praise himself, to approve of himself, to gratify himself, to congratulate himself, to give back to himself symbolically the value of what he thinks he has given or what he is preparing to give. The temporalization of time (memory, present, anticipation, retention, protention, imminence of the future; "ecstasies," and so forth) always sets in motion the process of a destruction of the gift: through keeping, restitution, reproduction, the anticipatory expectation or apprehension that grasps or comprehends in advance. (*Given Time* 14)

Since the gift is given "at the limit," where economic and philosophical speculations leave off, it is always secret, hidden. The true gift cannot be claimed or housed.

The gift is the (non)manifestation of what Derrida calls "radical hospitality" or "sacred hospitality," terms which do not simply describe the dialectical opposite of hospitality-as-invitation. Not unlike the passages that, in *House of Leaves*, disturb the family home, this other hospitality haunts and disturbs the specular framework of conventional hospitality: "what belabours and concerns hospitality at its core, what works it like a labor, like a pregnancy, like a promise as much as like a threat, what settles in it, within it, like a

Trojan horse, the enemy (hostis) as much as the avenir, intestine hostility, is indeed a contradictory conception, a thwarted conception, or a contraception of awaiting, a contradiction of awaiting itself" ("Hostipitality" 359). In sacred hospitality, it is not that the host refuses to wait for and on a guest. The phrase "contraception of awaiting" describes an arrangement that is difficult to conceive because it involves the sudden, unexpected coming of an other which disrupts the host's lookout position. Coming "beyond or before the invitation" ("Hostipitality" 360), this other throws techniques of reception into crisis. It is so unanticipated and surprising that it cannot be received on proper terms or conceived in proper terms, either before or after its arrival. Indeed, to say that such a terribly strange stranger arrives is not to say that it becomes fully present on the scene. Instead, its appearance is, paradoxically, always a sort of no show, a "this is not for you." Like the gift, which, to be a gift, must never show up or be presented as such, this stranger's arrival ruptures hospitality's system of exchange and accountability. It enacts an "intestine hostility" to hospitality. The other is so *totally other* that the host can contract no alliance, secure no guarantee of compensation. It is, more or less, what Derrida calls a "visitation," that which crosses thresholds unbidden and unannounced, blurring the distinction between living and dead, presence and absence. Haunting the host's premises as well as hospitality's economic premise, it also blurs the distinction between host and guest. For this reason, Derrida also refers to this stranger by the French term "hôte," a word that means both guest and host.

Sacred hospitality thus demands the impossible, namely that one be receptive to an other that exceeds the binds and bounds of receptivity:

> If, in [conventional] hospitality, one must say yes, welcome the coming, say the "welcome"; one must say *yes* there where one does not wait, *yes*, there where one does not expect, nor await oneself to, the other, to let oneself be swept by the coming of the wholly other, the absolutely unforeseeable stranger, the uninvited visitor, the unexpected visitation beyond welcoming apparatuses. If I welcome only what I welcome, what I am ready to welcome, and that I recognize in advance because I expect the coming of the hôte as invited, there is no hospitality ("Hostipitality" 361-62).

What does it mean that the host is "swept by the coming" of the hôte? The phrase hints that the unforeseen and untenable (non)appearance of this "wholly other" is a messianic matter and that the terms "visitation" and ghostly "hôte" represent an effort – an always halting, erring effort – to name the coming of God. Not coincidentally, Derrida's example of "hospitality *par excellence*" ("Hostipitality" 372) is God's unexpected visit to the ninety-nine-year-old Abraham to inform him that, impossibly, his wife will bear a son, Isaac. This surprise announcement of a conception that contradicts standard anticipations of birth and death is a "contraception of awaiting" which sweeps away any reasonable, economic-minded response. Abraham and his wife, Sarah, laugh at the announcement, hardly a calculated return.

As an archetypal example of a host "swept by the coming," Abraham is also a subject of Derrida's study *The Gift of Death*, where the focus is on God's later, equally unexpected appearance in Genesis to announce to Abraham that he must sacrifice his son. Here again Abraham is placed in a relation beyond all rational accounting. There is no assurance he will get anything back, not least his son, for putting Isaac to death. Like a gift, the death is not presented to Abraham as a present that, once delivered to God, secures a reciprocal, equivalent gesture. It is as though God communicates the following to Abraham, though without saying so: "I give you this death to do. It is for you to do, but it is not for you to expect anything in return. This death is [not] for you." Derrida writes that what God gives, as hôte, is the gift of an immeasurable goodness which marks a "Christian 'reversal'" (*Gift* 40) of Platonism. In Plato's famous allegory of the cave, the true philosopher employs reason to emerge, over time, from the shadows – the underground passages – of the world of appearances and, after a period of logical adjustment, to look directly at the sun, to understand the Good. Sacred hospitality challenges the essentialist logic of solar in-sight. God's goodness is given rather than grasped. Moreover, it comes from an "essence without essence" (*Gift* 29) which remains forever out of sight and beyond apprehension, even at the time of the coming of the hôte. As Derrida puts it:

> God is himself absent, hidden and silent, separate, secret, at the moment he has to be obeyed. God doesn't give his reasons, he acts as he intends, he doesn't have to give his reasons or share anything with us: neither his motivations, if he has any, nor his deliberations, nor his decisions. Otherwise he wouldn't be God, we wouldn't be dealing with the Other as God or with God as *wholly other [tout autre]*. If the other were to share his

> reasons with us by explaining them to us, if he were to speak to us all the time without any secrets, he wouldn't be the other, we would share a type of homogeneity. (*Gift* 57)

Unlike the familiar sort of guest, God is a hôte about which nothing is ever known. God is nothing of the sort.

Violating the techniques of reception that structure conventional hospitality, the hôte places the host in a position of subjection. Alluding to the title of Søren Kierkegaard's reading of God's Abrahamic visitations, Derrida suggests that to be swept by the tremendous mystery – the *mysterium tremendum* – that is this nothing-of-the-sort is, before all, to be subjected to fear and trembling. In contrast to the Platonic philosopher, whose destiny is, over time, to seize the truth by seeing the original Good, the host is seized by an all-seeing but obscure origin: "We fear and tremble because we are already in the hands of God, although free to work, but in the hands and under the gaze of God, whom we don't see and whose will we cannot know . . ." (*Gift* 56). God's gift of infinite love is given in secrecy so profound (Abraham can in no way discern why he is being called to put his son to death) that, before one knows it (even before the coming that conceals as it reveals), one is caught up in a "dissymmetrical alliance" (*Gift* 73). The host is always already taken hostage by the hôte. One is not at home in one's house. One shakes likes a leaf. One is possessed by a stranger that, paradoxically, remains beyond all reasonable relation. One is displaced and cast down. Perhaps it is not surprising then that in an effort to describe the impossible significance of the gift Derrida resorts to the metaphor of displacement:

> *Atopos*, as we know, means that which is not in its place (noon at two o'clock) and thus it means the extraordinary, the unusual, the strange, the extravagant, the absurd, the mad. Only an *atopic* and *utopic* madness, perhaps . . . could give rise to the gift that can only give on the condition of not taking place, taking up residence or domicile: *the gift may be, if there is any.* (*Given Time* 35)

What kind of place could, figuratively speaking, house such an atopic scene, such a scene of madness, such a scene where, even if the gift is given for you (*the gift may be*) it is not the kind of thing that gets left for you (*if there is any*)? Might such a place be a house of "leaves"?

II

Not coincidentally, the peculiar usher who meets "you" on the threshold of Danielewski's literary house is a displaced figure. Johnny Truant is an apprentice tattoo artist living a vagrant life in contemporary Los Angeles. The "Introduction" to *House of Leaves* is his testimony about coming into not-altogether-welcome possession of a densely layered, fragmented text. His story begins with an invitation, delivered at a point when he literally has no place of his own, while he is "couching it from Santa Monica to Silverlake looking for an apartment'" (xi). In the dead of night, his friend Lude, a hard-partying hairdresser, calls and asks him to "come over to his place" (xi). When Truant arrives, his host escorts him to the neighbouring apartment previously occupied by Zampanò, who, according to Truant, turns out to have been a stranger in his own right: "I never came across any sort of ID, whether a passport, license or other official document insinuating that yes, he indeed was An-Actual-&-Accounted-For person" (xii). On the premises of an unaccountable figure about whom nothing of "any sort" can be positively made, Truant is ushered toward a document made up of myriad scraps of paper couching passages which are "always branching off into other pieces" (xvii). Before he has a chance to familiarize himself with this errant text – one with no clear authorial or narrative origin – it visits him in a haunting fashion, though it is situated at a remove: "One thing's for sure, even without touching it, both of us slowly began to feel its heaviness, sensed something horrifying in its proportions, its silence, its stillness, even if it did seem to have been shoved almost carelessly to the side of the room" (xvii). Nevertheless, he decides to take the text with him. Without having read them yet, he decides to house the leaves, but his ability to do so depends on his framing them in economic terms. To play host, he must conceive of the text as a commodity, that which can be bound and assessed: "The thing became only a thing. So I took it home" (xviii).

Once he begins exploring the text's strange passages, he discovers them to be Zampanò's elaborate summary and analysis, replete with footnotes, of a documentary film titled *The Navidson Record*. The film is about a mysterious space that suddenly appears in a rural Virginia home into which a renowned photojournalist named Will Navidson has recently moved with his long-time partner, Karen Green, and their two young children. Zampanò's commentary and accompanying footnotes, which Truant stitches together, perhaps embellishes, and re-presents for the reader, appear after the "Introduction." The commentary references other close readings of the film (which are fictional, i.e. the product of Danielewski's imagination) and draws on writings from numerous disciplines (anthropology, psychology, religion, photography, architecture, etc.), some of which are fabricated by Danielewski and some of which are actual works. It is also marked by unusual, at times disorienting, typographical features: boxes; columns; textual collages; strike-throughs; blank spaces; appendices; an index, and multiple tiers of footnotes, including those made by anonymous editors of Truant's edition of the commentary. Among other things, these devices serve to illustrate the impossibility of navigating through the novel's passages to arrive at an authoritative understanding of *The Navidson Record*. There is no master text in Danielewski's *House*. Indeed, Truant's footnotes contain passages at times so lengthy and labyrinthine that it becomes difficult to tell what constitutes the novel's core text, the interior of *House of Leaves*.

However, Danielewski's commitment to formal displacement amounts to something more than a re-creation of postmodernism's preoccupation with the nature and status of representation. Instead, Truant's representation of Zampanò's representation of *The Navidson Record* may be read as a story about the displacements that mark the experience of radical hospitality. For the story concerns "a strange spatial violation" (24) that occurs in the Navidson-Green house. Returning from a wedding two months after they have taken possession of the property, they first discover a "peculiar addition" (28) off the master bedroom, a space not unlike a walk-in closet which, bizarrely, "lacks outlets, sockets, switches, shelves, a rod on which to hang things, or even some decorative molding" (28). In what ways does this space represent a violation? Its presence would indicate that the house was entered without permission, that there was a visit made without invitation: "No one could deny there had been an intrusion" (24). To borrow one of Danielewski's favourite phrases, the space seemingly comes from "out of the blue," an occurrence that may partially account for why, in certain editions of the novel, the word "house" always appears in blue[2]. On the surface, there is no sign of forced entry, and nothing material is missing or destroyed. In other words, the anomalous space constitutes a violation of the very concept of intrusion. Instead of wreaking destruction, the intrusion results in a construction of some sort, though given that the space is defined by what it lacks – given that its presence is defined by a kind of absence – to call it a "construction" is not to name it properly.

Showing up with such impropriety, the strange space violates the laws of reception that govern typical hospitality. When he first moves into the house, Navidson sets up motion-sensitive cameras throughout its interior to capture "pearls of the particular" (10) on film, moments of ordinary domestic life he plans to edit into a project (indeed, footage from the fixed cameras ends up in *The Navidson Record*). Mysteriously, however, the cameras – the host's prosthetic eyes – pick up no evidence of the intrusion: "Only their [the family's] exit and re-entrance exists on tape. Virtually a week seamlessly elided, showing us the family as they depart from a house without that strange interior space present only to return a fraction of a second later to find it already in place, almost as if it had been there all along" (28). Though there are technologies mounted to receive even an unwanted guest, the space appears so unexpectedly and shockingly that there is no way to be there, in time, to register the arrival. The family can establish no safe lookout position. Karen draws on photos to support their contention that, in the time before their leave, they saw nothing there, but the space itself is given before there is time to record the giving of the space. Like a gift, it appears in a time out of time, in a nick of time:

> wherever there is time, wherever time predominates or conditions experience in general, wherever *time as circle* . . . is predominant, the gift is impossible. A gift could be possible, there could be a gift only at the instant an effraction in the circle will have taken place, at the instant all circulation will have been interrupted and *on the condition* of this instant. What is more, this instant of effraction (of the temporal circle) must no longer be part of time. (*Given Time* 9)

If the cameras could capture the intrusion in time, they would illuminate the origin of a cryptic space which appears only as an impossible hole in the house and an impossible hole in time, a space that is a hole-y space. The cameras' record would allow the host, after a period of time for reflection, to respond reasonably to the coming. It would confirm the circle of exchange that defines ordinary hospitality. However, the space's in-firmity makes it so that the family is unable to enter such a circuit: "it was so odd no one knew how to respond" (24).

Like Derrida's "contradictory conception," Danielewski's "peculiar addition" is an otherness that haunts the constructs of speculative philosophy. Seemingly situated within the house, the strange space cannot be domesticated or brought in line. The failure is made graphic when Navidson, in the role of anxious host-turned-carpenter, seeks to square the exterior dimension of the house with the interior and literally extends a fishing line through the space to take a measurement. The line confirms only "the confounding impossibility of an interior dimension greater than an exterior one" (55). In other words, the line reveals an *atopos*, a displacement of space which cannot be accorded its proper, mathematically correct place. Like a host possessed, Navidson then extends more lines, inviting two experts – Tom, his fraternal twin and a house builder by trade and Billy Reston, a paraplegic engineer friend – to account for the discrepancy. However, it remains an errant space, a truant space. Despite Navidson's hospitable efforts to put the foreign at home, the house itself seems to wander off – to leave the premises – in incalculable ways. The first "addition," which appears on the second story of the house, is followed by the appearance, on the first story, of a "dark doorless hallway'" (57) that then, as explorations reveal, opens up into an unfathomable labyrinth of rooms and corridors, ascents and descents. Yet to say "opens up" is not entirely accurate, as the labyrinth expands and contracts without warning, defying all attempts to extend a familiarizing welcome: "Absolutely nothing visible to the eye provides a reason for or even evidence of those terrifying shifts which can in a matter of moments reconstitute a simple path into an extremely complicated one" (69).

Just because these shifts are described as "nothing" to the eye does not mean there is nothing at all to them. In fact, it is first important to note that the word "nothing" appears with great frequency in the novel[3]. At various points, Danielewski cleverly gives voice to scholars, real and faux, who equate "nothingness" with sheer emptiness or utter absence. In a fabricated book Zampanò footnotes titled *Red Cross Faith*, the space in the house is described as "'this twisting labyrinth extending into nowhere'" (99). In a "partial transcript" of interviews conducted by Karen Green with experts who view footage of the house, the (real) literary critic Harold Bloom says the following: "A lifeless, soulless place. Godless too. Milton's abyss pre-god or in a Nietzschean universe post-god" (359). The expert readers give voice to an assumption that it is possible to rescue from the house's shifting passages a masterful or fundamental meaning, even if the meaning turns out to be the total lack of meaning or "absolutely nothing."

Danielewski's depiction of expert (Red Cross!) faith in the idea that the house's signs refer to a stable signified is a critique of the humanist allegiance to what Mark C. Taylor, in his book *Erring*, calls "the ontotheological network" (105). The humanist subject seeks to sort through modernity's increasingly complex network of shifting signs in order to locate an abiding Truth. The ultimate goal of this sorting project is to possess total knowledge of self and world, to illuminate the dark places, to get to the centre of the labyrinth and slay the monster. According to Taylor, the semiotic belief in original, authoritative Meaning present beyond the shadowy realm of signs is related to the Christian belief in God as the original Author/Creator present beyond the shadowy realm of the material world:

> God, or His substitute, appears either overtly or covertly to be the final meaning of the word. Put differently, God is, in effect, the "transcendental signified" that grounds the structure of signification. . . . The point to be stressed is that some notion of the transcendental signified is required by any referential system that gives priority to the signified over the signifier. While not always explicitly named God, the transcendental signified functions as the purported locus of truth that is supposed to stabilize all meaningful words. (105)

The humanist subject views this all-knowing, all-seeing God as a model of self-possessed Being; however, this God is also threatening because it is totally other. While the subject seeks to make itself the independent, divine centre of all things through seizure and subjugation of everything other than itself, God, as transcendental signified, is a difference that cannot be reduced to the same. God cannot be claimed in the name of the human. God is nothing of that sort. God is, in this respect, not for you. The humanist subject aims to make itself at home in itself and in the world, but faced with God as transcendent Other it feels dis-possessed, out of joint:

> God and self, master and slave, engage in a life-and-death struggle that is inspired by the "absolute fear" that grows out of "the first encounter of the other as *other*." The meeting establishes a "specular relation" in which the "eyes" of the other initially appear to dispossess the "I" of the self. . . . By forcing the self outside of itself, the disruptive stranger discloses the subject's estrangement. (*Erring* 23)

Humanism equates the power of knowing with the power of seeing. Rational reflection and speculation enable one to see through ephemeral surfaces and grasp eternal verities. As a "disruptive stranger," God challenges such optical logic. In this context, it makes sense that in *House of Leaves* the narrator who hosts this scandalous guest is a blind man.

In Zampanò's text, the disruptive spaces that haunt Navidson's house resemble nothing so much as a gift. Like a gift, they withdraw even as they are given. They are, paradoxically, remote and proximate, what he calls "that vast abrupt" (87). Or as Truant puts it, in describing his editorial work on the leaves Zampanò left behind, "The elusive is still here with me" (326). The spaces are neither clearly inside nor outside the house, neither property nor anti-property, neither something nor nothing. No wonder, then, that one of the explorers eventually invited in by Navidson warns, "'Don't take nothing for granted here'" (126). The house's passages are so secret that it is impossible for any character to represent them. To figure the passages would be to identify the gift as a present and as a presence (even if of complete absence). It would then be possible, in good time, to compose a response, to deliver a counter-gift, to direct a return. With the gift no longer a disruptive force, the host would not be estranged from itself. The host would be self-present. As Zampanò indicates, the passages cannot be drawn into a self-orienting system: "Resistance to representation, however, is not the only difficulty posed by those replicating chambers and corridors. As Karen discusses, the whole house defies any normal means of determining direction" (90).

To represent the gift would be, by virtue of speculative work, to claim the gift. Tellingly, despite all the video technology employed in explorations of the passages, the camera's specular power cannot frame them. Holloway Roberts, the gun-toting "professional hunter and explorer" (80) whose team is brought in to explore the space, puts it this way: "'It's impossible to photograph what we saw'" (86). The impossibility of reception is also apparent in the fact that communications devices fail to work in the spaces: "how quickly all their transmissions deteriorated" (95). However, as impenetrable as the passages are, it is not the case that nothing can be made out. There is an "inimitable growl, like calving glaciers" (123) which causes much fear and trembling and whose source is never determined. Moreover, the one repeatedly visible feature in the passages is the ash-coloured appearance of the walls, a feature reflected in the "Black & White" edition (and some "2-Color" edition volumes) of *House of Leaves* by the fact that the word "house" always appears in a greyscale or ashen-looking font. When Holloway's team explores the spaces, one of his assistants takes "wall samples" that Zampanò describes as a "black-ashen substance" (118); later, after Holloway takes leave of his senses and murders one of his team members during the exploration, Karen directs authorities of the law to what Zampanò describes as "that all consuming ash-walled maze" (318). But if the space is a gift, why would it be marked by ash? What kind of gift is ash? And how is it all consuming?

Like the word "nothing," the ash may be read as a trace of transcendental otherness. Not something and not nothing, ash is marginal, residual matter associated with death. The sheriff whom Karen calls in compares entering the house's strangeness to "standing in a gigantic grave" (319). Since God, as transcendent Other, estranges the self from itself, the humanist dedicated to achieving an independent, unified selfhood views God as a threat to its integrity and, indeed, to its life: "From the perspective of individuals who are struggling to establish their autonomy, the wholly other is manifest as the shadow of death – eternal death. . . . 'The death of God,' therefore, signifies not only the death that God suffers but also the death that is God's or that God is. *God is death, and death is absolute master*" (*Erring* 23). Not coincidentally, the absolute master initially shadows forth in the novel as an opening off the master bedroom, "almost as if it had been there all along" (28). The gift of the space is a sign of the

unbridgeable gap between self and God. The gift of the space is the
gift of the death of God. In a halting fashion, Navidson almost says as
much in a letter he writes to Karen as he prepares to re-enter the space
a final time, even after two deaths have occurred there:

> Do you believe in God? I don't think I ever asked you that one. Well I do
> now. But my God isn't your Catholic varietal or your Judaic or Mormon or
> Baptist or Seventh Day Adventist or whatever/whoever. No burning bush,
> no angels, no cross. God's a house. Which is not to say that our house is
> God's house or even a house of God. What I mean to say is that our house is
> God.
> XXXXXXXXXXXXXXXXXXXXXXXXXXXXXXXXXXXXXXX
> XXXXXXXXXXXXXXXXXXXXXXXXXXXXXXXXXXXXXXXX. (390)

The line of Xs is more than an extended typographical sign of
affection, though it appears in what is, among other things, a love
letter. Like ash, X can be a mark of death . . . a symbol used to label
material toxic or to cover the eyes of the departed. Assuming the Xs
are not Truant's editorial signal of a missing section or Zampanò's
editorial decision to ink out a portion of the record, they might also be
read as Navidson's impulse to cross out his theological speculation.
Interpreted this way, they are a gesture of self-consumption, a sign
that he wants to swallow his words. As he goes on to say, "Pretty
crazy you have to admit. I just made God a street address" (390). In
other words, the Xs are an indicator that one's responses to the gift of
God's death are bound to fail, to go astray, to do no more than scratch
the surface. They suggest something is going to be missing. They
amount to an admission of error and also of errancy. Such erring is
evident in the irony that while Navidson claims God's alterity to be so
radical it cannot be signified by the sign of the cross, he draws on a
cross-like signifier – the X – to show he cannot sort out the "no thing"
that is God. The excessive line of Xs thus helps explain why, in the
novel, Johnny Truant is both a wanderer and a tattoo artist, a drifting
imprinter of the superficial who admits to cherishing the blind man's
errors:

> "Zampanò himself probably would of [sic] insisted on
> corrections and edits, he was his own harshest
> critic, but I've come to believe errors, especially
> written errors, are often the only markers left by
> a solitary life: to sacrifice them is to lose the
> angles of personality, the riddle of a soul"(31).

III

In *House of Leaves*, the issue of how to respond to the death of God is a crucial matter in that it is intimately linked to a broader concern about responsibility. Given the increasingly far-reaching influence of fundamentalist ideologues whose claims of responsibility are underwritten by an assumption that God is on their side, this concern is not an insular one. It is an indication that if one wishes to classify *House of Leaves* as postmodern, one should not bury it alongside postmodern works seen as embodying a hermetic or even nihilistic sensibility. Or, rather, it suggests that there should be no wake for this text without there being a sensitivity to the death (of God) that haunts, like a visitation, its premise.

The novel's deconstruction of the concept of hospitality serves as a critique of the irresponsibility inherent in every totalizing system of thought. This critique is most evident in the account of the explorations of the house conducted by Holloway and his team. Holloway is recruited by Billy Reston after Navidson gets lost in the cryptic spaces for a time and is asked by Karen not to re-enter it. An expert summons another expert. Equipped with a rifle, video cameras, tents, spools of line, neon markers, and a hypermasculine demeanour, Holloway is an archetypal penetrator of recesses and solver of riddles. Part spelunker, part detective, part colonizing force, he is brought in to plumb the house's tremendous mystery, to lay claim to the fundamental truth[4]. On entering the hallway, the first words out his mouth are "'How far back does it go?'" (82). Though there is no small irony intended given how blindly it proceeds, the team's days-long exploration is referred to, by Zampanò, as "epic progress" (98).

The summons for Holloway would not have been made, however, were it not dictated by Navidson's own drive, made manifest in his photojournalism, to examine and record the dark spaces: "'I think it is unreasonable of her [Karen] to expect me not to investigate'" (73). In his career, this investigative streak has caused him to seek out and photograph scenes of appalling grimness; he has captured on film the war-torn, the famine-ravaged, the plague-infested: "tank drivers in Cambodia, peasants hauling empty canisters of nerve gas to the side of the road, children selling soda near body bags smeared with red oil-soaked clay, crowds in Thailand, a murdered man in Israel, the dead in Angola" (367). While such work, might, from one point of view, be considered responsible (in that it focuses Western attention on such scenes), Susan Sontag, in her landmark study *On Photography*, argues that even the most earnest documentary photography is governed by the humanistic imperative of reducing all difference to the same:

> Whatever the moral claims made on behalf of photography, its main effect is to convert the world into a department store or museum-without-walls in which every subject is depreciated into an article of consumption, promoted into an item for aesthetic contemplation. . . . Bringing the exotic near, rendering the familiar and homely exotic, photographs make the entire world available as an object of appraisal. . . . The most heterogeneous subjects are then brought together in the fictive unity offered by the ideology of humanism . . . . The photographic purchase of the world, with its limitless production of notes on reality, makes everything homologous. Photography is no less reductive when it is being reportorial than when it reveals beautiful forms. By disclosing the thingness of human beings, photography transforms reality into a tautology. . . . Despite the illusion of giving understanding, what seeing through photographs really invites is an acquisitive relation to the world that nourishes aesthetic awareness and promotes emotional detachment. (110-11)

The taking of a photograph is not the giving of a gift. The photograph places the other neatly within an exchange economy by converting otherness to something appropriate and appropriable. The other becomes *for you*, the photographer and the consumer of the photograph. As opposed to the "all-consuming" and all-but-unpicturable foreignness of the space in Navidson's house, the stranger in a photograph is a familiarized guest, an "object of appraisal." To see the other through the lens of the camera is, invariably, to approach the other in a hollow way. It is, in effect, to abandon one's responsibility to the otherness of the other.

This abandonment of the other – this blindness to the other – is apparent in Zampanò's description of Navidson's work. At one level, Navidson's photography blinds him to his abandonment of those others closest to him, namely his family. His early response to his abode's pregnant abyss is an eagerness to go off into the unsettled territory and shoot it, regardless the cost: "Navidson finds himself constantly itching to leave his family for that place . . ." (82). Wanting to enter the house's impossible near distance, he threatens to repeat opening up the distance between him and Karen that led them to buy the house. At another level, his heretofore exclusive dedication to photographing other people – "there does not exist a single frame without a person in it. . . . Navidson religiously studied others" (367) – is an expression of humanist faith in the project of denying differences by collecting them, of transforming "reality into a tautology," of remaking everyone else in the image of the self. As Zampanò puts it, Navidson's images are sometimes "daring to suggest a whole" (367). His pictures of the labyrinth have this same flattening effect: "His camera, no matter the circumstances, manages to view the world – even this world [of the house] – with a remarkable steadiness as well as a highly aesthetic sensibility. . . . Only the images Navidson shoots capture the otherness inherent in the place" (64). To capture the other ostensibly involves reaching out to the other through the camera's technology of reception. What it really involves, however, is reaching out to seize the other. The goal is to make sure that the other, unlike the hôte, does not surprise.

Like Navidson's photojournalism, Holloway's exploration is an effort to deny the gift of the death of God. His dream, shared initially by Navidson, is a thoroughly self-aggrandizing one. It amounts to nothing less than a desire to achieve a kind of God-like status:

> Holloway warms to discussions of success, especially to the idea of, to use Navidson's words, "going down in history." Perhaps Holloway imagines himself joining Navidson's world, what he perceives as a place for the esteemed, secure, and remembered. Nevertheless, what these short clips [from *The Navidson Record*] do not show is the paranoia growing within him. As we are well aware, future events will ultimately reveal how much Holloway feared Navidson would get rid of him and thus deprive him of the recognition he had spent a lifetime trying to obtain, the recognition the house seemed to promise. (91)

The fantasy of placing the self at the centre of attention for all of history is a fantasy of denying death. Re-membered for good, one transcends all disintegration, all loss. One never trails off, never leaves home. Not coincidentally, Zampanò suggests that this fantasy underwrites Navidson's obsession with taking pictures: "Navidson wanted to use images to create an outpost set against the transience of the world. No wonder he found it so impossible to give up his professional occupation. In his mind abandoning photography meant submitting to loss'" (23). Moreover, this fantasy is a humanist one that involves re-placing God as the centre of all with the self as the centre of all. Holloway is the one who will spread light on the deep and (re-)create the house in his name. So, for instance, when his team enters the domestic wilderness they attempt to take possession of the space by assigning names to the unmapped terrain: the Anteroom, the Great Hall, the Spiral Staircase[5].

According to Taylor, humanism's drive to deny death and make the self divine is irresponsible because its commitment to total assimilation and/or negation of the other becomes, at its most extreme, commitment to a totalitarian position:

> The effort to master "absolute fear" leads to "absolute terror." In fleeing death, the self unknowingly rushes into its arms. The psychology of mastery and the economy of domination issue in a radical form of consumption that reduces everything to ashes by igniting flames that spread to become a (the) holocaust... (32).

The violence Holloway perpetrates within the house is an instance of "absolute terror." With his explorations yielding nothing definite and his energy exhausted, he wanders off into the dark, only to return and shoot his two team members, killing one of them. The riddle that is Danielewksi's labyrinth allows for the possibility that humanism's all-consuming drive is reflected in the "all consuming ash-walled maze"[6]. The tape Holloway makes of his final moments – a document reproduced in *The Navidson Record* – reveals that, even as the house's shifts and growls begin to produce a sense of dread, his narcissism makes no room for an incorporable otherness. In the moments leading up to his suicide, he has the camera turned on himself, and his thoughts are, almost exclusively, focused on himself: "Parts 4 [ ]6,[ ], 10 & 11 centre on Holloway's reiteration of his identity" (335). He goes so far as to convince himself the growl is evidence of something out there that is oriented toward him. If he can't consume the other, the other must be trying to consume him: "It's following me. No, it's *stalking* me. . . . But it won't strike. It's just out there waiting. I don't know what for. But it's near now, waiting for me, waiting for something. I don't know why it doesn't [   ] Oh god . . . Holloway Roberts. Menomonie, Wisconsin [chambering a round in his rifle] Oh god [   ]'" (335). He speaks the name of God even as he seeks to deny the death that is God, even as he tries to possess death's otherness by taking his own life.

Significantly, however, the brackets in these passages are signs of words that have gone missing from Zampanò's text but that remain in action on the page by virtue of the brackets. In a footnote, Truant indicates that "Some kind of ash landed on the following pages, in some places burning away small holes, in other places eradicating large chunks of text. Rather than try to reconstruct what was destroyed I decided to just bracket the gaps – [   ]" (323). This ash differs from the ashes of the holocaust. It is not the sign of a system of domination bent on reducing the other to absolutely nothing. It is the remainder of a writing event that, like the giving of a gift, remains forever missing from view. This ash is the trace of the missing in action that is God. The echo of radical alterity is heard in the title of Holloway's video, which, altered by ash, appears as "The Ho[ ]ly Tape." It is also heard in the voice of the mythical Echo. According to Zampanò, "Divinity seems defined by echo" (46). In the most popular version of the myth, Narcissus's self-absorption causes Echo's body to be consumed by the fires of unrequited love. In another version, Pan dismembers Echo for refusing his advances and buries all of her except her voice. In both versions, her body goes missing, but her voice, originating from an unidentifiable origin, is not negated by the narcissism; it remains in action. Moreover, even though Echo is able to do nothing more than repeat words she has just heard – Hera punishes her for having helped Zeus in one of his sexual escapades – her voice is not mere duplication. It is not more of the same. Instead, it is an errant version of the original, like the bracketed blanks that keep interrupting the text. Tinged with her sorrow, the voice expresses an irreducible difference that makes it haunting, like a visitation. As Zampanò says, "Echo is an insurgent" (41).

In Navidson's case, the issue of how to respond responsibly to the other that is always missing in action is dramatized through his relationship to Delial, a starving Sudanese girl whom he photographed being stalked by a vulture in a field of rocks. Just after he takes the picture, she dies in his arms as he tries to find help. The photograph wins him a Pulitzer Prize. The concept of awarding a prize for the image reinforces Sontag's notion that photography "invites an acquisitive relation to the world." Navidson takes or prises the girl's picture; the world is apprised of her plight through the shot's perhaps startling but ultimately emotionally distancing aestheticism; he earns a prize for it. In addition, he is the one who gives the figure the name Delial, though he keeps it to himself until Karen discovers it inscribed on the back of the print. The sequence of seizures transforms the girl into a possession or "article of consumption," a transformation reinforced by the fact that he hangs a print of the photograph in the house, one that comes from his "personal collection" (368). While Navidson is unable to forget her death, his decision to mount the image in his home is an effort to deny her death. Just as one who suffers the loss of another may symbolically incorporate that other so as to postpone the grieving process, he literally incorporates her into his house. By hosting her in this fashion, he keeps her alive.

Nevertheless, even before the house appears haunted Navidson is haunted by Delial. In a video journal entry included in *The Navidson Record*, Karen reports that in the dead of night the girl's name gets called out: "I got up to get a blanket and when I came back he was talking in his sleep: 'Delial.' Just like that. Out of the blue" (17). Without the host's intention or attention, a disruptive guest appears, in absentia, on the scene. Much later, in his letter to Karen after they leave the house and separate, Navidson writes that what occupies him, and what brings on the blues, is not that his house is occupied by a mysterious vacancy but that he is experiencing missing and that the missing is bound up with the absent figure that comes back to life in his dreams: "that poor little girl in this god awful world i miss her I miss delial i miss the man i thought i was before i met her . . ." (393). What is missing here? At one level, he may be acknowledging that he missed the girl, or was blind to her otherness, the moment he set out to take her picture. At another level, though, he is helplessly re-creating the trauma of her death, an expression of his conviction that he missed the chance to save her. In other words, he feels responsible for her death. He is haunted by the belief that he abandoned her by shooting her image before going to help: "it doesn't matter if she was already ten minutes from dying i took threem [sic] minutes to snap a photo should have taken 10 minutes taking her somewhere so she wouldn't go away like that . . ." (392). Earlier in the novel, he imagines that he might be able to make up for this missing by entering the house's abysmal spaces, over Karen's objections, to rescue Holloway's team: "Navidson has finally been granted the opportunity he has been waiting for all along. . . . 'I waited too long for Delial. I'm not going to do it again'" (101-02). The rescue mission is underwritten by the logic of exchange that governs hospitality. Bringing the team back from the grave in time gives him the "opportunity" to bury the figure to which he can never respond in time. By making sure the invited explorers return safely to the familiar part of his home, he could be quit of the hôte that takes him hostage, seizes him in his sleep. He could pay off the gift of her death. He could kill her off for good. He could go back to feeling like a fully responsible person, "the man i thought i was."

Navidson's determination to conduct the rescue is irresponsible not only because, as Karen argues, the authorities should be called in (which would mean, among other things, that he wouldn't leave his family again), but also because it is governed by a belief that forgiveness is possible. He wants to be forgiven for the perceived abandonment, and, along a more secret path, he wants to be able to forgive Delial for the loss of "the man i thought i was." However, according to Derrida the conventional notion of forgiveness is, like the conventional notion of hospitality, based on the economics of self-interest:

> One must [*il faut*] ask for forgiveness but even if one must [*il faut*] forgive, one must do so without knowing, without having or pretending to have the assurance. "I beg your pardon" is a decent statement – "I forgive you" is an indecent statement because of the haughty and complacent height it denotes or connotes. Who am I, who do I pretend to be to thus grant myself the right to forgive? ("Hostipitality" 389).

The granting of forgiveness is a speculative act that is always both self-initiated and self-directed. One acts with a knowingness that, no matter how well intentioned, makes one blind to the otherness of the other. By contrast, true forgiveness entails giving to and for the other "without knowing." It is giving to the other that which would not be marked by calculation of effect or measure of accountability. It is a not [knowing] for you. As Derrida points out, the impossibility of such extension and reception is highlighted in the case where giver and receiver are separated by the boundary of death:

> How could the living forgive the dead? What sense and what gift would there be in a forgiveness that can no longer hope to reach its destination, except inside oneself, toward the other, that is welcomed or rescued as a

narcissistic ghost inside oneself? And reciprocally, how can the living hope
to be forgiven by the dead or by a specter inside itself? ("Hostipitality" 387)

Thus, forgiveness cannot be given by the self or the other. It can be
given only by the absolutely Other – the deathly Other – whose giving
can never be known, whose gift it is impossible to receive properly:

> If forgiveness can be asked for by me but granted only by the other, then
> God, the God of mercy, is the name of he who alone can forgive, in the
> name of whom alone forgiveness can be granted, and who can always
> abandon me, but also – and this is the equivocal beauty of this word
> *abandonment* – the only one to whom I can abandon myself, to the
> forgiveness of whom I can abandon myself. ("Hostipitality" 389)[7]

Navidson's return to the house the day after writing Karen the
letter in which he speaks of the house as God is a re-entry that, like the
one made soon after by Karen, may be read as an example of such
responsible abandonment. When he goes home this time, he goes
home with a difference. He goes home at the beginning of the novel
with the belief that he can earn forgiveness from Karen for being
absent from home so often, something he hoped not just to acquire
but, selfishly, to capture on film by "turning reconciliation into a
subject for documentation" (10). The letter that prefaces his second
homecoming begins as follows: "I don't ~~deserve~~ expect your
forgiveness. I'm leaving tomorrow XXXXXXXX though I plan to
return. But who knows, right?" (389). The not-altogether-cancelled
word "deserve" suggests an inner conflict about whether Karen's
forgiveness is even possible. Soon after, he registers that his intended
journey will be, from her point of view, unforgivable: "No excuse
huh? Guess I'm just another bastard abandoning XXXX woman and
kids for a big adventure. I should grow up, right?" (389). However, it
is not at all clear that his decision to revisit the house is a mere
repetition of his previous photojournalistic exploits. He does bring
video and still cameras along with "survival gear," but, as Zampanò
indicates, the time leading up to the return is marked by paradoxical
calls, a call to be with his family and a call to respond to the Other.
The latter call produces an experience of fear and trembling: "He
grows quieter and quieter, often wakes up seized by terror, and
through Christmas and the New Year starts eating less and less.
Though he frequently tells Reston how much he longs for Karen and
the company of the children, he is incapable of going to them. The

house continues to fix his attention" (397). Literally displaced by the house, Navidson is also, paradoxically, held hostage by it. The house has him in a fix. He is swept by the coming of the hôte, by the "impenetrable sweep of the place" (387).

Zampanò details the "great deal of speculation" (385) done by scholars on why Navidson chooses to go back, but what these experts overlook is that his re-entry subverts, in a responsible fashion, the very concept of expertise. As Zampanò cryptically suggests: "People always demand experts, though sometimes they are fortunate enough to find a beginner" (329). Navidson's reason for re-entering his house is shrouded in secrecy, like the Xs that he uses in his letter to Karen and the Xs that Zampanò uses to indicate certain architectural passages encountered on the final journey in the house. He is not clearly abandoning his family for "a big adventure," nor is he clearly resigning himself to death; he says he plans to return, but who knows. Just as the house's otherness remains a secret, so Navidson's reason remains a secret. The final homecoming exceeds the reader's speculations. This no-thing for the reader is dramatized toward the end of Navidson's bewildering journey, one which leaves him in the house with all but nothing (no food, cameras, etc.). Near death, he illuminates his way by burning a copy of a book he has carried with him called *House of Leaves*. The book burns down to ash, and yet the house's tremendous mystery is still not revealed. What remains for the reader is not nothing. Like the "ash [that] peels off into the surrounding emptiness" (467), what remains is the nonknowledge of Navidson's faith[8]. In this regard, he is like Abraham, a figure seized by the unexpected, overwhelming arrival of the hôte who then embarks alone on a journey toward death (the death of his son) and who keeps the reason for his journey to himself. As Derrida points out, what the Abraham story passes on is not knowledge of some sort about Abraham's faith but rather that Abraham's faith is structured by secrecy, both God's secrecy about the reason for the command to kill Isaac and Abraham's secrecy about the command:

> Our faith is not assured, because faith can never be, it must never be a certainty. We share with Abraham what can't be shared, a secret we know nothing about, neither him nor us. To share a secret is not to know or to reveal the secret, it is to share we know not what: nothing that can be determined. What is a secret that is a secret about nothing and a sharing that doesn't share anything? (*Gift* 80)

Before he knows it, Navidson emerges from the house in Karen's arms after she goes into the house and, without explanation, finds him. In other words, Navidson's survival is a gift, one that bears the mark of death since from then on he walks with a limp, like Jacob after he wrestles with the angel. Karen survives as well, but what do the two of them share in their survival? She is described early on as "the standard bearer of responsibility" (60), but when she first confronts the fault in the house, not to mention the fault in their relationship, she too is possessed by a desire to know, by a rage for certainty; she asks the real estate agent "who could be responsible for 'this outrage'" (29). Her re-entry embodies an altered responsibility in that it is the expression of a willingness to entertain, as far as possible, Navidson's otherness as well as her own (an otherness related, at least in part, to abandonment she experienced as a model, as a figure that, like Delial, was turned into an object). His re-entry likewise embodies this altered responsibility in that it shows a willingness, as much as possible, to entertain the other on the other's terms – to abandon oneself to the Otherness of God, the otherness of death, the otherness of the death of Delial. However, toward the end of Zampanò's commentary on *The Navidson Record*, in a chapter that, according to a late list of "Possible Chapter Titles" (540), might be called "Faith," the two find themselves suddenly outside the house, in the front yard. Despite their new responsiveness and responsibility, they cannot presume to have gained total security. They have not illuminated the truth of the other. To presume to be able to do so would be the height of irresponsibility. They respond to the other, but within an impossible place where they can't remain. They can never be perfectly at home with the other or in the other. They are exiled, marginalized, set adrift, made truant. What they share is what they don't know. By emerging from the house as a starving figure held in the arms of another, Navidson re-creates the figure of Delial, but he does not represent her on his terms. Instead, he is sharing what he doesn't know about her. He passes on the secret of her otherness. It is just such death-bound secrecy that Danielewski passes on throughout the secret passages of his novel. Such passages appear, with all their faults, as an important expression of responsibility to the impossible. And they are [not] for you.

Notes

---

[1] Throughout the novel, Truant's narrative, which for the most part takes the form of footnotes to Zampanò's text, is presented in Courier font. Writings attributed to Zampanò and to (fictional) anonymous editors of Truant's edition of Zampanò's text appear in Times New Roman. While Truant's font teases the reader with the idea that he is simply a courier of Zampanò's otherwise dead letters, the difference between fonts imperfectly masks the problem of determining the extent of the editor's authorial role in delivering a project to publication.

[2] On the novel's copyright page there appears "A Note On This Edition" which identifies four possible editions of the novel: "Full Color," "2-Color," "Black & White," and (the fabulous?) "Incomplete." In the Full Color edition, house always appears in blue. In the 2-Color edition, house might or might not appear in blue (in my copy, a 2-Color edition, it does not). Where it is printed, the blue of the "house" might also be read as a hypertext link of sorts. Given the novel's dense intertextuality and the fact that it was first published online, this association does not exactly come out of the blue. The blue also suggests that the house's ruptures and shocks are architectural re-creations of traumatic experience, both personal (e.g., Truant, Navidson, and Green each suffer from having in some way been abandoned as a child) and national (i.e., the bloody history of the Jamestown colony, which was located perhaps near the grounds of the house; see pages 408-415). Haunted by shades of these horrific experiences, the house is a house of sorrow, a house of blues. In an essay on *House of Leaves*, Katherine Hayles offers yet another interpretation of the colour, linking it to one of Danielewski's myriad interests, namely the technology of filmmaking: "If we read the blue color as an evocation of the blue screen of a movie backdrop onto which anything can be projected, then the text is attempting to project into this space the linguistic signifiers of everything in the world, as if attempting to make up through verbal proliferation the absolute emptiness of the House as a physical space" (792).

[3] Following is a brief catalogue of "nothing" in the novel, one that could, in the spirit of Zampanò's penchant for listmaking, be greatly extended (see the entry for "nothing" in the novel's index). The word is used to describe the house's architectural passages: "'There's nothing there. Beware'" (4); "Nothing there provides a reason to linger" (119); "the impenetrable wall of nothingness looming around the Spiral Staircase" (155); "'In those endlessly repetitive hallways and stairs, there is nothing for us to connect with'" (167). It is used to describe Truant's unsettled response to working through the passages of Zampanò's manuscript: "Nothing has happened, absolutely nothing, but I'm still having problems breathing" (26)"; "Except these days nothing's obvious" (326). It is used to describe the visual recordings made by those who eventually enter the passages of the house; Navidson calls them "Nothing of consequence" (418). It even appears in the final entry of an appendix labelled "Various Quotes"; the passage is taken from the film *Cool Hand Luke*: "Yeah well, sometimes nothing can be a real cool hand" (656). By playful, self-reflexive extension, each of the above examples may also be used to describe the novel as a whole.

⁴ Chapter IX of *House of Leaves* presents a curious typographical feature that highlights how the house's passages deconstruct imperialist principles of domination and conversion. Pages 119-145 display a series of boxes, one on each page, which contains a staggering catalogue of architectural and engineering elements not found in the house's passages. Crammed with names of designs, instruments, fixtures, and building materials, the boxes might be considered a version of the wonder cabinets that became popular in Europe in the late sixteenth century. Since each even-numbered page in the series displays, in reverse, the same text as the preceding page, the reader is made aware that each textual leaf has a front and a back, an effect that lends the boxes a materiality and depth. In *Mr. Wilson's Cabinet of Wonder*, an account of a contemporary Los Angeles museum (The Museum of Jurassic Technology) which draws on the tradition of wonder cabinets (and which, like *House of Leaves*, revels in blurring the distinction between the authentic and the fabricated), Lawrence Weschler describes how the rage for cabinets that displayed artefacts considered strange and exotic was the result of European explorers' contact with radically different others: "The point is that for a good century and a half after the discovery of the Americas, Europe's mind was blown. That was the animating spirit behind, and the enduring significance of, the profusion of *Wunderkammern*" (80). The act of showcasing the marvellous was, at one level, the sign of an imperative to possess the other. However, it was also an acknowledgment of an inability to know the other. Like Danielewski's secret passages, the objects housed within the cabinets' domestic space continually challenged credulity and comprehension. As Weschler puts it: "the sense of wonder afforded a steady undertow to any simple, straightforward advances in positivist certainty" (89). Danielewski cultivates this sense of wonder by altering the idea of displaying astounding objects. His boxes exhibit an astounding collection of objects absent from the house. Wonderfully, his graphic cabinets put the missing on display. Not by accident, one of the books referenced in Zampanò's long bibliographic list of "literary hauntings" on pages 133-35 is *Mr. Wilson's Cabinet of Wonder*.

⁵ In effect, then, Holloway and Navidson are like rebellious sons in competition to overthrow and murder the father. Their aim is not simply to navigate the will of God; their aim is to usurp the will of God, to carry out the death of the death of God. This murderousness explains Zampanò's curious description of Navidson's seemingly well-intentioned attempts to solve the riddle that the inside of the house measures slightly longer than the outside: "No matter how hard he tries – and Navidson tries six consecutive times in six consecutive [film] segments – he cannot *slaughter* that tiny sliver of space [my emphasis]" (30). Navidson even bears a physical likeness to Oedipus, the archetypal solver of riddles and committer of patricide. Oedipus has swollen feet, the result of their having been bound when he was abandoned as a child – that is, forced to leave the house. Navidson, also abandoned as a child, has self-described "'rotten feet" (83), the result of a childhood skin condition that erupts again as he rages to know what pollutes his pastoral vision of family life in rural Virginia, his early "near idyllic impressions of a new world" (17).

⁶ Another way to interpret the all-consuming quality of the house's passages is to read it as descriptive of the novel's attempt to incorporate other media within its pages. Katherine Hayles points out that the novel's author and characters

continuously appropriate material which has been represented in one medium and re-present it in another medium (e.g., Danielewski re-presents collages, photographs, audio transmissions, etc. in his leaves; Zampanò re-presents the film *The Navidson Record* as a written commentary). This remediation work produces what she calls a "technotext," a print text that seeks to internalize other recording devices and to reproduce their material effects: "As if learning about omnivorous appetite from the computer, *House of Leaves*, in a frenzy of remediation, attempts to eat all other media. This binging, however, leaves traces on the text's body, resulting in a transformed physical and narrative corpus" (781).

[7] Danielewski makes graphic the madness of imagining that forgiveness could be granted otherwise than by God in a letter Truant receives from his institutionalized mother (627). Written before he discovers Zampanò's text, the letter is the mother's plea to be forgiven for having scalded him with burning oil when he was a child, a traumatic event she insists was an accident (and a trauma that helps explain why Truant becomes a tattoo artist; his profession involves making up or remaking the skin). At the beginning of the letter, the plea appears as a manic, literally strung-out repetition of the phrase "Please forgive me." Toward the end of the letter, the plea is transformed into a series of overlapping stamped blocks, each imprinting strings of "Please forgive me." Toward the centre of the bizarre collage, the print collapses into an indecipherable mass of black ink, superimposed on which is the word "give," clearly visible in a large font. Since the mother could not have produced this dizzying effect when she composed the letter, one might speculate that what appears on the page is Truant's reproduction of the document. After all, the stamps are the typographical equivalent of tattoos. Regardless of who is responsible for the letter's look, the print roughly illustrates the impossibility of forgiveness. The central "give" might express the mother's self-centred demand for forgiveness or her insistence that her son give up the idea that the scalding may not have been an accident. The "give" might also express Truant's demand that she give out the truth about the scalding or that she at least give up her request for forgiveness. Finally, since it appears within a virtual whirlwind of ink, the "give" might represent the intrusion into the text of a radically obscure, transcendent voice, like the voice of God which appears to Job from within a whirlwind. In other words, the "give" might be an imperfect representation of the hôte's disorienting demand that the self give itself over – abandon oneself – to its inscrutable, illegible Otherness.

[8] Danielewski alludes to the knotty connection between nonknowledge and responsibility in an interview with Larry McCaffery and Sinda Gregory. The allusion appears in the course of his claim that the novel denies the reader the possibility of establishing a knowing perspective on the text since every part of it may be seen as having already been interpreted – i.e. filtered, mediated, re-presented – by another (e.g., Zampanò's interpretation of Navidson's documentary; Truant's work on Zampanò's commentary; the anonymous editors' work on Truant's edition). Interestingly, he alludes to the interpreter as an intruder of sorts, the exegetical equivalent of an uninvited guest: "In *House of Leaves* you're always encountering texts where some kind of intrusion's taking place. The reason? No one – repeat no one – is ever presented with the sacred truth, in books or in life. And so we must be brave and accept how often we make decisions without knowing everything. Of course, this

poses a difficult question: can we retain that state of conscious unknowing and still act, or must we, in order to act, necessarily pretend to know? (121).

Works Cited

Danielewski, Mark Z. *House of Leaves*. New York: Pantheon, 2000.

Derrida, Jacques. *The Gift of Death*. Trans. David Wills. Chicago: U of Chicago P, 1995.

—. *Given Time: I. Counterfeit Money*. Trans. Peggy Kamuf. Chicago: U of Chicago P, 1992.

—. "Hostipitality." In *Acts of Religion*. Ed. And Intro. Gil Anidjar. New York: Routledge, 2002.

Hayles, N. Katherine. "Saving the Subject: Remediation in *House of Leaves*." *American Literature* 74.4 (2002): 779-806.

McCaffery, Larry and Sinda Gregory. "Haunted House – An Interview with Mark Z. Danielewski." *Critique* 44.2 (2003): 99-135.

Sontag, Susan. *On Photography*. New York: Anchor Books, 1977.

Taylor, Mark C. *Erring: A Postmoderrn A/theology*. Chicago: U of Chicago P, 1984.

Weschler, Lawrence. *Mr. Wilson's Cabinet of Wonder: Pronged Ants, Horned Humans, Mice on Toast, and Other Marvels of Jurassic Technology*. New York: Vintage, 1995.

9

Turncoat:
Why Jonathan Franzen Finally Said "No" to Po-Mo

Robert Rebein

> Simply to write a book that wasn't dressed up in a swashbuckling, Pynchon-sized megaplot was enormously difficult. I spent years trying to somehow make it work before I realized this thing's dead, and no matter how terrifying it is to let go of that kind of plotting, I have to let go.
>   –   Jonathan Franzen (Interview with Donald Antrim)

Early in his career, the novelist Jonathan Franzen was the darling of an older generation of writers and critics, all loosely associated with the narrative strategies and avant-garde stance of literary postmodernism. Indeed, in his first two books, *The Twenty-Seventh City* (1988) and *Strong Motion* (1992), Franzen often seemed to be striving specifically to fulfil this promise – to become, along with his friend David Foster Wallace, the next great po-mo writer. But with the publication of his long-awaited third novel, *The Corrections* (2001), and in a series of essays published in national magazines between 1996 and 2002, Franzen dramatically changed his tune, turning his back on postmodernism and siding instead with a realist tradition that includes such writers as Saul Bellow, John Updike, and Alice Munro.

Readers familiar with Franzen's early work were quick to note the change, some seeing in it the mea culpa of a misguided young writer who had finally come to his senses, while others, especially those still committed to the po-mo cause, tended to view the move as a cynical grab for money and fame. And indeed, the novel's publication in September 2001 turned out to be a carnival of hype and controversy, with talk show host Oprah Winfrey at first choosing *The Corrections* for her TV book club, then reneging on the offer after

Franzen expressed misgivings at having been chosen. In the media frenzy that followed, Franzen was accused (among other things) of being both a disingenuous sell-out and an elitist snob. A short time later, the novel won the National Book Award, igniting a second round of hoopla and ritualistic bloodletting. In the midst of this, it was easy to overlook the fact that Franzen's ideas about fiction writing and its role in the postmodern world had been evolving for the better part of a decade, and what seemed to the public like an overnight change was in fact a slow bleed.

But the truth is often stranger than the lie, and in this case, Franzen's rejection of postmodernism turns out to be far more interesting and instructive than either his critics or his champions would have us believe. Indeed, it might even be said that Franzen himself did not deliberately make the change so much as he surrendered to it; that he carried the po-mo banner as long and as far as he could, abandoning it only when it became clear that to carry it any farther would be to cease to write altogether; that ultimately his rejection of postmodernism was rooted as much in crisis and despair as in calculation or an underdeveloped sense of loyalty.

For the sake of clarity, however, I would like to advance the following reasons for the change: Audience; Illness; Loss of Faith; the Importance of Place (or Family); and Character. These were the issues haunting Jonathan Franzen in the years leading up to his transformation from Young, Hip Po-Mo Writer to Purveyor of "Tragic Realism" (about which, more later), and they continue to define his work today.

I

Before I get to the first of my areas, however, it's worth pausing a moment to consider the question of why a writer of Franzen's background, ambition, and realist-leaning tendencies would ever sign on with the po-mo program in the first place.

The short answer to this question may be stated in four digits: 1959. That's the year Franzen was born to middle-class parents in a Chicago suburb, and what it means in literary terms is that his coming-of-age as a writer – that crucial period during which his tastes and tendencies were formed – took place in the mid- to late-1970s, the absolute highwater mark of literary postmodernism. Thus after four years at Swarthmore College, when the young Franzen began to look around for models of how to be taken seriously as a white, male writer, the names he inevitably came across were those of Gaddis and Pynchon, DeLillo and Gass, Coover and Heller and Burroughs and Hawkes, etc. These were the writers who "kept showing up together in anthologies and in the respectful appraisals of contemporary critics," Franzen recalls, and to a man they "shared the postmodern suspicion of realism, summarized by the critic Jerome Klinkowitz: 'If the world is absurd, if what passes for reality is distressingly unreal, why spend time representing it?'" ("Mr. Difficult" 103). Thus began a fifteen-year period, stretching from his early twenties well into his late thirties, during which Franzen worked tirelessly to "join the guild" of literary postmodernism ("Mr. Difficult"103).

An aura of sophistication and avant-garde cool surrounded the early postmodernists, and Franzen bought into this aura despite the rather alarming fact that he didn't particularly *like* the work of any of these writers with the exception of DeLillo. "I liked the *idea* of socially engaged fiction," he notes: "I was at work on my own Systems novel of conspiracy and apocalypse, and I craved academic and hipster respect of the kind that Pynchon and Gaddis got and Saul Bellow and Ann Beattie didn't. But Bellow and Beattie, not to mention Dickens and Conrad and Bronte and Dostoyevsky and Christina Snead, were the writers I actually, unhiply enjoyed reading" ("Mr. Difficult" 103). As this quote amply illustrates, literary postmodernism appealed to Franzen primarily on the level of *style*; and not the style of the work, either, but the style of the writers themselves, the *stance* they took vis–a-vis what he increasingly saw as a sick and corrupt social order. In interviews and essays, Franzen has repeatedly emphasized the fact that he grew up in a household dominated by adults whom he was in the habit of trying to impress with his own "adult" behaviour. Thus, when discussing the authorship of his first two books, Franzen has a tendency to describe himself as at once very young ("I was about 13, in some ways, when I wrote the first book. Approximately 18 when I wrote the second") and very old ("that's what the first book, *The Twenty-Seventh City*, was: a conversation with the literary figures of my parents' generation. The great sixties and seventies Postmoderns" [Interview with Donald Antrim]). Rather than explore his own material, which he had yet to discover, he took a powerful shortcut and "adopted a lot of that generation of writers' concerns – the great postwar freak-out, the Strangeloveian inconceivabilities, the sick society in need of radical critique" (Interview with Antrim). He was "attracted to crazy scenarios" (a cabal from Bombay taking over the St. Louis police department, earthquakes in suburban Boston), and, like his literary forebears, he explored these scenarios through "large, externalized, heavily plotted dramas" overseen by an authorial presence characterized by its ironic detachment and low emotional temperature (Interview with Antrim).

And yet even in this early work Franzen was already showing signs of the realist writer hidden beneath all the po-mo machinery. Along with its absurdist plot and carefully rendered themes of conspiracy and apocalypse, *The Twenty-Seventh City* offers up as earnest a depiction of place and regional mannerisms as anything we might find in Chopin, Joyce, or Faulkner. (Indeed, like Faulkner, Franzen goes so far as to present readers with an actual *map* of his fictional world, lest they become lost amid all the references to Clayton, Ladue, and U City.) *Strong Motion* continues this drift toward realism, particularly in its second half, where Franzen's more rounded characters seem poised to escape the squirrel cage of his plot. But where another writer at this point might have shrugged off the early influences and allowed his newfound interests to carry him where they would, Franzen struggled mightily with what he saw as his responsibilities as a writer of "social" fiction. To Franzen, this meant a smart, thoroughgoing critique of contemporary culture, but the more he pursued such a critique, the more convinced he became that the stranger-than-fiction content and frenetic pace of contemporary culture would forever outstrip his efforts. It was the same problem Philip Roth had lamented thirty years before in his essay "Writing American Fiction";only now, with the advent of the Information Age, the stakes had grown considerably higher. In order to have his message heard, a novelist must compete not just with Hollywood or network TV, but with cable TV, video/DVD, and, increasingly, the Internet.

However, Franzen might have been able to stomach all this had it not been for the shock he experienced when *The Twenty-Seventh City* was published in 1988. Having assumed the mantle of Serious Po-Mo Artist, he fully expected that the "sick culture" he had set out to critique would stand up and take notice. It did – but not in the way he expected. Instead of long, serious discussions of the book's ominous conclusions about what it meant to live in a society defined by its apathy and materialism, he got questions about his youth, the size of his advance, how it felt to be on a national book tour, etc. He had set out to challenge and provoke; what he got instead was "sixty reviews in a vacuum" ("Perchance" (38). It was here, in the matter of the contemporary writer's tangled relationship with audience, that Franzen's first doubts about the efficacy of literary postmodernism began to emerge.

II

Anyone familiar with Franzen's public comments on literary matters will hardly be surprised to hear that audience is a crucial concern for him. Indeed, for a defender of the avant garde like Ben Marcus, Franzen the writer "has excelled most conspicuously at worrying about literature's potential for mass entertainment." This is a low blow, to be sure, but it is not altogether inaccurate. Certainly Franzen has taken every opportunity to bemoan the retreating cultural authority of literature in general and novelists in particular, and he has laid at least some of the blame for this decline at the feet of what he has called postmodernism's "fucked up" tendency to "punish" readers with "needless difficulty" ("Having Difficulty with Difficulty").

Franzen first and most famously wrestled with the problem of audience in his *Harper's* essay of April 1996, the unfortunately titled "Perchance to Dream: In the Age of Images, A Reason to Write Novels" (later collected as "Why Bother?"). Here Franzen concluded that the large, general audience that had supported the careers of writers like Fitzgerald and Hemingway in the 1920s and '30s (as well as, to a lesser extent, those of writers like Baldwin and Mailer a generation later) did not, properly speaking, exist any longer, having shrunk, splintered, and/or sequestered itself behind the walls of academia. "To the extent that the American novel still has cultural authority," Franzen complained, "it's largely the work of women," particularly women of colour like Amy Tan, Louise Erdrich, or Toni Morrison ("Perchance" 47). College-educated white men, secure in their cultural dominance, had long since given up on the reading of novels, preferring other, less demanding entertainments like televised sports or the acquisition of expensive gadgetry. "You ask yourself,

why am I bothering to write these books?" Franzen lamented in his
essay. "I can't pretend the mainstream will listen to the news I have to
bring. I can't pretend I'm subverting anything, because any reader
capable of decoding my subversive messages does not need to hear
them" ("Perchance" 44)

Meanwhile, Franzen's supposed models, the great po-mo
writers of the sixties and seventies, provided few answers to the
problem of audience. Their response had been to fake indifference or
retreat into endless "difficulty," and to Franzen these avenues began to
seem more and more like a sado-masochistic dodge. To take the edge
off his own hunger for an audience, he resorted for a time to writing
screenplays. But the market-driven, collaborative nature of the work
did not jibe well with his sense of himself as an uncompromising,
solitary artist. He tried journalism next, and was rewarded with the
large, attentive audience he had always craved. However, the problem
of how and where to find readers for his *fiction* remained.

It was at this point that Franzen's thinking about the whole
idea of audience underwent a critical shift. Rather than conceiving of
audience in the abstract, as something large and desirable that had
been lost, perhaps forever, he began to think of it in more concrete and
practical terms. "Audience," when you boiled the concept down,
meant nothing more nor less than "readers," and readers, as a group,
had far more in common with other readers (and with writers, too)
than they did with the culture at large. Seen from this perspective, the
gap between author and reader appeared to be shrinking, not
widening. "Instead of Olympian figures speaking to the masses
below," Franzen wrote in his *Harper's* essay, "we have matching
diasporas. Readers and writers are united in their need for solitude, in
their pursuit of substance in a time of ever-increasing evanescence: in
their reach inward, via print, for a way out of loneliness" ("Perchance"
51).

By identifying himself with rather than in opposition to
readers, Franzen had taken a large and decisive step away from the
aesthetics of literary postmodernism. As he ran it down in a 2002 *New
Yorker* essay ostensibly devoted to the career of William Gaddis, the
move amounted to a rejection of a "Status" model predicated on the
idea that authors are geniuses and readers exist mostly to confirm and
celebrate that fact, and a corresponding acceptance of a "Contract"
model whereby writers and readers work together in the creation of a

Idea of community

specific kind of "pleasurable experience," one that seeks "to sustain a sense of connectedness" and "to resist existential loneliness" ("Mr. Difficult" 100). According to the dictates of the Contract model, "a novel deserves a reader's attention only so long as the author sustains the reader's trust" ("Mr. Difficult" 100). If acceptance of such an idea meant burning his membership card in the guild of po-mo writers, then so be it.

In thus abandoning Status in favour of Contract, Franzen clearly hoped to gain new readers as well as to better deserve the readers he already had. And if sales are any measure of readers, he certainly accomplished that with *The Corrections*. However, to remark this is to invite the erroneous idea that Franzen's rejection of postmodernism was primarily a *strategic* move. In fact, as we shall see, that decision had as much to do with survival – as both a writer and a person – as with anything so pedestrian as increasing sales.

III

At the time of its publication in April 1996, Franzen's *Harper's* essay was widely viewed as a whiney, self-serving lament that did not always rise to the level of coherence. And in fact, there's a lot of truth to this assessment. Franzen acknowledges the first half in the essay itself, and he cops to the second in the introduction to *How to Be Alone* (2002), where he writes of the piece's "tenuous logic" and "tone of high theoretical dudgeon" (5). Having enjoyed some success and regained his mental equilibrium in the five years since he wrote the essay, he finds it hard to believe that he ever was this "angry and theory-minded person" who found it "apocalyptically worrisome that Americans watch a lot of TV and don't read much Henry James" (4). However, hē was that person, and the essay as a whole must be viewed in retrospect as "a stalled novelist's escape from the prison of his angry thoughts" (5).

That Franzen was "stalled" in 1996 is something of an understatement. He had begun work on his third novel shortly after his second was published in 1992. Following his usual method, he had spent a full year researching a raft of hot-button social issues, including race, drugs, prison life, insider trading, Internet boosterism, etc., that he hoped eventually to build a story around. But when he got into the actual writing, things did not go well. "I was torturing the story, stretching it to accommodate ever more of those things-in-the-world that impinge on the enterprise of fiction writing," he later wrote. "The work of transparency and beauty and obliqueness that I wanted to write was getting bloated with issues" ("Perchance" 40). Meanwhile his marriage was failing and his father had been diagnosed with Alzheimer's disease. The stable domestic life that had supported the composition of his first two books was breaking apart, leaving in its wake a chaos of uncertainty and change. It was perhaps inevitable that the book he was working on would change as well, taking off first in one direction, then in another. Years passed. Literally thousands of pages piled up. But the story itself stubbornly refused to cohere. He found himself assailed by doubt and despair. Should he scrap the story and start over? But how could he do that now, when he was already so far behind schedule? By the time he researched a new raft of topics and pieced together a workable plot, his interest in the new book might flag as well, and then where would he be? It did not help that the culture at large cared so little whether the cloud surrounding him lifted or not. Maybe it was true what people said, and the world had passed the novelist by. Maybe after five hundred years, the era of the printed page was indeed drawing to a close, and the time was not far off when the act of reading or writing fiction would become as obsolete and anachronistic as big game hunting or dressage riding.

In the *Harper's* essay, Franzen employs a number of different words in an attempt to describe the condition that plagued him during these years – "despair," "distress," "depression," "delusion," "isolation," "estrangement." Whatever one wished to call it, however, the result was the same: a deep and abiding inability to *believe* in what he was writing. Gradually he "began to think that there was something wrong with the whole *model* of the novel as a form of 'cultural engagement'" ("Perchance" 40-1). Wasn't such a notion just a tad grandiose? Wasn't it, in fact, somewhat *sick* to expect one's novel "to bear the weight of our whole disturbed society – to help solve our contemporary problems" ("Perchance" 49)? Eventually, under the pressure of this despair, Franzen quit writing fiction altogether, retreating into a long essay entitled "My Obsolescence." However, he could not finish that, either. "I was alone and unable to write fiction – unable, almost, to read a newspaper," he remembers in an essay from *How to Be Alone*. "I gave up. Just plain gave up. No matter what it cost me, I didn't want to be unhappy anymore. And so I stopped trying to be a writer-with-a-capital-W. Just to desire to get up in the morning was all I asked" (205).

As decisions go, this one was more instinctual than calculated or chosen; indeed, it was barely conscious. Simply put, Franzen's continued adherence to a theory of fiction writing that did not suit his temperament or talent had finally succeeded in making him physically ill. From this point on, only two paths were open to him: quit writing fiction altogether, or find a new way of writing it that would allow him to focus on those aspects of the craft that remained meaningful to him in the wake of his depression. Franzen concludes the *Harper's* essay:

> At the heart of my despair about the novel had been a conflict between my feeling that I should Address the Culture and Bring News to the Mainstream, and my desire to write about the things closest to me, to lose myself in the characters and locales I loved. Writing, and reading too, had become a grim duty, and considering the poor pay, there is seriously no point in doing either if you're not having fun. As soon as I jettisoned my perceived obligation to the chimerical mainstream, my third book began to move again. I'm amazed, now, that I trusted myself so little for so long, that I'd felt such a crushing imperative to engage explicitly with all the forces impinging on the pleasure of reading and writing: as if, in peopling and arranging my own little alternate world, I could ignore the bigger social picture even if I wanted to. ("Perchance" 54)

To lose myself in the characters and locales I loved ... It is interesting that Franzen resorts to cliché in describing this huge shift in his thinking as a writer. Certainly the softness of the conception, so obviously intentional, did not escape the notice of his critics. In his book *Late Postmodernism* (2005), Jeremy Green characterizes the shift as "a retreat from the political" (104) covered only partially by a corresponding "embrace of humanist platitudes" (95). What Franzen comes to call "tragic" realism, Green argues, "grows from the realization that life's essential problems, the problems with which great literature and art have always concerned themselves, cannot be overcome by new technologies or ideas" (94). Thus for Green, Franzen's big change turns out to be informed by nothing more nor less than a "deeply traditional notion of literature as quasi-religious solace" (96).

This is hardly earth-shattering news. Indeed, it is impossible to read Franzen's essays and interviews on literary topics without noticing the extent to which he relies on religious metaphor to describe his relationship with literature. The tendency was already strong in 1996, and it has only grown stronger in the years since.

IV

Case in point: in his 2001 interview with Donald Antrim, Franzen remarks that for him "art in general and literature in particular have basically replaced the Christianity of [his] parents' generation." More recently, in a review of Alice Munro's story collection *Runaway* (2004), Franzen pauses to ask, "Can a better kind of fiction save the world?" Almost certainly not, he answers. Then adds: "There is some reasonable chance, however, that it could save your soul."

In comments like these, Franzen aligns himself quite clearly with a Modernist tradition that includes writers as diverse in their beliefs as D.H. Lawrence, T.S. Eliot, and James Joyce. However, Joyce in particular would seem to provide the primary model. One of the major themes of *A Portrait of the Artist as a Young Man*, after all, is the way that a hollowed-out Catholicism might form the basis of a new priesthood of art. Franzen's embrace of this idea is at once more Protestant and more post-ironic and cool, but it is there all the same, and the fact that it is there becomes yet another reason for his ultimate rejection of the aesthetics of postmodernism.

Franzen first introduced the idea of a new religion of art in his *Harper's* essay, where he enacts a dramatic dialogue between himself and the Stanford linguist Shirley Brice Heath regarding her research into why people read "substantive works of fiction" (45). According to Heath, "strong work of fiction are what refuse to give easy answers to … conflict, to paint things as black and white, good guys versus bad guys" (49). Apropos of this, Franzen adds: "And religions themselves are substantive works of fiction" (49). Heath responds: "This is precisely what readers are saying: that reading good fiction is like reading a particularly rich section of a religious text. What religion and good fiction have in common is that the answers aren't there, there isn't closure" (49). Later in the essay, Franzen will define his notion of "tragic" realism by writing, "I hope it's clear that by 'tragic' I mean just about any fiction that raises more questions than it answers: anything in which conflict doesn't resolve into cant" (53). With this crucial formulation, Franzen attempts to separate himself from ideologues of every stripe, but in particular from those po-mo writers and critics whose beliefs have hardened into a rigid orthodoxy of cultural complaint.

Franzen's whipping boy for this kind of thinking turns out to be none other than his former idol, William Gaddis. In his *New Yorker* essay on Gaddis, Franzen describes his own acceptance of certain foundational po-mo ideas as a kind of religious conversion. "From a Congregationalist childhood I'd gone straight into a collegiate worship of art," he writes of his years studying literature at Swarthmore College ("Mr. Difficult" 104). By the time he was a senior, he'd given birth to an ambition to "create literary Art" of the kind praised by his professors ("Mr. Difficult" 103). "I took for granted that the greatest novels were tricky in their methods, resisted casual reading, and merited sustained study," he states. "I also assumed that the highest compliment this Art could be paid was to be taught in a university" ("Mr. Difficult" 103). Gaddis, whose "fanatical fervor" and "guilt-provoking authority" (104) earn him the sobriquet of "Mr. Difficult," becomes for Franzen a kind of High Priest of this particular brand of po-mo writing. As such, his life and works must be shown to be empty and without meaning if Franzen is to replace them with his own, reformed religion of art.

The job turns out to be not that difficult after all. Throughout the essay, Gaddis is portrayed as an angry but well-meaning fanatic committed to the po-mo idea of "formal experimentation as an act of resistance" ("Mr. Difficult" 108). He is a martyr of sorts, a false prophet and "purist of his faith" who throughout a long career steadfastly refused to give interviews or to otherwise connect with an outside world that might have saved him from his narrow views (105). "Strict prohibitions like this are a way in which threatened religious minorities resist the seductions of the majority culture," Franzen remarks; what mattered to Gaddis "was not the weak and fleshly artist but the afterlife" (105). However, adherence to this flawed faith dooms Gaddis to a life of meaningless and mechanical repetition. If *JR*, Gaddis's second novel, is "dedicated to the proposition that America sucks," Franzen writes, "the message of his third novel, *Carpenter's Gothic* (1985), is that it really, really, really sucks" (110). Of *JR* itself, which won the National Book Award in 1975, Franzen writes, "The first ten pages and the last ten pages and every ten pages in between bring the 'news' that American life is shallow, fraudulent, venal, and hostile to artists. But there has never been and never will be a reader who is unpersuaded of this 'news' on page 10 but persuaded on page 726" (109). In the ultimate in unintended irony, the novel itself "becomes as chilly, mechanistic, and exhausting as the System it describes" (109).

The hatchet job continues for several more pages, until finally the entire Gaddis oeuvre is summed up as "an encyclopedia of phonyness unparalleled in literature" (111). A few lines later, the former disciple widens his attack to include postmodernism itself, at the heart of which, Franzen contends, "is an adolescent fear of getting taken in, an adolescent conviction that all systems are phony. The theory is compelling, but as a way of life it's a recipe for rage. The child grows enormous, but he never grows up" (111).

The subtext for this statement, the particular testimony Franzen has to offer here, is the contention that he himself *has* grown up, and thus avoided the terrible fate of Gaddis and the other postmodernists. Where he once isolated himself and refused to discuss his work, he now sits for interviews and regularly publishes journalism and autobiographical essays. Where he once looked down his nose at readers, sneering at their childlike need to be entertained, he now joyfully embraces the role of entertainer. Where he once agreed that characters were little more than marks on a page, "feeble, suspect constructs" to be done with as author pleased, he is now able to speak of them with affection ("characters and locales I loved"), almost as if they were actual people.

It goes without saying that this, too, is a religion of sorts, that Franzen has cast himself not in the role of a faith-denier like Nietzsche, but rather in that of a faith-reformer like Martin Luther. "As a reader," he tells us, "I seek a direct personal relationship with art. The books I love, the books on which my faith in literature rests, are the ones with which I can have this kind of relationship" ("Mr. Difficult" 111). The dark, corrupt "Catholicism" of postmodernism (the formulation is Franzen's, not mine) has given way to a lighter, more honest and forgiving "Protestant"-style realism. It is a faith that will allow Franzen to pursue without guilt his interest in locale and character – to concentrate wholly, in his own words, on the business of "peopling and arranging" his "own little alternate world," trusting all along that the "bigger social picture" he used to worry so much about will take care of itself ("Perchance" 54).

V

Franzen once remarked in an interview that the most important experience of his life up to that point had been growing up in the Midwest as the son of middle-class parents much older than he was, parents whose lives of quiet desperation had supplied their son, whether they understood this or not, with a sort of window on the whole of twentieth-century American life (Interview with Donald Antrim). This is quintessentially *not* the sort of thing one would expect to hear from the super-hip, self-absorbed young writer Franzen is so often portrayed as being. Instead it is the confident, unassuming statement of a mature artist who has found his true subject at last. In Franzen's case, that subject turns out to be not America precisely, but rather the collision of the earnest, old-fashioned Midwest of his childhood years with the cool, "post-ironic" East Coast world of his adult life; not Society, exactly, but rather Family; not Conspiracy or Apocalypse (those twin bugaboos of the po-mo imagination), but rather "the sudden impingements of truth or reality on characters who are expending ever larger sums of energy on self-deception or denial" (Interview with Antrim). None of this was something Franzen had to stumble upon or invent. A strong interest in place and family had marked his work from the very beginning, and the newfound focus on character grew naturally out of these once the preoccupation with postmodernism was finally laid to rest. As Franzen once put it, "I feel like I'm essentially participating in ... a swing away from the boys-will-be-boys *Huck Finn* thing, which is how you can view Pynchon, as adventures for boys out in the world. At a certain point, you get tired of all that. You come home" (Interview with Antrim).

Franzen's abiding interest in place is a case in point. Few writers have taken this concept as seriously as Franzen does in his first novel. Indeed, with its gratis map and endless cataloguing of specific streets and neighbourhoods, *The Twenty-Seventh City* attempts to do for St. Louis what Joyce's books do for Dublin and Faulkner's for rural Mississippi. The novel abounds in place-specific sentences like this: "Although the streets of Webster Groves connect with those of its neighbors, and aside from Deer Creek to the north the town has no natural boundaries, its residents experience it as an enclosure, an area where Christmas can occur in safety" (264). Or this, from the same page: "Stopped at the Sappington Road intersection, by a Crestwood Plaza just lately closed for the night and tomorrow, drivers in neckties smile at other drivers in neckties, or do not, depending." There is a still, contemplative quality to these images that suggests a photographer who has spent many hours alone with his subject. The attempt is not to *create* a fictional world but rather to *document* one that already exists – to demonstrate a mastery or ownership of place.

It is a goal common to many first novels, but in the case of *The Twenty-Seventh City*, the attempt is both grander and more doomed. Grander because Franzen clearly believes that St. Louis's decline as a city, its fall from nineteenth-century greatness to twentieth-century mediocrity, is a subject bearing huge and tragic implications; more doomed because the gleeful, absurdist plot he has borrowed from Pynchon and imposed on this material (a cabal from Bombay takes over the St. Louis police department) cannot help but give readers precisely the opposite impression.

A less thoroughgoing interest in place is evident in Franzen's second novel *Strong Motion*, which is for the most part set in the Somerville and Cambridge neighbourhoods of Boston. Still, an important theme is introduced: that of exiles from the conformist Midwest seeking freedom in the cultural promised land of the East. This theme is no more introduced, however, than it is steam-rolled by the novel's Don DeLillo-inspired plot of conspiracy and apocalypse. Franzen's Midwesterners might *begin* the novel by having complex, personal reasons for gravitating to Boston, but once the earthquakes start up and faux newspaper accounts begin to point toward a Monsanto-style chemical company as culprit, it becomes all too clear that these characters exist for the sole purpose of turning the wheel of plot. They might as well be from Boston for all the difference it makes; just as, after a while, the novel itself might as well be set in Houston or San Francisco.

In *The Corrections*, by contrast, the subject of place is inextricably caught up with issues of individual and regional identity. The novel's primary settings in New York, Philadelphia, and fictional St. Jude vibrate with implications for characters and readers alike. When the Kansas-born and Depression-bred character of Alfred Lambert overhears Ohio railroad employees telling each other to "take it easy," for example, we are told that the "phrase seemed to Alfred an eastern blight, a fitting epitaph for a once-great state ... that parasitic

Teamsters had sucked nearly dry" (243). Alfred's son Gary, meanwhile, who lives in Philadelphia, cannot revisit his former home in the Midwest without being overcome with revulsion for the place, which in "its optimistic egalitarianism consistently failed to accord him the respect to which his gifts and attainments entitled him" (175). The tension of these opposed world views is felt not only *between* characters (for example, between Enid Lambert and her daughter Denise) but also *within* individual characters. Part of Gary Lambert may "hate" the Midwest, for example, but another part of him views his childhood there with nostalgia and longing. "It's like you're suddenly trying to make us act like it's 1964 and we're all living in Peoria," his wife Caroline complains. "'Clean your plate!' 'Wear a necktie!' 'No TV Tonight!' And you wonder why we're fighting! You wonder why Aaron rolls his eyes when your mom walks in the room!" (183-4). A similar tension exists in all the Lambert children. Huge portions of their mental lives are given over to a kind of endless regional squabbling, a continual comparison of Midwest and East on cultural, economic, and moral grounds. Gradually, over the course of six hundred pages, the tracking and dramatization of this debate becomes one of the novel's great thematic achievements.

A similar progression toward mastery marks Franzen's exploration of the theme of family in his novels. In all three books, a Midwestern family with grown children is put under a large pressure or stress that is at least partially the expression of changes in society at large. However, in the first two books, these pressures are expressed through big, external changes in the lives of the characters, most of which are outside of their control, while in *The Corrections* the changes are both internal and external, with the majority of them being the direct result of choices made by the characters themselves.

The most obvious example of the former scenario is to be found in *The Twenty-Seventh City*, where the stress affecting the Probst family occurs when its unhappy, suburbanite mother is secretly kidnapped by agents of the Bombay cabal, who try to make it appear as though she has left of her own accord. In *Strong Motion*, meanwhile, the outside force takes the form of a tainted inheritance of twenty-two million dollars that the mother in the novel, Melanie Holland, mysteriously refuses to share with her husband and children. Though somewhat contrived, either of these set-ups might provide the basis for an exploration of family identity, loyalty, and cohesion.

However, that is assuming that the plots of these novels flow from an initial situation involving rounded, complex characters, and as we have seen, that is decidedly not the way things work in *The Twenty-Seventh City* and *Strong Motion*. As a result, the theme of family becomes little more than a device for grouping characters whose actual responsibilities lie elsewhere. In *Strong Motion*, for example, Louis Holland's status as Melanie Holland's son plays little or no part in his larger role as Seeker of the Conspiracy, this despite the fact that Melanie stands to lose millions if the conspiracy her son seeks is uncovered. In the end, it is uncovered – although, oddly, not because of anything Louis does or doesn't do. Meanwhile, Louis's strained relationship with Melanie remains essentially unchanged from the beginning of the book right up to its rather flat and unsatisfying ending.

The family drama is handled much differently in *The Corrections*. Here the large, externalized plot we witnessed in Franzen's first two novels has been allowed to fall away, so that the focus of the book remains unremittingly on the Lamberts and their problems, which turn out to be far more internal than external. Alfred Lambert, the stoic, domineering patriarch of the family, is losing his mind to Parkinson's disease. Edith, his controlling, long-suffering wife, must meet this crisis largely on her own, because her children, Gary, Chip, and Denise, have long since escaped to Philadelphia and New York, where they face large and small crises of their own. And that's it: no cabals or earthquakes, no elaborate conspiracies threatening apocalypse. The crisis threatening the family comes quite literally from within Alfred Lambert's own body, spreading from there to his wife and children, each of whom must deal with it in their own way, bringing to it their own problems and memories and long-held grudges.

Of course, there is more than this rudimentary outline to a novel that features, among other happenings, a satiric Scandinavian cruise, a sado-masochistic lesbian romance, and a Lithuanian cell phone riot. But in *The Corrections*, these happenings are ornaments, as it were, not the tree itself. Structurally, the book takes the form of a series of interrelated novellas, each featuring a different member of the Lambert family. In this, it owes more to Faulkner's *The Sound and the Fury* or Erdrich's *Love Medicine* than to anything we might find in Pynchon, Gaddis, or DeLillo. In choosing such a structure, Franzen not only ensured that the subject of family would finally receive the attention it deserved, he also tipped the balance in his fiction away from plot and toward a thoroughgoing exploration of character.

VI

That postmodernism is hostile to character has long been recognized. One of the grand projects of Modernism in the first half of the twentieth century was a kind of textual mapping of human consciousness that the postmodernists, for their part, came to distrust. As Franzen described the prejudice in his Gaddis essay, "postmodern fiction wasn't supposed to be about sympathetic characters. Characters, properly speaking, weren't even supposed to exist. Characters were feeble, suspect constructs, like the author himself, like the human soul" ("Mr. Difficult" 103). In rejecting this notion, Franzen's work, most critics agree, offers a kind of correction or revision of the standard po-mo response to character. In his review of *The Corrections,* for example, James Wood argues that Franzen's novel proposes "a softened DeLilloism" that promises to retain the "tentacular ambition" of DeLillo's critique of culture while at the same time correcting that writer's "total lack of characterological depth" (35-6). For Wood, such a project qualifies as "an urgent task of contemporary American fiction, whose characteristic products are books of great self-consciousness with no selves in them; curiously arrested books that know a thousand different things ... but do not know a single human being" (36).

That assessment, harsh as it is, might well be applied to Franzen's first two novels. Consider, for example, the characterization of Martin Probst in *The Twenty-Seventh City*:

> Born in the very pit of the Depression, he had groped and bullied his way into some kind of light, demolishing and steam-rolling and building higher, building the Arch, building developments of the most youthful and prosperous nature, the golden years of Martin Probst. Inside, though, he was sick, and the city was sick on the inside too, choking on undigested motives, racked by lies. The conspiracy invaded the city's bloodstream while leaving the surfaces unchanged, raged around him and in him while he sat apparently unseen, uncounted, uninvolved, and it was right here, in this identity of his life with the city's life, that he could see himself disappearing. The more he was a figure, the less he was a person. (216-217)

These sentences contain, at best, notes for a fictional character. Everything is insisted upon or, worse, imposed by the author. Even the crucial identification of Probst with the city he helped build is handled in this way – from the outside and above, in the best po-mo style.

Compare this with Franzen's handling of Alfred Lambert in *The Corrections*:

> "I'll leave you alone for a minute," Denise said, "while I get the lunch going."
>
> He closed his eyes and thanked her. As if waiting for a break in a downpour so that he could run from his car into a grocery store, he waited for a lull in his tremor so that he could reach out and safely eat what she'd brought him.
>
> His affliction offended his sense of ownership. These shaking hands belonged to no one but him, and yet they refused to obey him. They were like bad children. Unreasoning two-year-olds in a tantrum of selfish misery. The more sternly he gave orders, the less they listened and the more miserable and out of control they got. He'd always been vulnerable to a child's recalcitrance and refusal to behave like an adult. Irresponsibility and undiscipline were the bane of his existence, and it was another instance of that Devil's logic that his own untimely affliction should consist of his body's refusal to obey him.
>
> If thy right hand offend thee, Jesus said, cut it off. (67)

There is much here that is abstract and delivered from above, but every word and image is filtered through a specific situation (a man with Parkinson's disease attempting to eat a plate of food his daughter has given him) and a particular consciousness (that of an isolated disciplinarian who secretly longs to connect with those around him). As readers, we come to know Alfred Lambert in a way we cannot hope to know Martin Probst.

Why? Because his actions are more natural and understated (steadying his hand, reaching for a plate, etc.), and in the course of them we are granted greater access to his thoughts? Yes, but that is only part of the difference. The characters in *Strong Motion*, Franzen's second novel, are considerably more dynamic and tortured – considerably more *conscious* – than those of *The Twenty-Seventh City*, and yet we finish that book feeling pretty much the same way about them as we feel about Martin Probst. There is that same lack of connection between the characters' histories and interior lives and their actions in the plot. Both are interesting, but they exist on separate planes, as it were. Thus, in *Strong Motion*, we follow with interest the Harvard seismologist Renee Seitchek's self-consciousness and incipient sado-masochism, her love of shopping and simultaneous hatred of those who love the same thing, her feelings of superiority toward her mother, and her humbling fear that she is becoming just like her, but these features of her interior life remain oddly unconnected to her role in the novel's plot. Like Louis Holland's strained relationship with his mother, they explain nothing and affect nothing. They are just there.

Ironically, it is only with *The Corrections*, the least self-consciously "social" of his novels, that Franzen manages to achieve his long-standing goal of writing a book that connects the personal and the social. The reason for this may have to do with the way the book was constructed, with Franzen first writing several drafts focused on hot-button social issues, and then, in revision, peeling back all those layers, until all he was left with was his characters and their problems. Having done that, he has said in an interview, he was surprised to find "all the formerly externalized conflicts to be inside the characters in the form of anxieties and desires" ("Only Correct").

For readers of the novel, of course, the experience is precisely the opposite. First we experience the characters in all their particularity – Alfred and his hallucinations, Enid and her Christmas obsession, Chip and his barely repressed hostility toward women, Gary and his determination not to become his father, Denise and her workaholic's lack of self-awareness – and only later do we begin to ask the big questions. What are the burdens we pass on to our children without even knowing we're doing it? Should a person be medicated just because he's unhappy or feels a sense of shame? How is success in America measured, in a practical sense? Is all this new technology really good for us? What does it mean to be a good daughter, mother, son, or father?

In *The Corrections*, these questions – and a score of others just as acute – are actively in play on almost every page. They are not forced on us or lowered from above on a rope of dazzling rhetoric. Rather they are *evoked*, brought to life first within the characters, and finally within us as readers. This is the great achievement of *The Corrections*, it seems to me. Indeed, it is one of the primary reasons the novel is not only Franzen's best work to date, but arguably the first great work of twenty-first century American literature.

VII

To what extent may Jonathan Franzen's defection from the ranks of po-mo writers be said to have *cultural* rather than merely personal causes? This is by no means an easy question to address, but a few observations may be risked by way of conclusion.

The first is that literary postmodernism has been losing ground to a revitalized realism since at least 1980, if not before. The trend has been obvious to anyone who has bothered to follow book publishing, mainstream reviewing, and the contents of syllabi devoted to contemporary American fiction over the last twenty years. More recently, it has begun to show up in the work of writers once hailed as second-generation (or even first-generation) postmodernists. I am thinking not only of Franzen, who is perhaps the most high-profile example, but also of less well-known writers like William T. Vollmann, whose work from *You Bright and Risen Angels* (1987) to *The Royal Family* (2000) clearly shows the pattern; or even of Don DeLillo, whose *Underworld* (1997) has been correctly hailed as a masterpiece of edgy realism. And when the captain himself abandons ship, what expectation can there be that any part of the crew will remain on board?

However, lest anyone believe that the trend in favour of realism is somehow cyclical, and that it is merely a matter of time before a new generation of American writers rediscovers and revitalizes the po-mo aesthetic, it should be pointed out that in the years since Franzen graduated from Swarthmore in 1981, hundreds of undergraduate and graduate programs in creative writing have sprung up in colleges and universities across America, and in these, the model held up to promising young writers is far more likely to be Raymond Carver than Robert Coover. As critics of the MFA programs have remarked so often, there is inherent in the workshop method itself an almost built-in prejudice in favour of realism. Until that changes, the odds of literary postmodernism making a comeback seem slight at best. Indeed, if the current trend holds, the generation of American writers that includes Franzen (born 1959), Vollmann (1959), Richard Powers (1957), Donald Antrim (1958), Rick Moody (1961), and David Foster Wallace (1962) promises to be the last to be directly influenced by the likes of a Pynchon or a Gaddis.

Even larger than the trend from postmodernism to realism, however, is the one from fiction to nonfiction – or indeed from reading to non-reading forms of entertainment. It used to be argued, by the postmodernists among others, that in losing its formerly large audience, fiction at least would be rewarded with a more literate one. However, few people hold to this quaint idea today. Instead, many of our most influential writers have come to believe that we are now living in a "post-literate" age in which the act of reading itself is being retooled or phased out altogether. In a *New Yorker* profile calibrated to appear in conjunction with the publication of his novel *The Human Stain* (2000), for example, Philip Roth flatly declares, "Literature requires a habit of mind that has disappeared. It requires silence, some form of isolation, and sustained concentration in the presence of an enigmatic thing" (Remnick 86). None of this is valued, let alone taught, Roth implies, in an era characterized by "the progression from the movie screen to the television screen to the computer" (86).

This is a bleak assessment, to be sure. But if Roth is correct, and the habit of mind required by even moderately serious reading is indeed disappearing, then what does this tell us about the habit of mind required by literary postmodernism, with its wilfully tricky plots, buried allusions, and uncompromising opacity? By this reckoning, the aesthetics of literary postmodernism have become an indulgence the contemporary writer can ill afford. To put it another way: when communication itself begins to be scarce, the value of clarity increases exponentially. Experimentation for its own sake declines dramatically, and the time arrives, as Franzen once wrote, "for form's dialectical counterparts, content and context, to return as vectors of the new" ("I'll Be Doing More of Same" 38).

Works Cited

Franzen, Jonathan. *The Corrections*. New York: Farrar, Straus and Giroux, 2001.
—. "Having Difficulty with Difficulty." *The New Yorker* Online Only 30 Sept. 2002. <http://www.newyorker.com/online/content/articles020930on_online only01>.
—. *How to Be Alone*. New York: Farrar, Straus and Giroux, 2002.
—. "I'll Be Doing More of Same." *The Review of Contemporary American Fiction* 16.1 (1996): 34-38.
—. Interview with Donald Antrim. *Bomb* 77 (Fall 2001) <http://www.bombsite.com/franzen/franzen.html>.
—. "Mr. Difficult." *The New Yorker* 30 Sept. 2002: 100-111.
—. "Only Correct." *Salon.com*. 7 Sept. 2001. <http://archive.salon.com/books/int/2001/09/07/franzen/index.html>.
—. "Perchance to Dream: In the Age of Images, A Reason to Write Novels." *Harper's* April 1996: 35-54.
—. "'Runaway': Alice's Wonderland." *The New York Times Book Review* 14 Nov. 2004. <http://www.nytimes.com/2004/11/14/books/reviews/14COVERFR.html>.
—. *Strong Motion*. New York: Farrar, Straus and Giroux, 1992.
—. *The Twenty-Seventh City*. New York: Farrar, Straus and Giroux, 1988.
Green, Jeremy. *Late Postmodernism: American Fiction at the Millenium*. New York: Palgrave Macmillan, 2005.
Marcus, Ben. "Why Experimental Fiction Threatens to Destroy Publishing, Jonathan Franzen, and Life as We Know It." *Harper's* Oct. 2005 <http:www.harpers.org/WhyExperimentalFiction.html>.
Remnick, David. "Into the Clear: Philip Roth Puts Turbulence in its Place." *The New Yorker* 8 May 2000: 76-89.
Wood, James. "Abhorring a Vacuum." *The New Republic* 15 Oct. 2001: 33-40.

10

Serving *Pi*(e) at the Wake of Postmodernism: Mathematics and Mysticism at the End of the 20th Century

Clayton Dion

All religions, arts and sciences are branches of the same tree. All these aspirations are directed toward ennobling man's life, lifting it from the sphere of mere physical existence and leading the individual toward freedom.

–   Albert Einstein, "Moral Decay"

They call it the "CSI effect." In legal circles this is the phrase applied to the problems of finding a conviction *without* forensic evidence (Willing A1). Since the appearance of *CSI: Crime Scene Investigation* in 2000, and the arrival of its two spinoff shows, *CSI: Miami* and *CSI: NY*, with their intensive examinations of the forensic evidence left at crime scenes, people now believe the truth is always out there, and readily accessible. As Gil Grissom reminds us each week, the answer is there, we just have to find the clues. But what if it's not? What if we don't have access to the popcan's perspective, or some fancy shot of a bullet as it makes its course through a human body? What if the necessary details just aren't there? What lawyers have found since these shows gained such popularity is that juries now expect and demand incredibly detailed forensic evidence; if none is available, the jury is now more likely to set the accused free under the assumption that if he or she was guilty, the clues would be there to provide the answer. The Answer, the one truth, a series of signs pointing us in a single direction that science can offer to explain the unexplainable: these are the new demands of the post-Postmodern world. Consider such other recent pop-culture phenomenons as *Numb3rs,* where each week a pop version of some new mathematical theory helps to locate a criminal's whereabouts. In a somewhat bizarre turn, the pairing of brothers Don and Charlie Epps on *Numb3rs,* is structured around the fact that Don, as an FBI agent, is interested only in the facts, while Charlie, a mathematician, is more concerned with abstract reasoning, probability and theories instead of a dogged adherence to "just the facts." Science is no longer seen as the study of, or the studying leading to, concrete facts about reality; it is now viewed as operating almost in a world of its own devising that only accidentally has a bearing on the world around us. So why this sudden renewal of interest in science, and specifically mathematics, to provide the one true answer to any given situation? And why now? In no small part, this is based on a merging of mathematics with spirituality at the end of the 20th century. Mathematics after Relativity and more so after the Quantum and Chaos theories, has been gradually moving toward the mysterious, embracing the unexplainable rather than trying to force an ultimate solution. Spirituality, on the other hand – having lost some of its hold on people as a result of its numerous conflicts with science – has started to make itself seem more scientific: Creationism is now "Intelligent Design" in scientific textbooks throughout the United States. In moving closer together, these two areas are influencing the creative process, inspiring literature and film to move in new directions.

It is no doubt unnecessary to note that such has not always been the case. The divide between science and spirituality has been vast and deep for some time. In the relatively recent era, we might trace this divide to the advances made in the 17th and 18th centuries by Galileo, Copernicus, and Newton. Not only did their findings lead to conflict with Biblical references, but so pervasive was science at this time, that it seemed as though the complexities of life were being reduced to mathematical formulas. This notion troubled artists of the time as well. At the end of Alexander Pope's *The New Dunciad*, Pope's narrator, situated in the court of Dullness, comments, "See mystery to mathematics fly" (647). In the 18th century, on the heels of a major scientific era which found Galileo revealing the true nature of planetary motion and Newton developing, essentially, modern mathematics and physics through to the 20th century, mathematics was seen as destroying the mysteries of life. Calculus was invented, optics were developed, and motion was reduced from a mystical, God-driven experience to an attractive power between two large bodies; gravity was unleashed on the world. Yet, in the last 100 years, the distance between mysticism and science has gradually been reduced and today they seem as closely aligned as perhaps they have ever been before. Not surprisingly, then, the artistic response has begun to highlight the consequences of this allegiance. In his article "Overcoming the Limit Syndrome," Gregorio Morales sums up this change claiming, "if it was science that constrained aesthetics within realism in the eighteenth century, then it is science that restores to art the grandeur, possibilities, and mysteries that were lost" (10).

This correlation in the 20th century begins with the advances to mathematics and physics created by Albert Einstein and his Theory of Relativity. As the theory generated further mathematical advances in the forms of Quantum and Chaos theories, the connection between science and spirituality only deepened. By exploring the philosophical underpinnings of these theories and examining the correlation of ideas in mathematics with those present in various religious discourses, it becomes evident that the world is now poised to accept or at least ponder the impact of the union of mathematics and spirituality. This connection is the basis for recent movies such as Darren Aronofky's 1998 film π in which a connection between mathematics and mysticism is examined as a way of understanding reality. Aronofsky suggests in his film that recent advances in mathematics and physics reveal an ordering, a structure that exists behind even the most random series of events. If such a structure exists, it may then be supposed that it reveals the presence of a divine hand. Relativity theory, with its suggestion that there may be a plurality of apparent truths despite a constant truth lurking behind them, might be seen as the mathematics of Modernism. Quantum theory, then, with its rejection of an absolute truth in favour of a system of essentially infinite possibilities, can be understood as the mathematics of Postmodernism. Finally, Chaos theory which looks at the randomness, the seeming chaos of a world comprised only of possibilities and once again tries to find an organization, a structuring principle that beckons to a higher Truth, seems ready to be the mathematics of post-Postmodernism. Aronfosky's film presents a quest through mathematical theories in search of a divine structure, a search that reflects the yearning for a new language, or a new understanding of language, that is more consistent with a multi-dimensional world. These various quests unite in the film and in the post-Postmodern aesthetic as ideas from mathematics, mysticism and literary theory, specifically deconstruction, reflect the desire for a new understanding of existence which requires a new form of expression, one that embraces the paradox of Chaos theory.

The confines of this paper make it impossible to explain fully any one of the mathematical theories under discussion here, much less all three. Rather than spend time providing a cursory glance at these complex ideas, I shall simply hint at some of the more surprising findings in each and use these to display the connections between these theories of the physical world and beliefs from the spiritual realm as they relate to π. Einstein's Relativity theory allows for the scientific possibility that a single event may be recorded in completely different ways (differences in the ordering of events or the size of an object) with neither report asserting dominance as the One True Answer. It would be impossible to determine whose account was correct in certain situations since, though they disagree, each version is equally valid. While many saw in Einstein's theories the possibility that anyone's perspective could be accurate, an idea that would lead to the notion of moral relativism, this is not a component of the theory. In fact, though a greater potential for differing viewpoints is embraced, Relativity theory suggests that "under certain conditions we can extract from different reports ... all the laws of physics ... It is for this reason that, by comparison to classical [i.e. Newtonian] physics, modern relativity is simple, universal, and, one may even say, 'absolute'" (Holton 131). So, while two people may record an event in two distinct ways, the truth of the event is never questioned; the discrepancy is attributable to their respective position, their frame of reference. Moreover, given either reference frame and recording, we can deduce the other's observations; an absolute remains behind the difference. It may be impossible to determine which observer is "right," but certain facts remain in place; the truth of the event is never completely questioned.

Also, Einstein's theories made links between previously distinct areas of science. The three-dimensional world we believed we inhabited was suddenly rendered four-dimensional as time attained the same status as the three dimensions of space, resulting in the portmanteau term "space-time." Even the language associated with Einstein's theories underscored the forged bonds, the links created between seemingly disparate realms. Moreover, the world was expanded to four dimensions although the language we used was rooted in a three-dimensional existence, an idea that would also create problems in literary theory, as discussed below. After Einstein, then, paradox is embraced, not as a problem that needs resolution, but as a component of the way the world really works while language was forced to adjust to a new reality, an adjustment that is still ongoing.

Initial reaction to Relativity was overwhelming though fraught with confusion leading to the assertion that there were only 12 people in the world who understood the theory. Beginning in 1919[1], the popular media would offer a new discussion of Relativity almost daily, many of which concluded by commenting on the impossibility of understanding the theory. In an edition of the London *Times* that featured an article from Einstein explaining Relativity, the editors also ran an article that stated: "We cannot profess to follow the details and the implications of the new theory with complete certainty, but we are consoled by the reflection that the protagonists of the debate, including even Dr. Einstein himself, find no little difficulty in making their meaning clear" ("Dr. Einstein's Theory" 13). Einstein rejected the claim that his theory was only capable of being understood by a few people. Yet, the difficulty of the theory presented a challenge to readers, daring them to try to understand, while also suggesting that there was some strange mystical knowledge contained there, ideas that only a select group had been shown in some inner sanctum. In fact, the very opacity of the theories aligns Relativity with the Modernist aesthetic, which praises difficulty as evidence of a greater truth and as a sign of development from earlier "simpler" understandings of the world. As T. S. Eliot notes in his 1921 article "The Metaphysical Poets," "poets in our civilization, as it exists at present, must be *difficult.* Our civilization comprehends great variety and complexity, and this variety and complexity, playing upon a refined sensibility, must produce various and complex results. The poet must become more and more comprehensive, more allusive, more indirect, in order to force, to dislocate if necessary, language into his meaning" (65). By altering physics from a concept taught to grade school children to a notion that even physicists had trouble comprehending, Einstein promoted, perhaps even helped establish, the Modernist desire for complexity and difficulty.

In addition to a new way to understand the physical world, ideas from Relativity quickly spread to other areas of thought, including religion. The connection between Relativity and spirituality was explored very soon after Einstein's theory reached the mainstream, transforming the physicist into something of a celebrity. Frequently interviewed by newspapers and magazines, Einstein was eventually asked to comment on the incredible interest being paid to a scientific theory; he offered:

> I believe quite positively that it is the mysteriousness of what they cannot conceive which places them under a magic spell. One tells them of something big which will influence all future life, of a theory which only a small group, highly learned, can comprehend. Big names are mentioned of men who have made discoveries, of which the crowd grasps nothing. But it impresses them, takes on color and the magic power of mystery, and thus one becomes enthusiastic and excited. ("Einstein Declares Women Rule Here" 9)

Einstein again alludes to the importance of the theory's difficulty, but it is this "magic power of mystery" which might speak loudest toward the initial interest in Einstein's theory outside of scientific circles, a harbinger of the renewed interest in mathematics amongst non-mathematicians.

Although developed roughly contemporaneously, Relativity would eventually cede the stage to the developments of Quantum theory, which reached its full potential after Einstein's Relativity theory. Under this theory truth is reduced to a series of possibilities. Rather than saying what is happening at the atomic level, we are left discussing the potentialities of exceedingly small bits of matter. On this level we cannot say with certainty what occurs, all we can determine is a series of probabilities; certain events, then, are simply more or less likely to happen. Also, Quantum theory saw the development of the idea of wave-particle dualism. Essentially, this states that an atom behaves like a wave when it is not being directly observed, so that it may exist in a multitude of locations, but it exists as a particle, in only one location, when we check on its position. It is, therefore, both a wave of possibilities and a unique particle at the same time. The paradoxes begun with Relativity theory were further enhanced just as the importance of the observer became more crucial.

With events replaced by possibilities, there remains a great potential for paradox and uncertainty under Quantum theory. One way of confronting this situation is with "the 'many-minds' and 'many-worlds' hypotheses, the latter most recently expounded by David Deutsch in his book *The Fabric of Reality*. On Deutsch's account of the quantum 'multiverse' every wavepacket collapse gives rise to every possible outcome and thereafter to an infinite series of further branching possibilities (or 'worlds') along with a likewise proliferating series of observer-relative conscious states" (Norris, *Philosophy* 122). This scientific theory advocates the bizarre notion that there constantly exist a myriad of different worlds, different potential existences occurring simultaneously and which we select to experience almost at random. As Werner Heisenberg states, "in quantum-theoretical terms: '(through) every act of perception we select one of the infinite number of possibilities and thus we also limit the number of possibilities for the future'" (qtd. in Norris, *Philosophy* 133). Science, from this perspective, involves choice as much as it does a recording of fact, while the unexplainable – even bizarre – is further entrenched in scientific discourse.

Further, Quantum theory also includes Heisenberg's uncertainty principle which states that it is impossible to know both the precise location and the precise momentum of any given particle. Uncertainty is now a scientifically accepted fact; mystery has been (re)inscribed into the workings of the world. When determining the position of a particle, one must take into consideration the observer who determines the location or the momentum of that particle. Power shifts, therefore, away from the suggestion that there is a single sentient being, a god, controlling the outcome of events. Instead, humankind quite literally takes control; reality is structured around the observation recorded. Truth is not "out there" waiting to be discovered, it is internal, waiting to be chosen. As Christopher Norris claims in *Philosophy of Language*:

> the lesson of quantum mechanics, according to [John] Wheeler, is that we inhabit a strangely 'participatory universe' and one that is subject to effects of retroactive causality over vast distances of spatiotemporal (or space-like and time-like) separation. In which case, the only way to resolve the quantum measurement problem is to . . . conclude that every act of observation brings about a 'choice' between various possible results whose consequences may extend to the entire past and future evolution of events on a cosmic scale. (122)

This choice is dependent on the observer. The power for generating truth is thus shifted from some external, omnipotent god and is placed squarely in the hands of humankind. Reality is, literally, a matter of choice.

In terms of the visual arts, for example, Relativity theory might be said to influence Modernist painters such as Pablo Picasso while Quantum theory appears to be behind the Postmodern theories of painters like Jackson Pollock. Consider a painting such as Picasso's *Les Demoiselles D'Avignon* or *Geurnica*; in these paintings – although new devices are used, new approaches that, it may be argued, seek to incorporate a fourth dimension into a three-dimensional existence[2] – there remains a concrete reality behind the pictures: a group of women posing, or the horrors of war, respectively. Although we are being asked to look at these standard images in a different way, an absolute reality is presupposed. Conversely, in any of a number of Jackson Pollock's paintings, we are confronted by dribbled paint, composed by an artist according to a balance and style in his own mind. Certainly there is an expression, an idea here, but we are not offered the sense that these canvases represent a discernable reality; we cannot say a Pollock painting is depicting war or a group of women, instead the balance or harmony of independent colours effects a purely aesthetic response. This outward rejection of concrete absolutes and, thus, Truth, nicely echoes ideas of Quantum theory. As Norris claims in *Against Relativism*,

> for [Jean-François] Lyotard contemporary science – or his favoured branches of it, those concerned with 'undecidables, conflicts, ... "fracta", catastrophes, pragmatic paradoxes', etc. – may be seen as embarked upon the same kind of enterprise that is currently pursued by avant-garde figures in the literary, visual and musical arts. ... This involves the idea of 'presenting the unpresentable,' of the sublime as somehow giving access to a realm of 'suprasensible.' (103)

In short, a new reality was formed via Quantum theory, one based on indeterminacy rather than causality, such that "The application of quantum theory to literature has attempted to create a space for freedom, extraordinariness, and imagination, where academic realism – that does not recognize the complexity of reality – is replaced by a version that is more transcendent" (Peñas-Bermejo 50). Rather than being freed from the shackles of realism, then, artists have been able to continue as realists. It is, after all, reality that has undergone the transformation; artists, as always, simply record that reality, even if, now, it has become more "transcendent," other-worldly, mystical.

Both Relativity and Quantum theories seem to open the door for a more spiritual outlook on life. Relativity theory, with its embracing of paradox and a plurality of voices, while rejecting the scientific realism of past centuries, reflects the same world we see in the work of the Modernists. Traditional "realism" was beginning to disappear, but the notion of an absolute Truth, of a higher spiritual plane which we should all aspire to, remained. Quantum theory, on the other hand, furthered the break with realism and replaced reality with a series of potentialities. No longer was there an Absolute Truth behind the scenes; the best we could hope for was, well, whatever we might choose. Humans were free to make their own destiny without waiting for the hand of fate or god. This rejection of a concrete truth was a further remove from realism; as such, it is consistent with the concepts of Postmodernist thought. Recently, though, science has taken a new turn and the artistic world is making use of these new developments. In his 1993 play *Arcadia*, one of Tom Stoppard's characters hints at this very shift:

> People were talking about the end of physics. Relativity and quantum looked as if they were going to clean out the whole problem between them. A theory of everything. But they only explained the very big and the very small. The universe, the elementary particles. The ordinary-sized stuff which is our lives, the things people write poetry about – clouds – daffodils – waterfalls – and what happens in a cup of coffee when the cream goes in – these things are full of mystery, as mysterious to us as the heavens were to the Greeks ... the smallest variation blows prediction apart, and the weather is unpredictable the same way. When you push the numbers through the computer you can see it on the screen. The future is disorder. (qtd. in Hawkins 2-3)

The suggestion here is that Chaos theory is the theory of the future and, indeed, Chaos theory is the latest approach to understanding a world that so often seems random and uncontrollable. This theory seems poised to guide the post-Postmodern world.

In Chaos theory scientists search for a pattern, an organizing principle behind even the most seemingly random series of events. The assumption underlying this theory is that there is something, some structure, organizing everything, and this structure can be ascertained, with enough effort. This organizing principle opens the door wide once again for the presence of a (type of) god. If even the output of a random number generator might contain an order, then there must be some guiding hand behind this. First developed, essentially, by Edward Lorenz's work on predicting the weather, Chaos theory examines the fact that even minute changes in initial circumstances can have huge effects on the outcome of a given system. Further, one of the most often cited examples from Chaos theory, and the title of a film loosely using the idea, is the notion commonly called the "butterfly effect." Under this example, a butterfly flapping its wings in Asia might generate a hurricane in North America. As Ian Stewart claims in *Does God Play Dice?*, "The flapping of a single butterfly's wing today produces a tiny change in the state of the atmosphere. Over a period of time, what the atmosphere actually does diverges from what it would have done. So, in a month's time, a tornado that would have devastated the Indonesian coast doesn't happen. Or maybe one that wasn't going to happen, does" (141). Chaos theory thus examines how small changes affect major outcomes; it searches for the order that underlies apparently random situations. Note also, that there is the presumption here that an event either was or wasn't "going to happen." Under this new scientific theory, there is a return to a sense of fate, a sense that we are travellers on a train waiting for the next moment to occur; absent is any suggestion that we simply select from a series of possibilities at any given moment and that we decide our own reality. In addition, with examples such as this, there is the underlying assumption that all life is connected in some capacity. If a butterfly flapping its wings can affect whether people live or die in Indonesia, then all life is interconnected, a notion that has strong ties to Eastern mysticism as well.[3]

The assumptions implicit in Chaos theory go hand-in-hand with those associated with post-Postmodern culture. Chaos theory maintains many philosophical components of the previous two theories (discussed above); the chaos of a quantum world unites with the paradoxical Absolute of a relativistic existence. In other words, the world of possibilities as presented in Quantum theory is maintained but it is maintained as the effect of limited human perception: "Basically, Chaos theory is a relatively new physics paradigm which supplants deterministic causality with a view of the universe as essentially unknowable (or unpredictable) on the local level, but easily grasped as a system" (Kundert-Gibbs, "Continued Perception" 367). Chaos theory, then, unites the unknowable with the knowable, the chaotic with the absolute and the scientific with the mystical.

This recent shift to the assumptions implicit in Chaos theory has begun to impact the wider cultural existence and this impact is only continuing to be developed. In her text *Strange Attractors*, Harriet Hawkins notes that recently there have even been t-shirts printed with ideas from Chaos theory emblazoned on them (10), and that "the manifest ubiquity of its relevance clearly accounts for the international vogue for chaos in popular culture and the fine arts as well as in specialized scientific publications. And to my mind, its ubiquity of appeal – across history, cultures, generations, genres, art and science – makes chaos theory of special perhaps crucial, and timely importance to our increasingly Balkanized world" (14). Hawkins goes on to state that "In a time of collapsing explanatory and ideological paradigms and certainties, a theory which stresses built-in unpredictabilities seems both necessary and congenial to a post-Newtonian, post-Freudian, post-Marxist and post-Postmodern world view" (15). While Relativity theory embraced greater complexity and Quantum theory rejected an authoritative truth, Chaos theory with its mingling of uncertainty and certainty into a paradoxical whole, will best be able to understand this emergent Age of Paradox.

This brings me to the issue of pi and, thus, π. In an effort to find an order behind the chaos there is frequent, almost obsessive, desire to calculate the value of pi to even more digits. Each new breakthrough in computing technology seems motivated in no small part by the desire to work out the ratio of a circle's circumference to its diameter to even more digits. With each new advancement, the researcher believes that a pattern must finally emerge; eventually, we will see where pi duplicates in value and becomes a "simple" iterative fraction. Yet, no pattern has yet to emerge; the digits remain seemingly random although we have the formula for this randomness. Within this number, then, we are offered chaos with a distinct structure behind it. As such, pi holds a mystical interest for mathematicians, seeming to offer the answer to the chaos that is revealed in the value.

This idea, with its connection to Chaos theory and the tie between mathematics and spirituality, is the driving force behind Aronofsky's π. In the film, a brilliant (or, quite possibly, mad) mathematician, Max Cohen (played by Sean Guillette), searches for patterns in everything from the stock market to the natural world. Drawing parallels between these seemingly disparate realms he believes that he will find the order behind the apparent randomness of life and be closer to locating some hidden truth about our world. Invoking ideas from Chaos theory, Max also hopes to solve problems presented in Jewish mysticism. Aronofsky overtly exploits the bond that had developed between these unlikely allies in the 20th century; in fact, when released, π carried the tagline "Faith in chaos." Religion, belief, and faith join forces with chaos, randomness, and lack of control in the search for a hidden structure – God. If one can make sense of the chaos and find the structure, Max believes, one might find God. Ultimately, Max's research generates a 216-digit number that everyone wants to possess, for this number is, we are informed, the true name of God; hence, Chaos theory, in the film, literally reveals God. An obscure, low-budget movie like π, shot in black and white film stock, should have quietly disappeared from art house cinemas in about a week. Yet, somehow, the film struck a chord with audiences and has turned into something of a cult classic, winning awards at prestigious festivals like Sundance and the Independent Spirit Awards.[4] The surprising popularity of this and other such films and TV shows, displays the cultural interest during this time in the confluence of math and spirituality.

Near the beginning of π, Max recounts an event from his youth; this story is recited again at the movie's conclusion, but with different implications. In the story, Max describes staring at the sun because he has been specifically told not to, and nearly going blind from the abuse his eyes endure. The story is presented as an explanation for both his mathematical ability and his chronic headaches. He claims, by staring at the sun "something crept in," a "something" that has made him the person he is today. The implication here is that Max has developed a higher consciousness from this connection with the cosmic energy, suggesting that his mathematical knowledge is infused with a divine presence, but also with the problems of a troubled mind. This early story suggests an interesting parallel with the beginnings of mathematical mysticism in the 20th century. If we view the beginning of the changes to our understanding of mathematics and its parallel with spirituality as arriving with Einstein, then this change was also achieved, in a sense, by staring into the sun. Einstein's Theory of Relativity was, effectively, validated by the results of the solar eclipse expedition in 1919 which confirmed the deflection of light waves by large bodies (i.e. the moon). For Max, staring into the sun creates a change in his being, he endures an individualized paradigm shift from Max Cohen, a young boy, to Max Cohen, a mathematical prodigy and true "seer." This rupture from a simple past to a complex present is suggestive of the beginnings of mathematical change and spiritual assumptions.

The connections between mathematics and spirituality presented in the film are numerous, and to a certain extent readily apparent: Max's practice of number theory is of interest to Lenny, a follower of the Jewish mysticism known as Kabbalah, who wishes to use Max's mind to understand the intricacies of his beliefs. However, the mathematics used in π offer a way of understanding a post-Postmodern world that is both scientific and spiritual, invoking ideas from Relativity, Quantum and Chaos theories, and ultimately implying that it is this final theory that hold the keys to the future. One of the central results of Einstein's Relativity theory was its revision of our understanding of time. Time had always been seen as a constant progress, a river we were caught up in and forced to yield to its whims. As such, time was always seen as something closely connected with God; only God knew the "true" time, an absolute construct that we could only hope to approximate. Instead, Einstein made time a dimension just like length, width and height; it was a dimension that was relative to the reference frame selected, just like the others, so the independence of time was abolished and replaced by Einstein's concept of space-time. Under Relativity theory, with time as a dimension, all times become eternally present; as Einstein claimed, "People like us, who believe in physics, know that the distinction between past, present, and future is only a stubborn, persistent illusion" (qtd. in McFarlane 126). This concept of time has strong parallels with the world of spirituality. In his text *The Tao of Physics*, Fritjof Capra cites Buddhist scholar D. T. Suzuki, who claims that "In this spiritual world there are no time divisions such as the past, present and future; for they have contracted themselves into a single moment of the present where life quivers in its true sense ... The past and the future are both rolled up in this present moment of illumination, and this present moment is not something standing still with all its contents, for it ceaselessly moves on" (179). Science and mysticism, then, developed an identical outlook on time.

Aronofsky's film, shot in grainy black and white and existing in a world that defies temporal confines, presents a sense of "timelessness." Even the computer Max uses is composed of parts from an old keyboard, hoses, and boxes that suggest a computer from the 1950s not the 1990s; however, it also contains a modern, high-tech microchip, consistent with contemporary computing technology. Old and new technologies mingle together to "create this timeless space," as Aronofsky describes it on a DVD commentary track. While this sense of a world outside of time invokes ideas of a Postmodern aesthetic, π also undermines the implications of that aesthetic by suggesting the possibility of a higher, absolute truth. Traces of both Modernist and Postmodernist ideologies remain, mingling and altering into a new whole. Also, the mixture of narrative development with Max's hallucinatory visions, creates the sense that the events we are witnessing may, in fact, be occurring inside Max's own mind, furthering the sense of a timeless presence. This timelessness puts us on a level closer to a god or some other being outside of time. If we can, scientifically, move within time, we would have greater control of our own destiny, correcting past mistakes and fixing future problems.

In addition to Relativity theory, π also juxtaposes Quantum and Chaos theories. These differing approaches to the world can be seen most clearly in the scenes involving Max and his mentor Sol Robeson. Robeson, not unlike Max, was once obsessed with finding patterns in seemingly random mathematical occurrences. Yet, while Max searches for a meaning, an order, behind the physical world, hoping to find something that will unite all components of that world, Sol sought to discover a pattern behind the digits in pi, before finally abandoning it as a futile project. Sol's rejection of the search for finding the hidden order, then, represents ideas linked more directly with Quantum theory. As he tells Max over a game of Go, "You need a break or you will get nowhere. There will be no order, only chaos." For Sol, these ideas are mutually exclusive: the world will either appear as chaos or, if Max is lucky, as ordered. Yet, under Chaos theory, the chaos *is* a kind of order. Having abandoned the hope, we might even say the faith, that an order will ever be revealed from his analysis of pi, Sol has accepted the quantum mechanical approach to the world where an absolute truth is impossible to determine. For Sol, life is chaotic; there is no hope of finding The Answer. Max disagrees, however, and questions Sol's commitment to finding a solution to pi, wondering in a narrative voice-over, "how could you stop believing that there is a pattern, an ordered shape behind those numbers" comprising pi. For Max, even rigorous mathematical analysis requires an element of faith, of belief. Max is rooted in a mathematical approach based on Chaos theory, deciding "there's an Answer in that number," referring to the 216-digit name of God that initially seems to be an anomaly. He has belief, faith that an Absolute will appear from the mists of chaos, and he justifies his faith even though he seems to go mad as a result.

Similar to Sol's abandoned search for the order behind pi, Max believes that an order will appear to explain the interconnectedness of life and uses the stock market as his data set. While Sol abandons his search accepting that one either has chaos or order, not both, Max believes that chaos and order intermingle. His search leads him to discover the 216-digit number name of God by accident as he searches for the structure, the order behind all life. That order, the film suggests then, is God. This search is based on Max's "assumptions," "1. Mathematics is the language of Nature. 2. Everything around can be represented and understood through numbers. 3. If you graph the numbers of any system, patterns emerge. Therefore there are patterns everywhere in nature." Searching for the patterns in nature leads Max to look for a pattern in the stock market, believing that these areas are connected. This idea has a direct correlation with John Leeland Kundert-Gibbs's analysis of Zen and Chaos theory as applied to literature in *No-Thing is Left to Tell*; he claims, "There is a very important branch of Chaos theory ... which is more concerned with the striking fact that Chaotic or highly complex systems ... can and often do produce order. ... The rich interaction of a multitude of elements in these disordered systems (which range from the stock market to the origins of life) allow 'the system as a whole to undergo *spontaneous self-organization*'" (42). To generate his analysis of the stock market which, he believes, will lead to an analysis of the patterns behind all of nature and life in general, Max routinely sits at his computer, announces a specific time, and then instructs himself, "press return." Once he does so his computer generates a new sheet of stock picks based on the initial conditions he has fed into the program. Max's actions suggest that there is something important about pressing return at a precise moment, a specific time that will cause the computer to yield "the solution." Yet, when Max first encounters the "sacred" number, he gives himself this instruction and is then temporarily distracted by a voice he believes he hears nearby. A few minutes later, Max remembers his mission and presses the return key, generating the glitch, the "bug," as Sol describes it, that is in fact the name of God. Beginning with such a small variation, only a few seconds of difference from the time when he was supposed to press return, Max generates a vastly different and surprising result. This is the butterfly effect in action.

With the invocation of each of the three mathematical theories discussed above, π highlights the developing bond between science and religion. By shifting its focus away from an absolute truth and toward possibilities and choice, and toward a scientific theory that emphasizes the role of the observer in actually creating reality, science moved further toward the mystical. As I suggested, behind Max's belief in Chaos theory and the suggestion that he can encounter a structure that is behind nature, the stock market and the world as a whole, is the inherent suggestion that all life is interconnected. If a butterfly flapping its wings can affect the weather on the other side of the globe, then we must accept that we are not completely autonomous, we are part of a global whole. Also, as Max believes, if the same structure governing the wind in the trees governs the flow of stock values (as is suggested in an early shot which blends these two images to suggest the potentiality of viewing the stock market as a component of the natural world), then all life, all "authentic" and "inauthentic" components of the natural world must function within that same structure. In fact these opposing labels are revealed to be a fiction. What we require, then, is belief; and it is belief which Max argues is required to find the hidden truth lurking behind our chaotic existence. What we require to understand modern mathematics, is also belief, a faith that somehow, the paradoxes have their place and that the whole will bind together in a manner that transcends logic.

For Max (as, we might assume, Aronofsky), understanding must include both physics and metaphysics, science and religion. Toward the end of π, Max finally understands that the number he has generated is actually the true name of God and when he realizes that his mathematics have led him to a new spiritual insight, he is allowed to enter a pseudo-dream state and see God. Max, may, however, see too much; the frequent references to Icarus and his own story of staring into the sun as a child and nearly losing his eyesight, suggest that there are prices to be paid for reaching too high, for trying to know too much; there are prices to pay for stripping life of its mystery. Some uncertainty becomes crucial to a complete understanding of the world. As Einstein, himself, claimed:

> The most beautiful thing we can experience is the mysterious. It is the fundamental emotion that stands at the cradle of true art and true science. He who does not know it and can no longer wonder, no longer feel amazement, is as good as dead, a snuffed-out candle. It was the experience of mystery . . . that engendered religion. A knowledge of the existence of something we cannot penetrate, our perceptions of the profoundest reason and the most radiant beauty, which only in their most primitive forms are accessible to our minds – it is this knowledge and this emotion that constitute true religiosity. (Calaprice 199)

Life, and our understanding of it, or so π and Einstein suggest, needs to maintain a link to the mysterious, to the unknowable. As Chaos theory (and thus, perhaps, the aesthetics of a post-Postmodern epoch) suggest, we can never fully understand the individual components of the world, although we can know the larger structure. There are limits then to our knowledge; uncertainty must be a component of life. We can take comfort in the knowledge that there is a structure, a design behind random events without having to know precisely how or why that structure functions the way it does. Pi may never reveal where it duplicates, we might never know why a pattern refuses to emerge, but we can rest comfortable in the knowledge that the order remains, the formula exists and a structure is present.

The structure behind π challenges us to reassess our concept of reality, how we perceive that reality, and how we know what to believe. Throughout the film, Max suffers from chronic migraines and has visions or hallucinations that make the entire film somewhat suspect: are the events we're seeing really happening or are they simply the "effects" of Max's mind? It is the central paradox of this film that it is impossible to determine whether the events are actually occurring or whether they are all or mostly hallucinations caused by a troubled mind. The film's form, then (like its content), suggests that life is much more complex than a series of either/or dualities. Life is not comprised of things that are either good or bad, short or tall; just like the image of yin and yang of Eastern spiritual philosophies, there are gradations, shades of each polarity blending into the other. This idea runs through mathematics, religion and literary theory. As N. Katherine Hayles claims in *Chaos and Order:*

> That chaos has been negatively valued in the Western tradition may be partly due . . . to the predominance of binary logic in the West. If order is good, chaos is bad because it is conceptualized as the opposite of order. By contrast, in the four-valued logic characteristic of Taoist thought, not-order is also a possibility, distinct from and valued differently than anti-order ... In chaos theory chaos may either lead to order, as it does with self-organizing systems, or in yin/yang fashion it may have deep structures of order encoded within it. (3)

Thus it is only by rejecting a language structured on dualisms, a language linked with a mathematics that no longer adequately describes our complex and chaotic word, that we might be able to adequately describe our existence in a four-dimensional world, a world more in line with Chaos theory than Newtonian mechanics.

This movement toward a multidimensional language has a grounding in the work of literary theorists, as well, including Jacques Derrida whose theories often invoke concepts from scientific disciplines. It is here that many of these ideas coalesce. As Kundert-Gibbs claims,

> In deconstruction, the centralized relationship between signifier and referent is destabilized by the marginalized force of the quasi-potential 'trace,' an interloping third element that exposes the necessary slippage between sign and meaning. However, [as N. Katherine Hayles claims,] 'When the center is empty – or has been emptied by discourse that claims to be marginal – there is no meaningful distinction between margin and center in terms of the power they exercise'... thus language is re-viewed as multiple – even 'multivalent' ... Here, too [ie. as with Chaos theory], what has been regarded under the old paradigm as a set of minor, fringe aberrations – small errors in transferring meaning from sign to referent – is moved to a central role, replacing a deterministic system with one that is chaotic but potentially richer in the resultant 'play' of language. (*No-Thing* 53).

The "freeplay" that Derrida reveals by identifying the absent centre behind language, becomes the chaos of the system; yet, this chaos is only apparent. A structure remains intact and, if not grounded in language, at least in the approach to language.[5] Christopher Norris, in his reading of Derridean deconstruction, highlights this concept when he claims that "it is often ... assumed that deconstruction in general, and Derrida's work in particular, is just another version of this postmodern 'turn' against the values of truth, reason, criticism, and conceptual analysis. However, that reading ignores ... where Derrida affirms the necessity – the 'absolute and principled' necessity – of thinking these issues through with the greatest possible rigour and precision" (*Deconstruction and the Unfinished Project of Modernity* 84). Norris makes this even clearer in the same work, claiming, "Derrida is routinely taken to assert that texts can be read however one likes. ... On the contrary, he has often been at pains to repudiate this 'anything goes' approach" (75). Not unlike Einstein's repudiation of those who claimed Relativity allowed anyone's perspective to be accurate, Derrida's concept of deconstruction does not allow for complete chaos. There is a method to his madness, so to speak, a guiding principle to the practice of deconstruction; this organization is the system which is knowable despite the chaos of the individual elements, as with Chaos theory.

Hence, the intermingling of Derrida and Chaos theory suggests the need for a language that can transcend the boundaries of our limited perspective by rejecting dualisms in favour of a multidimensional language with gradations rather than polarities. This latent idea which has its grounding in a Postmodern aesthetic just as Chaos theory has its roots in Quantum theory, is further advanced here. Not only is the distinction between opposites broken down to be replaced by shades in between (not either/or but a full spectrum) but these seeming opposites are forcefully yoked into a new unity ("space-time"). Chaos is order and order is chaos, paradoxically comprising a more mathematical-spiritual view of the world. Moreover, as above, small variations, minor distinctions which had been marginalized in the past are moved to a central position and given a prominence that is no less valued than the formerly crucial components of language and thought. The dislocation of spirituality to the margins by scientists and the dislocation of science to the margins by the spiritually-minded is undone as the bond between them grows and they unite into a more paradoxical yet complete whole. In *Against Relativism*, Norris claims, "there seems to be at least some warrant for [the] view that Derrida – along with Bohr, Gödel and other prophets of postmodernity – is engaged upon a wholesale undoing of those values (like the 'classical' truth/falsehood distinction) that once held sway in the discourse of the

Western natural and human science" (115). Abandoning such binary thinking leads to a new way of representing the world that is both more mathematical and more spiritual. No longer must we view even these discourses as separate realms (something is *either* spiritual *or* scientific), instead they may unite in a multivalent universe.

Thus, π refuses to provide solutions for us to the various questions it poses. Are Max's hallucinations reality? Does the number really reveal God? Is the world structured around an organizing principle that is knowable at large but unknowable in the details? Again, this advances the notion from Postmodernism in which in the absence of an order, a structure, we are left in a nihilistic world; instead, the freeplay itself, the chaos, includes a structure, an organization. Ultimately, unlike Postmodernism, in this new era the possibility of an answer is not denied; it is promised, it is just not provided for us. Similarly for π and for pi: in both we are left uncertain: we cannot be sure if Max is mad or brilliant (yet another dualism that is bridged here); we cannot be sure if pi will ever reveal a pattern or continue with seeming randomness forever. Yet, a solution is promised: we know the formula for pi; we know there is an order behind it even if we cannot determine its repetitive pattern when written out as 3.14....; and, in terms of the film, no answer can be given to the many questions it poses because the answer is simply yes and no at the same time. At the film's conclusion when Max recounts the story of staring into the sun again, another paradigm shift occurs; this time Max has seen God and relinquishes his compulsive need to understand all components of life. Instead, consistent with the ideas of Quantum and Chaos theories, Max needs to learn to accept that there are some aspects of life that must remain a mystery, a paradox without resolution. This idea has a grounding in various religious ideologies that strive to achieve inner peace by abandoning an obsessive devotion to the desires of the world. I certainly don't mean to suggest that Max's decision to drill into his own skull is a Zen-like release from the burdens of the world, but in the scene which concludes the movie, we find Max sitting calmly with little Jenna on a park bench, enjoying the wind blowing in the trees and claiming (or actually no longer knowing) that he cannot solve Jenna's math problem as he has released the devotion to mathematics and the desire to understand everything that had plagued him throughout the film. Instead of obsessing over number theory, Max enters "the 'void' .... or unity that gives birth to multiplicity [that] lies as the heart of Taoist thought and provides the basic 'concept' on which Taoists depend to achieve transcendence over the desires and drives of society and nature" (Kundert-Gibbs, *No-Thing* 24). In one of the final (possibly) dream sequences after destroying his computer, Euclid, Max finally finds himself in a white room, an inner sanctum where he confronts God. On the DVD commentary track, Aronofsky refers to this place as "the white void," suggesting that Max does achieve a final moment of transcendence. Here, Max quietly recounts the numbers that make up the 216-digit name of God one digit at a time. In this final release from the world, in this final connection with the divine, language itself breaks down and only the numbers remain. That number is not, also, uttered as one long number but as 216 individual numbers; the fragmentation, the deconstruction of existence, is realized as the line of numbers "can never be completely fulfilled or totalized" (Kundert-Gibbs, *No-Thing* 52). The indeterminacy remains within a system that has a solution, chaos remains in the individual analysis while order governs the system, language has an infinite freeplay within a finite field. The yin and the yang of life are actually one. This paradoxical unity of opposites under the guiding hand of Chaos theory is thus poised to influence art and culture in the years to come and form the basis of post-Postmodernist thought.

In Douglas Adams's novel *The Hitchhiker's Guide to the Galaxy* we are actually provided with the "The Answer" (121), the meaning of "Life, the Universe and Everything" (122). Since this is a comic novel and not a philosophical treatise, that answer turns out to be "Forty-two" (129), and what follows is a very bizarre quest not for an answer, but for a question: the question that, if properly asked, will broaden our understanding of life by knowing that the answer is 42. Not unlike the events in π, the hidden mysteries, the hidden truths of life are bound up in a number. By unlocking the code behind the number, by understanding pi, by knowing how 42 answers the ultimate question, humans might solve an enigma and know the Truth behind the chaos of their existence. While Adams suggests The Answer to life might be simpler than we think, just a 2 digit number, others have claimed that the truth is not just "out there" but "in here" and all around us. All life is interconnected into a unified whole where polarities no longer exist, dualisms dissolve into unity. Math and religion, science and literature, so often seen as enemies, might unite in a holistic world. In "Science and Religion," Einstein makes the assertion, "Science without religion is lame, religion without science is blind" (26). Each of the major mathematical theories of the twentieth century seem to obey this dictum. Indeed, Relativity, Quantum theory, and finally Chaos theory have moved science ever closer to the realm of spirituality. And, it would seem, as we stand on the brink of yet another epochal transition – a transition, that is, away from the apparent secularism and nihilism of Postmodernism and Quantum theory – we are witnessing a profound union of science and religion, doubt and faith, uncertainty and certainty, mathematics and mysticism.

Notes

[1] The year when a solar eclipse expedition effectively verified Einstein's theory.

[2] See Arthur I. Miller's *Einstein, Picasso: Space, Time, and the Beauty that Causes Havoc* for a full discussion of Einstein's influence on Picasso's style.

[3] There are numerous parallels between Buddhism, specifically, or Eastern mysticism, generally, and 20th century physics which also suggest not only a return to the spiritual, but to ancient Eastern philosophy rather than Western ideologies. Although a full evaluation is beyond the scope of this paper, this area also offers an interesting potential area of development for post-Postmodern literature which further develops the ideas discussed here.

[4] A similar theme is present in the pseudo-documentary *What the Bleep Do We (K)now!?* which also found a wider audience than many expected. This film cuts between snippets of interviews with various scientists discussing the impact of science on how we understand reality, and a narrative chronicling a few days in the life of Amanda (played by Academy Award winner Marlee Matlin). Essentially, as the scientists discuss new ways of perceiving the world, Amanda experiences these moments in her daily life.

[5] Derrida's approach to language in "Structure, Sign and Play in the Discourse of the Human Sciences" has several resonances with modern mathematics, particularly Einstein's theories. In his *Relativity*, Einstein notes that the theory advances on Newtonian concepts of the universe such that "We ... free ourselves from the distasteful conception that the material universe ought to possess something of the nature of a centre" (120). This awareness of the absent center would inform Derrida's approach to literary theory. Similarly, Einstein's theories present "the possibility of a 'finite' and yet 'unbounded' universe" (122), a concept that would only grow in popularity through Quantum and Chaos theories. This fact is transformed into an approach to literary analysis, again, when Derrida claims that "the nature of the field – that is, language and a finite language – excludes totalization. This field is in fact that of *freeplay*, that is to say, a field of infinite substitutions in the closure of a finite

ensemble" (886). The paradox of an infinite play within a finite field suggests the key role paradox plays in both mathematics and literature.

WORKS CITED

Adams, Douglas. *The Hitchhiker's Guide to the Galaxy. The Hitchhiker's Trilogy.* New York: SFBC Science Fiction, 2000. 1-153.

Calaprice, Alice, Ed. *The New Quotable Einstein*. Princeton: Princeton UP, 2005.

Capra, Fritjof. *The Tao of Physics: An Exploration of the Parallels Between Modern Physics and Eastern Mysticism.* Berkeley, CA: Shambhala, 1975.

Derrida, Jacques. "Structure, Sign, and Play in the Discourse of the Human Sciences." *The Critical Tradition: Classic Texts and Contemporary Trends*. Ed. David H. Richter. Boston: Bedford, 1998. 877-889.

"Dr. Einstein's Theory." *Times* [London]. 28 Nov. 1919: 13.

Einstein, Albert. "Moral Decay." *Out of My Later Years*. New York: Philosophical Library, 1950. 9-10.

—. *Relativity: The Special and the General Theory*. Trans. Robert W. Lawson. New York: Three Rivers P, 1961.

—. "Science and Religion. *Out of My Later Years*. New York: Philosophical Library, 1950. 21-30.

"Einstein Declares Women Rule Here." *New York Times*. 8 July 1921: 9.

Eliot, T. S. "The Metaphysical Poets." *Selected Prose of T. S. Eliot*. Ed. Frank Kermode. London: Faber, 1975. 59-67.

Hawkins, Harriett. *Strange Attractors: Literature, Culture and Chaos Theory*. Toronto: Prentice Hall/Harvester Wheatsheaf, 1995.

Hayles, N. Katherine, Ed. *Chaos and Order: Complex Dynamics in Literature and Science*. Chicago: U of Chicago P, 1991.

Holton, Gerald. *Einstein, History, and Other Passions*. Don Mills, ON: Addison-Wesley, 1996.

Kundert-Gibbs, John L. "Continued Perception: Chaos Theory, the Camera, and Samuel Beckett's Film and Television Work." *Samuel Beckett and the Arts: Music, Visual Arts, and Non-Print Media*. Ed. Lois Oppenheim. New York: Garland, 1999.

—. *No-Thing is Left to Tell: Zen/Chaos Theory in the Dramatic Art of Samuel Beckett*. London: Associated UPs, 1999.

McFarlane, Thomas J., Ed. *Einstein and Buddha: The Parallel Sayings*. Berkeley, CA: Seastone, 2002.

Miller, Arthur I. *Einstein, Picasso: Space, Time, and the Beauty that Causes Havoc*. New York: Perseus, 2001.

Morales, Gregorio. "Overcoming the Limit Syndrome." *The World of Quantum Culture*. Ed. Manuel J. Caro and John W. Murphy. London: Praeger, 2002. 1-34.

Norris, Christopher. *Against Relativism: Philosophy of Science, Deconstruction and Critical Theory*. Oxford: Blackwell, 1997.

—. *Deconstruction and the 'Unfinished Project of Modernity.'* London: Athlone P, 2000.

—. *Philosophy of Language and the Challenge to Scientific Realism*. New York: Routledge, 2004.

Peñas-Bermejo, Francisco Javier. "Quantum Literature." *The World of Quantum Culture.* Ed. Manuel J. Caro and John W. Murphy. London: Praeger, 2002. 47-70.

π *(Pi)*. Dir. Darren Aronofsky. DVD. Artisan, 1998.

Pope, Alexander. *The New Dunciad. Eighteenth-Century English Literature.* Eds. Geoffrey Tillotson, Paul Fussel, Jr. and Marshall Waingrow. Toronto: Harcourt Brace Hovanovich, 1969.

Stewart, Ian. *Does God Play Dice? The Mathematics of Chaos.* New York: Blackwell, 1989.

Willing, Richard. "'CSI Effect' Has Juries Wanting More Evidence." *USA Today.* 5 Aug 2004: A1+.

11

Derrida and the Ethics of Mourning After

Dawne McCance

> Isn't there always an element excluded from the system that assures the system's space of possibility?
> — Jacques Derrida, *Glas*

Apart from the texts of Greek philosophy, notably those of Aristotle written some five hundred years after the plays, only two decisive turns to Greek tragedy take place in the Western philosophical tradition: one at the end of the eighteenth century, another in our own time. In both cases, although the turn occurs at the very moment when a discourse of the absolute is on the rise, it bodes ill for totalising systems. Thus, at the end of the eighteenth century, the turn to tragedy made by Schelling and Hölderlin heralds the end of philosophical absolutes – just as Hegel is elaborating his speculative system, and invoking tragedy in its support. This paradoxical "double movement" is behind the title of David Farrell Krell's recent study, *The Tragic Absolute: German Idealism and the Languishing of God*. "'The tragic absolute,' as a title, wants to suggest a double movement in the work of a number of German Romantic and Idealist thinkers and writers," Krell explains. "On the one hand, for many of them Greek tragedy occupies a position of absolute importance, not only for their theories of literature and aesthetics in general, but also for their metaphysics and moral philosophy." On the other hand, the turn to tragedy made by these thinkers presages "the tragic fall of the absolute" in their work and in the tradition overall (1). Given this, Hegel's "last-ditch effort [. . .] to elevate comic over tragic poetry, and systematiccategorial philosophy over all poetry and art, was destined to founder" (*Tragic Absolute* 3).

If the unprecedented importance it has received in recent critical work serves as an indicator, tragedy has today sparked another turning. It is as if, as Miguel de Beistegui and Simon Sparks put it in their "Introduction" to *Philosophy and Tragedy*, "the Greeks can be seen to have thought more than we moderns" (7). Consider, for example, alongside Krell's text and many others: Tina Chanter's "Tragic Dislocations: Antigone's Modern Theatrics" (1998); Judith Butler's *Antigone's Claim: Kinship Between Life and Death* (2000); Luce Irigaray's *Speculum of the Other Woman* (1985) and *An Ethics of Sexual Difference* (1993); Carol Jacobs' "Dusting Antigone" (1996); Jacques Lacan's *Seminar VII, The Ethics of Psychoanalysis 1959-60* (1992); Nicole Loraux's *The Mourning Voice: An Essay on Greek Tragedy* (2002) and *Tragic Ways of Killing a Woman* (1991); Will McNeill's "A 'scarcely pondered word.' The place of tragedy: Heidegger, Aristotle, Sophocles" (2000); Martha Nussbaum's *The Fragility of Goodness: Luck and Ethics in Greek Tragedy and Philosophy* (1986); Kelly Oliver's "Antigone's Ghost: Undoing Hegel's *Phenomenology of Spirit*" (1996); Cecilia Sjöholm's *The Antigone Complex: Ethics and the Invention of Feminine Desire* (2004). From this list alone, it seems clear that *Antigone*, and Antigone, currently hold particular fascination, and that the draw of the play and of its tragic heroine has to do with the question of ethics. Carol Jacobs, for instance, asks: "Would a return to the specificity of the Greek heroine accomplish a redefinition of woman and her position in the question of the ethical?" ("Dusting Antigone" 895). If so, then the "question of the ethical" to be derived from the current return is not one that reaffirms the absolute. This is only to say that the "double movement" suggested by Krell's title is evident again today, when even as tragedy takes on absolute importance, it continues to unsettle absolutes: "the absolute right of kings, the absolute authority of churches, the absolute fraud of dogma" (*Tragic Absolute* 3) – and, not the least, the absolute sovereignty of modernity's subject. Given the neoconservative climate to which it comes, the current unsettlement is, needless to say, not without its "last-ditch" (many of them "Hegelian") detractors. Yet the demise of the absolute does not portend what Fredric Jameson (1991), for one, laments as "postmodern" dissolution and cultural collapse. On the contrary, just as for the thinkers of the late-eighteenth century the end of the absolute marked "the birth of a finite human freedom" (*Tragic Absolute* 71), so in our time, the turn through tragedy to the question of the ethical (and the question of the woman's, the animal's, the *other's* place in it) introduces new understandings of human freedom – and responsibility.

In the interest of exploring the contemporary turn and its potential significance for an ethics *after absolutes*, I will suggest in what follows that the "double movement" by which Krell characterizes the "tragic absolute" is akin to what Jacques Derrida calls the "double writing" of "deconstruction." In *Positions*, for instance, amid a discussion that involves Hegel, Derrida describes his strategy of deconstruction as, on the one hand, "a phase of overturning" of the binary oppositions that every philosophy of the absolute puts in place; and, on the other hand, and simultaneous with this dismantling ("*fall*") of the absolute, "the irruptive emergence of a new [set of] 'concept[s],'… concept[s] that can no longer be, and never could be, included in the previous regime" (41-42). One of these "new 'concepts'" is *trace*. I will approach Derrida's trace as an imparting of a tragic vision, and thus as a resource for our rethinking of ethical and political responsibility. To my knowledge, no sustained study has been done of the tragic dimension of Derrida's work or of his legacy, *as tragic thinker*, for issues of individual and communal responsibility. I offer my remarks as preliminary only, taking my cue for them from a Note to Chapter 9 of *The Tragic Absolute*, "A Small Number of Houses in the Tragic Universe," where Krell comments, only briefly, on the structure of the trace as what, in Derrida's view

> disturbs the continuity of the metaphysical tradition. Such a disturbance reveals a deeper continuity in our tradition than that represented by metaphysics, namely the continuity of tragic thinking, extending perhaps from the time of Gilgamesh to our own era (290 n6).

Trace as tragic thinking: might the "deeper continuity" revealed by the trace have import for a rethinking of ethical responsibility? I will proceed by way of reading Derrida's *Glas* as an instance of the contemporary turn to tragedy: thus, on the one hand, as a wake for Hegel's philosophy of the absolute; and, on the other hand, as proffering/performing a response to that which gets left out, removed or remaindered, when an absolute stakes its claim.

Passages

As an instance of tragic turning, as itself a staging of the fall of
Hegel's *savoir absolu*, *Glas* is a work on the family. "I have chosen to
draw on one thread," Derrida announces early in the Hegel column of
Glas. "It is going to seem too fine, odd, and fragile. It is the law of the
family: of Hegel's family, of the family in Hegel, of the concept
family according to Hegel" (*Glas* 4a). As it turns out, the thread is not
too fine. Indeed, as Derrida demonstrates through the "first gesture" of
his double, deconstructive strategy in *Glas*, the family is what ties the
entire Hegelian system together. So much so, that when the thread
unravels, the absolute undergoes a? tragic fall. We might well expect
the scene of this undoing to involve the Christian Holy Family, since
it enjoys such privilege in Hegel's history and philosophy. It is, after
all, because Christianity – where God becomes father and where a
trinitarian schema of return-to-self is established – is a religion of the
family that Hegel esteems it as *the* religion of spirit. Christianity
makes of spirit's return-journey through history an absolute Holy
Family scene, something that Judaism – a kind of Kantianism where
God remains abstract, does not become a father ("A father without a
son is not a father" [31a]) – could, Hegel says, never do. But no, it is
not the family of Christianity but of Labdacus, the tragic household of
Oedipus, that sets the stage for this tragic fall.

To begin drawing on the chosen thread, Derrida approaches
the family as, on one level and most obviously, a determinate moment
within Hegel's system, what the *Phenomenology of Spirit* and
Elements of the Philosophy of Right describe as the first moment of,
the entry moment into, the ethical world called *Sittlichkeit*. Here, an
important passage is made from abstract ["Kantian"] to actual freedom
and from animal to rational life. For although the family is the first
and most natural of *Sittlichkeit*'s three stages (family, civil society,
state), it does belong to ethical life, not to animal nature: "There is no
love nor family in physical or biological nature. *Logos*, reason,
freedom are love's milieu" (*Glas* 12a). The family – in turn a
syllogism comprised of three moments: marriage, property, education
of children – by producing sons, enables the leap to be made beyond
the confines of the hearth into free rational subjectivity, citizenship
and *Sittlichkeit*'s highest moment, the nation-state. Only sons make

this passage. Daughters are remaindered; they remain behind, preparing to become wives and tending to the toilette of the dead. To the woman falls the work of mourning and of memorialising the man's corpse, so that a final passage might be made by the male, through death, into the universality of spirit: "Entrusting with death, the guarding of a marrowless body, on the condition that the woman erect his burial place after shrouding the rigid corpse (unction, bandages, etc.), maintaining it thus in a living, monumental, interminable surrection" (143a). The woman, after death, is not raised into universality. "In herself: under the earth, but the night of the subterranean world is the woman, Hegel specifies" (143a). The woman, as contained by the family, as pure singularity, when she dies, simply decays underground. In Hegel's system, "the woman is the middle (*Mitte*)" (170a) that disappears.

Might Hegel's high praise for Sophocles' *Antigone* have to do with its portrayal of just this account of the ethical world? Might Hegel see the play as enacting his own philosophy of the family, with all of the oppositions his familial passage entails? And praise the *Antigone* Hegel does, as "the most magnificent and satisfying work of art of this kind" (*Aesthetics* Volume II, 1218). In several places in *Glas*, Derrida reminds us of how many hierarchical oppositions are organized by the Hegelian family, as itself belonging to singularity, and as enabling the male's passage into universality: "To this great opposition (the law of singularity/the law of universality) is ordered a whole series of other couples: divine law/human law, family/city, woman/man, night/day, and so on" (*Glas* 142a). Hegel apparently reads *Antigone* as dramatizing these dialectical oppositions, man against woman, light versus darkness, the law of the city in conflict with the law of the family. Thus, Sophocles' play, he says in the *Aesthetics*, is

> one of the most sublime and in every respect most excellent works of art of all time. Everything in the tragedy is logical; the public law of the state is set in conflict over against inner family love and duty to a brother; the woman, Antigone, has the family interest as her 'pathos,' Creon, the man, has the welfare of the community as his. Polynices, at war with his native city, had fallen before the gates of Thebes, and Creon, the ruler, in a publicly proclaimed law threatened with death anyone who gave this enemy of the city the honour of burial. But this command, which concerned only the public weal, Antigone could not accept; as sister, in the piety of her love for her brother, she fulfils the holy duty of burial. In doing so she

appeals to the law of the gods; but the gods whom she worships are the underworld gods of Hades [. . .] the inner gods of feeling, love, and kinship, not the daylight gods of free self-conscious national and political life (Volume I, 464).

Miguel de Beistegui and Simon Sparks suggest that the tragic turning within German philosophy at the end of the eighteenth century is best thought of as a *passage*, precisely because, for the thinkers in question, "tragedy was itself envisaged as passage" (1). This is surely the case for Hegel, and for the reason that, as Derrida's reading in *Glas* makes evident, tragedy is a family affair, an enactment, for Hegel; not only is it an enactment of the passage entailed in *Sittlichkeit*'s first moment, but also, and importantly, of the familial structure of passage itself. The Hegelian family, in other words, more than a determinate moment, is a structure: "his propositions are structural" (*Glas* 165a). "The *Aufhebung*, the economic law of absolute reappropriation of the absolute loss, is a family concept" (133a). The structure is of course evident in the relieving union of opposites in Hegelian marriage: the wife, drawn up into the light by her husband's seed, falls back and disappears in the movement that sets his spirit free in a son. As Derrida suggests, "The union of opposites, of man and woman, has the form of a syllogistic copulation" (170a). The "copulative" structure, and with it, Hegel's opposition of the sexes, is put in place again with the transition to higher education, a transition that is a family relief: in bringing the family circle to a close, it accomplishes the family's end (the loss of itself as nature, the regaining of itself as spirit). Education, as Derrida puts it, is "a constituting/deconstituting process of the family, an *Aufhebung* by which the family accomplishes itself, *raises itself* in destroying itself or falling (to the tomb) as family" (13a). Always, in every passage – throughout Hegel's philosophy of history and of nature, throughout his entire system – a middle (a woman, a body) disappears, and the *oikos*, economy of the house, is rehearsed again.[1] It is in this sense, finally, that for Derrida in *Glas*, the Hegelian history of spirit "is a family history" (256a): the family is put back in place each time one of Hegel's syllogistic circles closes, with each passage of spirit through history. In short, "The whole system repeats itself in the family" (20a).

"Enter(s) on the scene Antigone" (145a). Hegel, I have suggested, is drawn to her story as dramatizing this familial passage through which spirit attains self-reconciliation-beyond-catharsis, as what Miguel de Beistegui calls a "figurative expression of the speculative" (12). And yet, as Derrida points out,

> Antigone's parents are not some parents among others. She is the daughter of Oedipus and, according to most of the versions from which all the tragedies take their inspiration, of Jocasta, of her incestuous grandmother. Hegel never speaks of this generation *moreover* [de plus], as if it were foreign to the elementary structures of kinship. (165a)

Hegel never speaks of Antigone as introducing *an excess* to his familial schema. Nor does he mention the words uttered by Antigone in Act One of Sophocles' play, expressing her desire "to lie down" with Polynices, her brother, "my loved one," as lover with beloved. Quite the contrary, in the *Phenomenology of Spirit* (and in a section where he cites *Antigone*), Hegel declares the brother-sister bond to be the highest degree of naturalness to which the feminine can attain, precisely because it is free of desire (274-75). Since they are of the same blood, the brother and sister, Hegel says, "do not desire one another, nor have they given to, or received from, one another this independent being-for-self" (274). In a system where the war between the sexes is "not one war among others," but rather, as Derrida puts it, "*the* war" (146a), the sister and brother would then relate to each other without desire and thus "without entering into war" (149a).

There is much more to say on this than I can venture here, and on the anomaly, *unmentioned by Hegel*, that Antigone is for this exemplary brother-sister bond, for his family and for his familial schema of passage. Suffice it to conclude that, in Derrida's reading, she is a figure *in excess* of Hegel's "kinship structures," by virtue not only of her incestuous heritage but also of her desire. A sister who desires her brother: "Is this possible? Does it contradict the whole system?" (149a). Does Antigone introduce the possibility of desire without war? Of desire not determined as phallic virility?[2] Of sexual difference without opposition? Of a "remain(s) of nonreturn" (148a)? Antigone cannot be assimilated; she thwarts the closing of the syllogistic circle. "Like Hegel, we have been fascinated by Antigone," Derrida muses, "by this immense impossible desire that could not live, capable only of overturning, paralyzing, or exceeding any system and history, of interrupting the life of the concept, of cutting off its breath" (166a). But why is Hegel fascinated with what would cut off the phonocentric passage of *Sa*'s return-to-self?[3] Why, in turning to tragedy, does he turn to the very figure who would overturn the absolute? Might it be that, while inadmissible in it, Antigone "assures the system's space of possibility" (162a)?

> The effect of focusing, in a text, around an impossible place. Fascination by a figure inadmissible in the system. Vertiginous insistence on an unclassable. And what if what cannot be assimilated, the absolute indigestible, played a fundamental role in the system, an abyssal role rather, the abyss playing an almost trans- (151a).

It is at this point that Derrida interrupts the left column of *Glas* with some twelve pages of correspondence pertaining to the relationship between Hegel and his sister Christiane. As important as are the parallels between Christiane and Antigone, and not the least where an inadmissible and inassimilable desire for the brother – *an other desire* – is concerned, we cannot consider them here. My summary point is this: Antigone, for Derrida reading Hegel, is a figure of remains; a woman who would be remaindered but does not disappear/cannot be sublated. "Antigone remains in the middle [. . .] She is the figure of the fall" (174a).

Remains

I have argued elsewhere[4] that *Glas* can be read as a family rebus. For in its typographical design, the book is a layout of the Hegelian familial structure: on the left is Hegel himself, the philosophical father; on the right, Genet, the poet who takes on his mother's name; and between these two, the father and the mother, Derrida, the bastard son. The question, of course, as Derrida puts it, is this: "Is there a place for the bastard in ontotheology or in the Hegelian family?" (*Glas* 6a). The columns, philosophy on the left and poetry on the right, do not confront each other as two discrete terms of a dialectical opposition. For each column is tattooed with "judas" pockets; cut open by these incisions and by insertions, some of which go on for several pages, the two columns leak their contents into each other and spill undigested material into the middle space. Derrida once remarked that *Glas* "is neither philosophy nor poetry. It is in fact a reciprocal contamination of one by the other, from which neither can emerge intact" ("Deconstruction and the Other" 122). Needless to say,

Hegel's elevation of philosophy over poetry is destined to founder here, for what constitutes the middle of *Glas* cannot be raised or made to disappear. The book introduces what Derrida in *Positions*, discussing the second gesture of his dual movement of deconstruction, refers to as "a new concept of writing," a "bifurcated writing," which not only "brings low what was high" but also "releases the dissonance of a writing within speech, thereby disorganizing the entire inherited order and invading the entire field" (42). The second gesture releases "undecidables" which, Derrida says, "can no longer be included within philosophical (binary) opposition, but which, however, inhabit philosophical opposition, resisting and disorganizing it, without ever constituting a third term, without ever leaving room for a solution in the form of speculative dialectics" (43). In Derrida's notion of the "undecidable," we have, David Krell suggests, a contemporary instance of the tragic vision (*Tragic Absolute* 70). One term for the undecidable is *trace.*

If there were a definition for it, *trace* would be a middle that does not disappear, that the Hegelian system, try as it might, cannot either erase or resolve into a transcendent third. Trace would be a remains: "A sensible remain(s) [that] prevents the three-stroke engine from turning over or running smoothly" (*Glas* 252a). I can read Antigone as a figure of the trace, so understood, and *Glas* as tragic affirmation. For although it is by way of the trace, Antigone, that Hegel's absolute undergoes tragic fall, the alterity that this process releases – designating what Rudolph Gasché calls the "irreducibility of the Other with respect to the self" (187) – introduces the *possibility* of a non-oppositional response to difference. Trace presses on us the question of whether the determination of difference as opposition, as a threat to be tamed ("consumed"), is ethically or politically *responsible.*[5] Trace does not come on the scene *after* as some "postmodern" contamination of self-presence, some "collapse" of a previous coherence. Rather, trace gives the lie to the positing of pure origin or full presence, bidding us to acknowledge that what remains preceded the myth of the purity of origin and has in fact been in place all along. "What is odd about remains, remainder, or remnants," Krell notes, "is that they appear both to undergird and to undermine the system. What endures and lasts, what *remains* after everything else has come and gone, after all accident and caprice are done, is the very essence of things" (*Purest of Bastards* 151). At the same time, "What remains is precisely what passes, decomposes, and in the stench of its corruption – the green spots of decay on its exquisite hands – elaborates the very definition of what is *inessential* for philosophy" (153). It is through this inessential – through such a bastard figure as that of Antigone – that Derrida countersigns the Hegelian *Sa*, making *Glas* a text of remains, "crypting the signature so that it becomes impossible to spell it out" (Spivak 24); and, in so doing, ensuring that the signifier cannot give way to a signified. Ultimately, then, "The debris of d-words is scattered all over the pages" (24).

As a book of remains, of "the *remains* of absolute knowing" (*Purest of Bastards* 150), *Glas* is a labour of mourning – for an Hegelian philosophy of the absolute and for the sacrificial, "familial," structure through which such phallocentric philosophy assimilates difference. Not so much a discourse as a *work of mourning*, a "taking part in it" (Derrida, "By Force of Mourning" 142), *Glas* stages the absolute's tragic fall, its death knell sounding back and forth between the two columns, inscribing a passage that is not a relief and that denies resolution into an idealized self-presence. A performance of "mourning's default" (Derrida, *Memoirs* 3), then, *Glas* works against that "*possible mourning*" (*Memoirs* 6) which would, repeating Hegel's familial structure, interiorize the other. Its drama is of an "impossible mourning" that, letting alterity be, "either refuses to take or is incapable of taking the other within oneself" (*Memoirs* 6).

Notes

---

[1] In *Medusa's Ear*, I consider the prevalence of the man/woman binary throughout Hegel's *Philosophy of Nature*, where such dichotomies as light/darkness, conscious/unconscious, active/passive, life/death, are everywhere evident and determinative for Hegelian botany and biology. My point, however, is to argue that all of these binaries come to rest on the opposition of speech/muteness: "We see this in the plant (flower) that he dwells on at length in his *Philosophy of Nature*, and that he opposes to the animal in much the same way that he opposes woman to man. Indeed, since, according to Hegel, '[t]he difference between man and woman is the difference between animal and plant; the animal is closer in character to man, the plant to woman' (207), we might look to the *Philosophy of Nature* for a difference between the family's male and female – as well as for an instance of (the familial) passage as *passage into voice*, into the 'reverberating interiority couple that voice and hearing form' (*Glas* 250a). For at every point in his discussion of the animal and plant, Hegel poses the difference between them as the difference between what possesses, and what lacks, a voice. 'Voice,' he says, 'is the high privilege of the animal, which can

appear wonderful; it is the utterance of sensation, of self-feeling. The animal makes manifest that it is inwardly for-itself, and this manifestation is voice'" (*Philosophy of Nature* 354). I cite this at length, in part because of the importance that the opposition of speech and muteness has for Hegel's system, and for all questions of ethics that we might bring to it; and in part because this is a matter I am unable to explore in the present chapter. What must be noted, though, is that the passage from plant to animal is the *passage into voice*; the passage from animal to human is the upward *passage into speech*. Yet, muteness remains the law of the woman who (like the plant) belongs to singularity only and who lacks the man's capacity for self-relation. Derrida's analysis of the ethical importance of phonocentrism is highly relevant here, as is his linking of phonocentrism to phallocentric mastery in Western philosophy, including the traditions of modernity from which contemporary ethics is derived.

[2] One point that needs to be opened here at length is the relation Derrida draws out in *Glas* between "virility," (phallic) desire, and war in Hegel, and the ethical implications of that. For instance, while explicating Hegel, Derrida writes: "A people that fears war reverts to animality; it wishes to save its life, its natural and biological health; but it alters its spiritual life and its ethical health.[…] So war would prevent the people from rotting; war preserves 'the ethical health of peoples,' as the wind agitating the seas purifies them, keeping them from decomposing, from the corruption, from the putrefaction (*Fäulnis*) with which a 'continual calm (*dauernde Stille*)' and *a fortiori* a 'perpetual peace' would infect that health. In this putrefaction, this return to inorganic nature, the people would lose its name and face, its shape (*Gestalt*), its form. No longer would a people stand up straight" (*Glas* 101a).

It is interesting and important that Derrida turns to "the question of the animal" in Hegel at just this place in *Glas*. See also Derrida's discussion with Elisabeth Roudinesco, "Violence Against Animals," in *For What Tomorrow . . . A Dialogue* (2004): 62-76. Here he notes that, in Hegel, where "the" animal is at stake, the question of "the" woman is raised as well.

[3] *Sa* is Derrida's siglum in *Glas* for Hegel's *savoir absolu*, absolute knowledge or absolute spirit. David Farrell Krell points out that "*savoir absolu* can be heard in French as *s'avoir absolu*, absolute self-having or self-possession, so that the goal of absolute knowing and the fantasy of perfect presence to self appear to be indistinguishable" (*Purest of Bastards* 151).

[4] See *Medusa's Ear*.

[5] The oppositional model of difference continues to hold sway in contemporary ethics and bioethics, whether of the dialectical or analytical sort, where "persons" are defined as minds and not bodies, as essentially conscious minds, and only as such, as claimants of full moral rights. The model is sexist and adversarial, and it counts "the" animal out. And as Derrida points out, the model implies a "carnivorous virility" that, among other things and as I mention in my first note above, "ingests" the materiality of the written or spoken signifier. Ethics, here, comes down to "eat-speak-interiorize," as Derrida explains in "'Eating Well,' of the Calculation of the Subject."

Works Cited

Butler, Judith. *Antigone's Claim: Kinship Between Life and Death.* New York: Columbia UP, 2000.

Chanter, Tina. "Tragic Dislocations: Antigone's Modern Theatrics." *Differences* 10. 1 (1998): 75-98.

de Beistegui, Miguel, and Simon Sparks, eds. *Philosophy and Tragedy.* London and New York: Routledge, 2000.

de Beistegui, Miguel. "Hegel: or the tragedy of thinking." *Philosophy and Tragedy* Eds. Miguel de Beistegui and Simon Sparks. New York: Routledge, 2000. 11-37.

Derrida, Jacques. "By Force of Mourning." Trans. Pascale-Anne Brault and Michael Naas. *The Work of Mourning.* Eds. Pascale-Anne Brault and Michael Naas. Chicago: U of Chicago P, 2001. 139-164.

—. "'Eating Well,' or the Calculation of the Subject: An Interview with Jacques Derrida." Trans. Peter Connor and Avital Ronell. *Who Comes After the Subject?* Eds. Eduardo Cadava, Peter Connor and Jean-Luc Nancy. New York: Routledge, 1991. 96-119.

—. *Memoirs for Paul de Man.* Trans. Cecile Lindsay, Jonathan Cullter, Eduardo Cadava, and Peggy Kamuf. New York: Columbia UP, 1989.

—. *Glas.* Trans. John P. Leavey, Jr. Lincoln and London: U of Nebraska P, 1986.

—. "Deconstruction and the Other: An Interview with Richard Kearney." *Dialogues with Contemporary Continental Thinkers.* Oxford: Manchester UP, 1984. 107-26

—. *Positions.* Trans. Alan Bass. Chicago: U of Chicago P, 1981.

—. and Elisabeth Roudinesco. *For What Tomorrow . . . A Dialogue.* Trans. Jeff Fort. Stanford: Stanford UP, 2004.

Hegel, G. W. F. *Elements of the Philosophy of Right.* Trans. H. B. Nisbet. Ed. Alan W. Wood. New York: Twayne Publishers, 1991.

—. *Phenomenology of Spirit.* Trans. A. V. Miller. Oxford: Clarendon Press, 1977.

—. *Aesthetics: Lectures on Fine Art.* Volumes I and II. Trans. T. M. Knox. Oxford: Clarendon, 1975.

—. *Philosophy of Nature: Being Part Two of the Encyclopedia of the Philosophical Sciences (1830).* Trans. A. V. Miller. Oxford: Clarendon , 1970.

Irigaray, Luce. *An Ethics of Sexual Difference.* Trans. Carolyn Burke and Gillian Gill. London: The Althone, 1993.

—. *Speculum of the Other Woman.* Trans. Gillian Gill. Ithaca: Cornell UP, 1985.

Jacobs, Carol. "Dusting Antigone." *Modern Language Notes* 111 (1996): 889-917.

Jameson, Fredric. *Postmodernism or, the Cultural Logic of Late Capitalism.* Durham: Duke UP, 1991.

Krell, David Farrell. *The Tragic Absolute: German Idealism and the Languishing of God.* Bloomington and Indianapolis: Indiana UP, 2005.

—. *The Purest of Bastards: Works of Mourning, Art, and Affirmation in the Thought of Jacques Derrida.* University Park, Pa.: Pennsylvania State UP, 2000.

Lacan, Jacques. *Seminar VII: The Ethics of Psychoanalysis 1959-60.* Trans. D. Potter. London: Routledge, 1992.

Loraux, Nicole. *The Mourning Voice: An Essay on Greek Tragedy.* Trans. Elizabeth Trapnell Rawlings. Ithaca and London: Cornell UP, 2002.

—. *Tragic Ways of Killing a Woman.* Trans. Anthony Foster. Cambridge, Mass.: Harvard UP, 1991.

McCance, Dawne. *Medusa's Ear: University Foundings from Kant to Chora L.* Albany: State U of New York P, 2004.

McNeill, Will. "A 'scarcely pondered word.' The place of tragedy: Heidegger, Aristotle, Sophocles." *Philosophy and Tragedy.* Eds. Miguel de Beistegui and Simon Sparks. London and New York: Routledge, 2000. 169-189.

Nussbaum, Martha. *The Fragility of Goodness: Luck and Ethics in Greek Tragedy and Philosophy.* Cambridge: Cambridge UP, 1986.

Oliver, Kelly. "Antigone's Ghost: Undoing Hegel's *Phenomenology of Spirit.*" *Hypatia* 11, 1 (Winter 1996): 67-90.

Sjöholm, Cecilia. *The Antigone Complex: Ethics and the Invention of Feminine Desire.* Stanford: Stanford UP, 2004.

Spivak, Gayatri. "*Glas* Piece: *A Compte Rendu.*" *Diacritics* 7. 3 (2004): 22-43

12

Postmodernism and the Crisis of Belief:
Neo-Realism vs. the Real

Clayton Crockett

We live in a time of counter-enlightenment, and in some ways what has been called postmodernism signifies this reactionary counter-enlightenment. At the same time, however, we must distinguish between postmodern theory and a broader postmodern condition. Postmodern theory is a largely American phenomenon, a broadly literary, cultural and political reading of French post-structuralism. Jean-François Lyotard and Jean Baudrillard are exceptional figures in that they are primary French philosophers who use the term postmodernism. According to Lyotard, postmodernism refers to a situation of incredulity toward all meta-narratives.[1] This incredulity to any meta-narratives constitutes a crisis of belief, or a situation marked by theoretical discord. According to Gregg Lambert, a literary theorist who writes about Lyotard in his *Report to the Academy*, "the trouble with consensus, simply put, is that it is dead" (104). The death of consensus leads to a state of permanent war, at least at the level of conceptual language.

Postmodernism has come to signify a variety of philosophical, literary and cultural discourses inspired by contemporary French Continental philosophy. The key insight that provides a family resemblance among these theories concerns their anti-foundationalism. Anti-foundationalism concerns the lack of foundations, or at least any consensus regarding the proper foundations of our theoretical discourses. Whether it goes by postmodernism, post-structuralism, deconstruction, or some other name, this particular kind of deconstructive, anti-foundationalist theorizing is passing, or past, and yet it lives on in spectral fashion, as

Derrida has analysed in *Specters of Marx*. According to Derrida, even if deconstruction is dead, or its moment has passed, it continues to haunt our language and our thinking – it constitutes a "hauntology."[2] We are witnessing the passing of postmodernist theory in its original, classic sense, however much it continues to be relevant and/or true.

According to Samir Amin, "postmodernist discourse is an ideological accessory that, in the end, legitimizes liberalism and invites us to submit to it" (19). Although I think this judgment is extreme, Amin draws attention to the "culturalist retreat" to which some forms of postmodern discourse contribute, that fails to seriously engage with the Reality of the postmodern condition (20). The postmodern condition, insofar as it serves as a name for the contemporary historical, cultural and/or political situation, is now a new or neo-realism, which is fundamentally religio-political and brutal in its effects. On the one hand, Italian neo-realism, as it developed after World War II, constitutes a complex and nuanced approach to reality through cinema. According to Gilles Deleuze, neo-realism "invented a new type of image" to register the encounter of cinema with the world, called a "fact-image" (*Cinema* 1). For Deleuze, this neo-realism serves as a catalyst for what Deleuze calls in his influential work on cinema a "time-image." The time-image is a break or cut that disables the more common movement-image, and it allows cinema to assemble itself as a brain. Despite this productive aspect of cinematic neo-realism, I am using the term in a more explicitly political and polemical way, following the work of Kenneth Waltz.[3] Political neo-realism is a theory of international relations that emphasizes structural relationships of state political power and its inevitable violence.

Beyond specific genealogies, which could also be produced for the term postmodernism itself,[4] I use the word neo-realism broadly to refer to the new realism that dominates our political, philosophical and aesthetic intellectual discourses. In a political sense, neo-realism is an ideological name for the convergence of economic neo-liberalism and political neo-conservativism, resulting in a hegemonic American neo-imperialism. Neo-realism is neither simply a reaction against nor a result of postmodernism, but a complex cultural and theoretical phenomenon that in certain respects "succeeds" postmodernism. That is, certain interpretations of postmodernism are deployed in the service of neo-realism, as Amin points out, although he uses the more traditional name liberalism. At the same time, other understandings of postmodernism provide critical tools to resist neo-realism, and this is the strategy I will develop using Deleuze and Žižek and their respective understandings of the Real.

Neo-realism, like postmodernism, is essentially non-foundational, because it is grounded upon a virtual reality of images, as the theoretical insights of Jean Baudrillard and Paul Virilio help us understand. Reality is precisely in question, because we are inundated with images. Neo-realism is the result of an ideology or a propaganda that frames reality for us in a schizophrenic fashion because it selects images to deploy according to a powerful but derivative logic.

If one is to resist neo-realism and its effects, one strategy is to argue that reality really is conventional, or as Baudrillard puts it, there is nothing but simulacra. That is, there is no real object or idea before or behind the images that we perceive. A simulacrum is a copy of a copy, where a copy is a copy of an original. A simulacrum, in Platonic terms, is thus worse than a copy, but for Gilles Deleuze in *Difference and Repetition*, the "triumph of the simulacra" overcomes the traditional model of representation that posits an original and a copy (128). Baudrillard's conception of simulacra derives directly from Deleuze, but whereas Deleuze views the affirmation of simulacra in *Difference and Repetition* as a liberation, Baudrillard's embrace of simulacra is more cynical and ironic. Baudrillard attempts a desperate affirmation of simulacra, hoping against hope that championing hyperreality will somehow loosen its grip or unravel its web of interpenetrating images.

If simulacra are all that exist, then there is no prior reality to copy, but all copies are copies of copies, or simulacra. Reality is eclipsed by hyperreality. In his book, *Simulacra and Simulation*, Baudrillard mentions Disneyland as an example, because "Disneyland exists in order to hide that it is the 'real' country, all of 'real' America that *is* Disneyland." That is, "Disneyland is presented as imaginary in order to make us believe that the rest *is* real, whereas all of Los Angeles and America that surrounds it are no longer Real, but belong to the hyperreal order and to the order of simulation" (12). We are bombarded with images, and we no longer possess the ability or the confidence to peel away the virtuality in order to penetrate to the core reality, and this is the postmodern condition. Baudrillard cannot fully cure himself of his nostalgia for the Real, however much he forswears it. In *America*, Baudrillard expresses awe at the achieved utopia of the United States, but there remains a certain horror in his affirmation: "the US is a paradise....mournful, monotonous, and superficial though it may be, it is paradise." He struggles to penetrate "the mystery of American Reality" by regarding it with the "same enthusiasm which Americans show for their own success, their own barbarism, their own power" (100). This enthusiasm is cynical because it doubles a naïve and primitive "American" enthusiasm with a forced repetition, a repetition from the perspective of European "knowing better" that wishes to divest itself of this awful self-knowledge.

The problem is that even with "better" or more consistent arguments for constructivism, this position loses out to a more appealing neo-realism that is able to appropriate the language of cultural relativism and graft powerful emotional, political and religious appeals – fundamental appeals – onto it. Baudrillard's postmodernism is now in some ways a nostalgic postmodernism, because it appeals to a time and a sensibility where theoretical arguments about hyperreality could be imagined to be persuasive, like the second half of the twentieth century.

An alternative strategy is to make a desperate appeal to the Real, a Real that is being manipulated and distorted in sinister ways by neo-realists, neo-fundamentalists and neo-conservatives. This is the position of Paul Virilio, who is an incredibly lucid and powerful theorist who provides tools to understand the reconstruction of perception and vision by sinister forces in order to develop and enhance a war machine. In Virilio's work, the mechanism for the production of images is a motor. In *The Art of the Motor*, Virilio explains that our technology invades and explodes our bodies, creating a new physiology. According to Virilio, "technology is no longer exploding a long way away from the body, it is exploding inside the body," specifically in the form of miniaturization or nanotechnology (113). Technologies invade the body, transforming our physiology, altering our perception and self-perception in dramatic ways. We are experiencing "the motorization of the living being," which is the breakdown of the distinction between organic and machinic (111). The motorization of humanity involves the production and intensification of images designed for the representation and control of complex processes, including images of the brain.

Virilio emphasizes the negative, dystopian aspects of these processes, particularly the interaction of military and information technology and their complicity in war. From the "simultaneous invention of gunpowder and printer's ink," he affirms, to a similar connection between

> the machine gun and the camera, nitrocellulose and film, radar and video – but also between the *trick effects* of the depiction of actual events in graphic illustration, photography, film and television and good old fashioned camouflage…[we are] no longer able to tell *where Reality begins or leaves off* (*Desert Screen* 43).

Virilio argues that the technical creation of images screens us from Reality, and screens us from ourselves, and this is both an aesthetic and a military project. The most important aspect of the vision machine is the speed of its motor, a speed that approaches the speed of light and overwhelms critical or self-conscious thought and reflection. Authoritarian forces benefit from the proliferation of images that confuse and disorient thinking. As Virilio explains in *Desert Screen*, his reflections on the first Gulf War of 1991, "no politics is possible at the scale of the speed of light. Politics depends upon having time for reflection" (43).

According to Virilio, the technological construction of a vision machine serves these authoritarian and anti-democratic purposes. In *The Vision Machine*, Virilio provides a genealogy of the technologies of perception and memory across modern Europe. He argues that symptoms of dyslexia and amnesia are the product of the standardization of ways of seeing, which constitutes a "progressive disintegration of a faith in perception founded in the Middle Ages." This disintegration of natural perception fulfils itself in the twentieth century "death of art," which represents "the zero degree of representation" (16-17) Paradoxically, the proliferation of images induces a breakdown in perception, and brings about blindness, a blindness caused by the overwhelming intensity of the speed of light. The vision machine is an autonomic, inhuman entity that bypasses thought and reflection. Human reflection is cut out of the loop, in order to perfect and extend authoritarian control, which is the thesis of Manuel De Landa's book, *War in an Age of Intelligent Machines*. In this context, it is interesting to consider the February 2005 *New York Times* story, "Military Predicts Robot Soldiers in Decade," which seems to confirm the pessimistic picture Virilio portrays. A representative of the Pentagon's Joint Forces Command is quoted as saying "the lawyers tell me there are no prohibitions against robots making life-or-death decisions" (*New York Times*).

Virilio harbours a more explicit nostalgia for the Real than Baudrillard does, and that allows him to assess the Real transformations of thought and life in our world. In no way do I want to discount the significance of Virilio's insights, but at the same time, this nostalgia, explicit in Virilio and disavowed but implicit in Baudrillard, works against the ability to challenge the reigning ideology of the postmodern condition, neo-realism. The only alternative Virilio can offer is a naturalized understanding of perception and vision tied to an essentialized body that has largely disappeared, while Baudrillard admits that he can offer nothing.

In the remainder of this chapter I will present two further alternative understandings of the Real that suggest more promise for opposing neo-realism. For Gilles Deleuze, the Real is directly produced by an event, and this is a variant of constructivism, but is not easily trapped within linguistic signifying webs. The production of the Real is the effect of an event, which Deleuze theorizes in his book, *The Logic of Sense*. Read from the standpoint of Deleuze and Guattari's Capitalism and Schizophrenia project, especially *Anti-Oedipus*, where desire is inherently revolutionary, we can understand how the event is unconscious in a specifically Lacanian manner, but it is not petitioned but directly produced. In addition to drawing attention to the Real in Deleuze's work itself, I want to suggest a series that runs from Spinoza through Deleuze to the work of Antonio Negri that assembles a revolutionary materialist ontology that counters neo-realist and capitalist ideology.

An alternative viewpoint on the Real that also can be used to oppose neo-realism can be found in a more speculative metaphysical ontology that is inspired by psychoanalytic theory, and in this context I will take up the thought of Slavoj Žižek. Žižek represents a distinct but complementary political possibility of a Lacanian psychoanalysis wedded to a theoretically sophisticated post-Marxism. Here the Real is opposed to Reality, and "deconstructs" in its operation because it can always be tied back to fantasy, or the shift between symbolic Reality and the imaginary fantasies of neo-realists. The Real works against Realism in critical and political fashion, but not in a naïve way, because psychoanalytic theory provides theoretical resources to think the Real beyond and against the deployments of neo-realism. In contrast to the series Spinoza-Deleuze-Negri, the series that runs from Hegel through Lacan to Žižek (and also to a certain extent, Alain Badiou) composes a speculative, metaphysical ontology. For Hegel-Lacan-Žižek, the Real is a subtractive gap, the swerve or shift from Reality posited as thing in itself to symbolic, linguistically mediated Reality. Rather than simply decide upon one of these two alternatives, I would like to hesitate, but I will offer some reflections and suggestions about how to frame an alternative at the end of the essay.

In this essay, I am reading both Žižek and Deleuze in relation to Lacan. The thought of Lacan represents a decisive event for twentieth-century theory. Even though an encounter with Lacan has been substantially missing in the English-speaking world, we are seeing the political and ontological implications of Lacan's work unfolded in the philosophies of Badiou and Žižek. Lacan's reading of Freud provides a significant basis for French post-structuralism and post-modernism, and it inspired Louis Althusser to conduct a parallel reading of Marx. According to Althusser, just as Freud developed a "topographical model without center, in which the various instances have no unity other than the unity of their conflictual functioning," Marx before him "abandoned the bourgeois individual myth that thought the nature of society as a unified and centered whole, in order to think every social formation as a system of instances without center" (121). In other words, the significance of Freud and Marx is that both think in terms of conflict rather than unity, and dissolve the centered whole of the individual (Freud) and society (Marx).

Although Lacan did not explicitly focus on Marx, his interpretation of Freud provided important resources for re-reading Marx, for Althusser and others, including Deleuze. In many ways, the central chapters of Deleuze and Guattari's *Anti-Oedipus* read Marx and Freud (along with Nietzsche) against some of the conclusions of Freud and Lacan, specifically Freud's theory of the Oedipus complex. According to Deleuze and Guattari, the Oedipus theory contains the revolutionary force of Freud's thinking within the bourgeois family. On the other hand, "the first thesis of schizoanalysis is this: every investment is social, and in any case bears upon the sociohistorical field" (342). To truly read Marx and Freud together in a revolutionary way, is to conceive a "libidinal economy" that is at once social, political and individual.[5] I will return to the beginning of *Anti-Oedipus*, in order to show how Deleuze and Guattari interpret Lacan's notion of the Real, but first I want to return briefly to Lacan, in order to explain his terminology of the Real, the imaginary and the symbolic.

Lacan's work is important for understanding Continental philosophy and theory, especially thinkers not limited to the discourses of phenomenology and hermeneutics. Although Deleuze does not usually use Lacanian language in his work, and was very critical of Lacan, his writings have resonance with Lacan's ideas. Slavoj Žižek, on the other hand, affirms Lacan as his primary inspiration, and the significance of Žižek's work is to inscribe Lacanian psychoanalytic theory directly into philosophical thinking. At the same time, Žižek applies Lacanian insights to film and other aspects of popular culture in suggestive and brilliant ways. In order to understand Žižek's conception of the Real, and also to see how I am constructively appropriating Deleuze's philosophy for a different, but complementary understanding of the Real, I want to briefly lay out Lacan's threefold schema of categorization.

According to Lacan's later thought in the 1970s, the Imaginary, the Symbolic and the Real constitute a triangle or a knot.[6] In his early work in the late 1930s and 40s, Lacan works to isolate and distinguish what later became known as the imaginary, as it is expressed in the imago or ideal self created out of a narcissistic "mirror stage."[7] Out of this effort comes the ethical emphasis on language as a symbolic Reality, expressed in his famous Rome discourse, "The Function and Field of Speech and Language in Psychoanalysis," delivered at a psychology congress in Rome in 1953.[8] In his early work, the Real is usually described as intrinsically inaccessible, a brute unknowable x. During the later 1950s, Lacan shifts toward a more direct interest in theorizing about the Real, beginning with Seminar VII on "The Ethics of Psychoanalysis" in 1959-1960, which names "das Ding" or the Thing as the term that minimally designates the Real, insofar as it can be symbolized in language.[9] As Lacan becomes more pessimistic about symbolic language, he moves toward a more heightened emphasis on the Real as a significant and distinct register. One result is that the attempt to express the Real takes the form of mathematical and topographical formalizations, which makes Lacan's later work extremely dense and difficult to read. One way to describe the trajectory of Lacan's thought is to say that he shifts from a primary concern with the boundary between the imaginary and the symbolic in his earlier work, to a more explicit concern with the border between the symbolic and the Real in his later work.

Lacan's typology can also be elaborated on the basis of objects that can be respectively associated with these three registers. In the case of the Real, as mentioned above, the Thing is the object that best expresses the Real, but Lacan does not consistently use this term in his later work, and in some ways women's jouissance functions to refer to the Real in *Seminar XX*. In any case, the Real cannot be directly or adequately symbolized as an object, because "the Real can only be inscribed on the basis of an impasse of formalization" (93). The symbolic is fundamentally associated with the Other, which refers not to a person but to a concretisation of the social order. In order for language to function, it necessarily refers to an Other, which means that it is inter-subjective or inter-textual and not direct or unmediated in its activity. Lacan provocatively declares that desire is the Other's desire, which means that your desire is never simply your own, but personal identity is constituted by symbolic forces, meanings, assumptions, suggestions, etc. The Other is also where Lacan locates the Freudian Unconscious, which is not simply an individual id, but rather a social function that structures human desire through linguistic symbolization. Finally, in the context of the imaginary register, Lacan locates object a, or *objet petit a*, which means the objectification of a portion of social Reality into a phantasmatic entity, a little other (*autre* in French) that encapsulates a portion of the big Other (A, or *Autre*). Object a is imaginary because it is a fantasy to believe that one can approach or grasp an object directly, unmediated by the entire social structure and Reality of language. An object a represents a single part that stands in for the entire whole universe of symbolic Reality, at least if we understand it correctly. Finally, it is important to understand that these three registers never exist separately: they always occur in relation to each other, and in *Seminar XX* their inter-relationship forms a Borromean knot. Also, we can only approach the interaction of the three registers from the standpoint of the symbolic language, which skews the relationship towards the symbolic, even if Lacan's later work is oriented more towards the Real.

In his later work, Lacan seems not so much hopeful about the opportunities of touching the Real as he is pessimistic about the possibilities of symbolic language. Žižek follows Lacan's later thinking about the Real, but he qualifies Lacan's pessimism based upon his understanding of the potentiality of Lacanian thought to short-circuit the workings of capitalist ideology in a practical and Real way. In many ways, the heart of Žižek's reading of Lacan, and his understanding of the Real, occurs in Žižek's appropriation of Lacan's distinction between phallic jouissance and woman's jouissance in *Seminar XX*. According to Lacan, Woman as such does not exist, at least in relation to symbolic representation, which is necessarily phallic. Insofar as "everything revolves around phallic jouissance," Lacan declares that "woman is defined by a position that I have indicated as 'not whole' (*pas-tout*) with respect to phallic jouissance" (7). Jouissance refers to the limit of desire, as opposed to symbolic language. Symbolic language is inherently phallic, because it is sustained by masculine desire. According to Lacan, "the phallus is a signifier…that is destined to designate meaning effects as a whole," by lifting the veil of what is unknown to symbolic discourse (*Écrits* 579). Beyond the limits of desire, however, jouissance can touch upon the Real, and here Lacan calls it woman's jouissance. Woman's jouissance, which does not "exist" in ordinary, conventional terms, is "not whole" or not-all. Lacan later associates woman's jouissance with God, at least an understanding of God expressed by certain mystics (*Seminar XX* 76-77).

In *Tarrying with the Negative*, Žižek reads Lacan's understanding of sexual difference into the Kantian sublime. On an initial Kantian reading of Lacan, "the Real is the *Ding-an-sich*, the inaccessible substance," and *das Ding* lies beyond the limit Kant prescribes for phenomenal knowledge (35). On the other hand, "what actually breaks down in the Sublime is the very notion that, behind the field of phenomena, lies some inaccessible positive, substantial Thing" (38). The sublime represents the passage from Kant to Hegel, which is also a passage back into Kant: "We do not pass from Kant to Hegel by filling out the empty space of the Thing…but by affirming this void as such, in its priority to any positive entity that strives to fill it out" (39).

The dialectic between Kant and Hegel, whose point of contact is the sublime, concerns "the paradoxical dialectic of the Limit and its

Beyond." The Beyond refers to masculine phallic jouissance, which is based upon the logic of an exception that lies beyond the limit. Masculine logic works by positing an exception that paradoxically maintains the limit. The Kantian Thing-in-itself is viewed as a mysterious, transcendent substance that lies somewhere beyond the phenomena that appear to human intuition and can be comprehended by human understanding. The Limit, however, refers to the not-whole or not-all of woman's jouissance, which affirms the priority of the limit over the beyond: "Lacan's point is the logical priority of the not-all to the All, of the Limit to what lies Beyond" (*Tarrying* 58). The feminine not-all draws attention from the beyond back to the limit, the limit as void. The Real initially appears to be something beyond the symbolic order, as an exception to the symbolic, but this is a limited, and ultimately incorrect understanding of the Real. Žižek follows Lacan's thinking about woman's jouissance in order to show that the Real is in fact the limit, the not-all or not-whole, which is what allows the conception of a beyond-the-limit in the first place.

Or so it appears. Technically, however, and this is what *The Puppet and the Dwarf* clarifies, the Real is actually the shift in perspective from the Beyond to the Limit, or from the first, masculine perspective to the second, feminine perspective. And paradoxically, it is this insight that not only illuminates the "correct" relationship between Kant and Hegel, but also reveals the perverse core of Christianity. In the crucifixion of Christ, the reversal of the death of Christ as God into the resurrection that expresses God's grace is not an additional event. Rather, "the intervention of Grace is not something distinct from the preceding loss, but is this very loss, the same act of self-renunciation, conceived from a different perspective" (*Tarrying* 170). This reflection upon death of God, which is at the same time the infinite grace and mercy of God, opens up the theo-philosophical understanding of the Real in *Tarrying with the Negative* that is later fleshed out in *The Puppet and the Dwarf*.

In *The Puppet and the Dwarf*, Žižek is clearer about the precise nature of the Real, even though it is the same understanding that appears in *Tarrying with the Negative*.

> The Real is thus simultaneously the Thing to which direct access is not possible and the obstacle that prevents this direct access; the Thing that eludes our grasp and the distorting screen that makes us miss the Thing.

> More precisely, the Real is ultimately the very shift of perspective from the first standpoint to the second (77).

Again, the first standpoint can be correlated with masculine phallic jouissance, the understanding that the Real is the Thing that lies beyond the symbolic, whereas the second, the Thing as obstacle or limit, conforms to the feminine logic of the not-whole as expressed by Lacan in *Seminar XX*. Ultimately, neither standpoint is exactly the Real, even though the feminine standpoint of the limit is more correct than the masculine one. The Real is rather the shift, the dynamic movement from one to the other, which creates what Žižek calls a "universal singular," a "singular that appears to stand-in for the universal" (65).

The process that generates the Real is the result of a short-circuit or subtraction, which brings about "the identification of the non-part with the Whole" (*Tarrying* 65). The movement from the beyond, the Thing as beyond, to the limit, the Thing as the obstacle that prevents access to the beyond, re-inscribes the Real within phenomena, but not as imaginary object a. Rather, the universal singular is the opposite of object a, a singular universal where the point is that a part does substitute or stand for the whole. Here a non-part is identified with the whole, or a phenomenon expresses the Real insofar as it is not-all, or paradoxically, not-whole. It is the movement back from the beyond to the limit that characterizes the Real, not the movement from limit to beyond in a more conventional understanding of transcendence.

Žižek again refers to Hegel, even though his reading cuts against the more standard, accumulative and masculinist reading of Hegelian Spirit. According to Žižek's understanding of Hegel, "it is not possible to choose the 'true meaning' directly. That is, one has to begin by making the 'wrong' choice," and then by means of the dialectic "the true speculative meaning emerges only through repeated reading, as the aftereffect (or byproduct) of the first, 'wrong' reading" (83). We have to posit an initial, "wrong" meaning, and this meaning only becomes wrong in relation to the later, "true" meaning, but the correct meaning is not immediately available. The true meaning shows itself as the intensification of the obstacle to the Thing beyond the limit. And this is the key to understanding Christianity's relation to Judaism. According to the initial, necessary but wrong standpoint, Christianity represents an advance upon Judaism because it posits love (*agape*) as beyond the restrictive and deadly Jewish Law. This is wrong, but only by following the dialectic from the masculine beyond to the feminine limit does the "true" interpretation emerge: Christian love is precisely the intensification of the law itself. "The problem with the law is not that it does not contain enough love," Žižek writes, "but rather, the opposite one: there is too much love in it..." (117). Love is not beyond the law, but affirms the law itself as limit.

In Žižek's work, then, the Real is the shift from beyond to limit, and this limit or void constitutes subjectivity, for humans and for God. Žižek writes about Christianity as an atheist, but he uncovers a profound Christian logic that works against neo-realism. Neo-realism in its inherent masculinity violently insists upon the limit in order to uphold the nature and value of the beyond that transcends the limit. Neo-realism in its neo-traditionalist and neo-fundamentalist forms differs from neo-liberalism in that it directly says what it believes, but this belief is the result of a powerful repression that disavows the progression to the feminine standpoint. The truth is that neo-fundamentalism is not-all, but it clings to its belief with a paranoid fervour. Attention to Žižek's formulation of the Lacanian Real allows one to understand precisely in what way the Real disables Realism, emasculates it, and renders it inoperable.

Gilles Deleuze represents an alternative understanding of the Real, but one that I think is compatible with Žižek's, in that both are incompatible with neo-realism. Deleuze understands the Real as the result of a process of material production, rather than speculative subtraction. The production of the Real is the becoming of an event, as Deleuze articulates the concept of an event in *The Logic of Sense*. By way of a complex encounter with Lewis Carroll's *Alice in Wonderland*, Deleuze suggests two series, a series of sense and language that Carroll's work explores, and a series of bodies that cannot be connected to sense in any direct manner. Sense occurs along a surface, whereas bodies have depth. The conception of an event is caught up in the superficial and paradoxical logic of sense: "the event is sense itself" (22). Events are surface effects of sense and language, which means that they are symbolic rather than Real, in Lacanian terms. *The Logic of Sense* is more structuralist than *Anti-Oedipus* in that events are associated completely with sense and language, but even so Deleuze is already striving to understand how the event extends beyond sense.

According to Deleuze, "events are like crystals, they become and grow only out of the edges, or on the edge" (9). The edge of sense is where events occur, by means of an extension of sense. In a way, the event precedes sense, which means that it is unconscious. Later in *The Logic of Sense*, Deleuze opposes Antonin Artaud's schizophrenic language to Lewis Carroll's logic of sense in a way that prefigures *Anti-Oedipus*. Here Artaud's "poles of depth" form a primary order in contrast to Carroll's secondary organization of sense and language, even though the two series cannot meet up and "have nothing in common." Deleuze declares that Artaud's work is more valuable than Carroll's, but nonetheless Carroll remains the "master and the surveyor of surfaces" (91). Sense concerns meaning and language, whereas depth concerns bodies in their passion. These two series do not connect up with each other, but the impossible passage from sense to body occurs in and through the event. Deleuze is straining towards an understanding of the event, or a schizophrenic language, that connects up with the other series of bodies.

Even though technically an event must always be associated with sense, it possesses a special relationship to body that allows it to reach beyond sense. In writing about Joe Bousquet, Deleuze claims that Bousquet "apprehends the wound that he bears deep within his body in its eternal truth as a pure event" (*Logic* 148). A pure event is a kind of wound, as Deleuze affirms, every event is "a kind of plague, war, wound, or death," because it occurs in relation to body (151). The event creates or produces sense because it is capable of connecting up with body and transfiguring body into sense. Once it is expressed, "the splendor and the magnificence of the event is sense" (149). But this is the result, the result of a univocalization of being which the event communicates to language in its becoming, that is, in its being an event.

In *Anti-Oedipus*, Deleuze and Guattari emphasize the productive nature of desiring machines, which directly produce the Real. Desire is not inherently imaginary, based upon the fantasy of what the subject who desires lacks; rather, "desire does not lack anything." According to Deleuze and Guattari, "the Real is the end product, the result of the passive syntheses of desire as autoproduction of the unconscious" (26). In naming the production of the Real by desiring machines an event, I am stressing the continuity between *The Logic of Sense* and *Anti-Oedipus*, and also showing how Deleuze, with the aid of Guattari, moves away from the symbolic, structuralist reading of events as pure expressions of sense, toward an explicitly productive understanding of an event in relation to bodies. Here is Deleuze's turn toward the Real, which mirrors that of Lacan in the early 1970s.

Desire produces the Real, and this is a social production rather than an individual one: "social production is purely and simply desiring production itself under determinate conditions." This is true to such an extent that "there is only desire and the social and nothing else" (29). Deleuze and Guattari criticize Lacan's separation of desire from the Real, and its relegation to a purely symbolic order. Schizophrenic language provides a way to radically question the bourgeois model of symbolic Reality that is based upon forms of neurotic disavowal, and their method of schizo-analysis pushes capitalism to and possibly even beyond its limits.

> They ask:
> Wouldn't it be better to schizophrenize – to schizophrenize the domain of the unconscious as well as the sociohistorical domain, so as to shatter the iron collar of Oedipus and rediscover everywhere the force of desiring-production; to renew, on the level of the Real, the tie between analytic machine, desire and production? (53)

The unconscious is not imaginary or symbolic, but "it is the Real in itself." Oedipus serves as the name for that which organizes and controls – represses – the productivity of the desiring-machines.

How do these desiring-machines work? Deleuze and Guattari claim that every "object" "presupposes the continuity of a flow" which the machine interrupts in order to produce an object (6). They write that "every machine, in the first place, is related to a continual material flow (*hylè*) that it cuts into" (36). Apparently, production is subtractive in a manner similar to Žižek's speculations. If the material flow is the Real, then symbolic Reality subtracts from the Real in order to produce an object. On the other hand, and as we saw with Žižek, the Real is the process, not the material flow that is posited beyond the productive workings of the machines. Every machine is a machine of a machine, which means that every machine both interrupts but also re-establishes a flow or continuity of material processes: "In a word, every machine functions as a break in the flow in relation to the machine to which it is connected, but at the same time is also a flow itself, or the production of a flow, in relation to the machine connected to it. This is the law of the production of production" (36).

Žižek's language is more negative, whereas Deleuze and Guattari's is more positive, but they approach a similar or at least a complementary position. The masculine beyond refers to the flow in itself, apart from the productive desiring-machines, whereas the limit concerns the desiring-machines themselves, which directly produce the Real. In Žižek's terms, then, the Real is precisely the shift in perspective from the beyond (material flow) to the limit (machinic production). For Deleuze and Guattari, this language is too idealistic, so they collapse the gap between the machines and the material flow, as well as that between the second perspective and the gap between the two perspectives, even though they respect the gaps, interruptions and cuts that are necessary for the desiring-machines to be productive. In the language of *The Logic of Sense*, to associate an event as the Real with body is to posit a beyond or a depth underneath language and sense. But in tying the event to sense, Deleuze draws us back to the event as limit. We can read the Deleuzian Real as event in the shift from body to sense (in *The Logic of Sense*) or from material flow to machines of production (*Anti-Oedipus*). To shift from Žižek's notion of the Real to Deleuze or Deleuze and Guattari's understanding of the Real requires a twist of a quarter-turn, a slightly vertiginous swerve, but one that "fits" with Žižek's if slightly adjusted.

As I indicated earlier, we could construct two competing series, one that is more explicitly materialist that runs from Spinoza through Marx to Freud and then Deleuze and Guattari. From this standpoint, we could also read the work of Antonio Negri (and his works co-written with Michael Hardt – in some ways *Empire* and *Multitude* "repeat" Deleuze and Guattari's *Anti-Oedipus* and *A Thousand Plateaus*) as a contemporary extension of this materialist series. In a materialistic ontology, the Real is directly produced as an event, even though this production is, strictly speaking, unconscious. On the other hand, a more speculative series runs from Hegel through Marx to Lacan and Žižek, as well as Alain Badiou. Here is a metaphysical, subtractive ontology, where the Real is revealed by the gap between being and an event, to use Badiou's terms.[10]

For pragmatic purposes, based upon their resources to oppose to neo-realism, I am more interested in the compatibility and the convergences than the differences between these two perspectives. Both views of the Real refuse neo-realism and its naïve/cynical ideology. I do not wish to "decide" which one is right, but instead to set up a productive opposition that can be considered in Žižekian terms. Thinking Žižek's thought in meta-philosophical terms, we could suggest that the Real is not to be identified with either position, but it is the gap or shift between the two. This shift in perspective is what Žižek calls a parallax view.[11] What I would question is any necessary progression between one viewpoint and the other; that is, either one can occupy the position of beyond or the position of limit, depending on the context. The particular view is in some respects arbitrary, but it is the event of insight that moves beyond the beyond, back to the limit, an understanding of the Real that produces Real effects, creates and distributes sense according to a different articulation. This shift and its effects can also be understood as the only real freedom that remains in a world characterized by increasingly fascist and bio-political forces of domination and control.

In conclusion, neo-realism can be seen as a response to the crisis of liberalism, which is at bottom a crisis of belief. At its core, neo-realism betrays a combination of nostalgia and cynicism: cynicism about the contemporary liberating potentialities for living and thinking, and nostalgia for previous eras in which such possibilities were presumably possible. I call neo-realism an ideology because it posits a gap between belief and the Real, such that belief becomes subject to cynical and/or nostalgic manipulation. Michel Henry contrasts ideology with authentic Marxist praxis in his study of Marx, in reference to the gap between theory and practice: "The fundamental reference of theory to practice, against the background of their essential difference, opens up the place in which ideology resides…" (159). According to my understanding of the Real in both Žižek and Deleuze (and Deleuze and Guattari), there is no gap between belief and the Real. For Žižek, there is a gap, but it is within both belief and the Real, whereas for Deleuze and Guattari there is no gap because there is only direct production of the Real as event.

In one of his late works, *Cinema 2: The Time-Image*, Deleuze diagnoses the contemporary crisis of thought as a crisis of belief. In our contemporary world, "it is because this world is intolerable that it can no longer think a world or think itself" (170). The world is experienced as intolerable because the link between humanity and the world has been broken. Modern philosophy, from Pascal to Nietzsche, replaces the model of knowledge with that of belief, but belief in the world is incredible. The easiest solution, the temptation, is to imagine an other world, a different or transformed world in which belief would be possible. But according to Deleuze, belief must be "belief in this world, our only link," and this is the goal of modern cinema as well as contemporary philosophy: "Restoring our belief in the world – this is the power of modern cinema (when it stops being bad). Whether we are Christians or atheists, in our universal schizophrenia, *we need reasons to believe in this world*" (172). Unfortunately, most of our beliefs make us feel like we are living in a bad movie, or at best, a pretty good one. Cinematic narratives script ideological scenarios manipulated in order to control our perception, thoughts, desires and actions, as Virilio has shown. Deleuze calls cinema back to its revolutionary potentiality, to its ability to film the Real, to produce the Real through film, which is connected to our ability to perceive, know and believe in Reality in a postmodern world whose proliferation of images creates autism and schizophrenia. The restoration of belief in the world in no way concerns the use of processes of Realism to lend verisimilitude to fantastic daydreams about winning the lottery, marrying a prince, or being saved by angels, aliens or the United States Marines.

The crisis of liberalism is a crisis of belief, ultimately a crisis of belief in the Real, which brings about a loss of belief in the world. Postmodernism both contributed to and responds to this crisis of belief, and various strands of postmodern theory can be designated as neo-liberal. Many intellectuals are bound to liberalism based upon strong feelings, a love of liberalism that consists in an affirmation of its humane liberal values, and an appreciation of its material advantages for Western elites living in a global capitalist world. To a certain extent, this choice means blinding oneself to the destructive economic effects of neo-liberalism and its "free" trade, which has destroyed environments and economies in a process that Amin calls "pauperization" (39). Other intellectuals have bravely sacrificed their sentiments and followed the crisis of liberalism to its end, and following Carl Schmitt or Leo Strauss embraced various forms of neo-conservativism, either idealistically or cynically, or both. Wittingly or unwittingly, neo-conservativism is now a tool of the American imperial machine, which is engaged in permanent war in order to defend its interests, which are extending military power and concentrating wealth for the ultra-capitalists making the decisions. Finally, some thinkers, like so many people struggling with and against contemporary capitalism, have become neo-traditionalists, usually of a religious variety. Neo-traditionalism deploys neo-realistic interpretations of past time periods in order to offer resistance to or reforms of contemporary ideas and practices. Religious traditions offer important resources for thinking and acting, but they are also being manipulated into an ideological spectacle (Christianity vs. modern secular atheism, Islam vs. modern values of freedom and democracy, Christianity vs. Islam, etc.) that serves to obscure the Real sources of conflict and suffering.

My call, in attending to the revolutionary nature of the Real, and the revolutionary implications of the thought of Žižek and Deleuze, is to refuse these options, liberal, conservative or traditionalist, in the guise of their "neo" versions. In addition, it is to refuse to simply choose between Žižek and Deleuze, or rather, it is to choose that "between." We must become much more radical thinkers, as Marx suggests – "to be radical is to grasp things by the root" (251). We need an almost unimaginable *hijra*, a breaking of the bonds with global capitalism and its neo-realist ideology. We need a new, anti-capitalist Ethics that would stitch together body and spirit, rich and poor, world and humanity along the limits of an earth whose resources are increasingly limited, before it is too late, at least for us. No more neo's, not now, not ever!

Notes

1 See Lyotard's *The Postmodern Condition.*
2 See Derrida's *Spectres of Marx,* pages 109 and 161.
3 See Waltz's *Theory of International Politics* and Keohane's *Neorealism and Its Critics.*
4 See Anderson's *The Origins of Postmodernity.*
5 See Lyotard's *Libidinal Economy.*
6 See Lacan's *Seminar XX,* page 94.
7 See Lacan's *Écrits,* pages 75-81.
8 See *Écrits,* pages 197-268.
9 See Lacan's *Seminar VI,* pages 43-56.
10 See Badiou's *Being and Event.*
11 See Zizek's *Parallax View.*

Works Cited

Althusser, Louis. *Writings on Psychoanalysis: Freud and Lacan*. Trans. Jeffrey Mehlman. New York: Columbia UP, 1996.

Amin, Samir. *The Liberal Virus: Permanent War and the Americanization of the World*. Trans. James H. Menbrez. New York: Monthly Review, 2004.

Anderson, Perry. *The Origins of Postmodernity*. London: Verso, 1998.

Badiou, Alain. *Being and Event*. Trans. Oliver Feltham. London: Continuum, 2006.

Baudrillard, Jean. *America*. Trans. Chris Turner. London: Verso, 1988.

—. *Simulacra and Simulation*. Trans. Sheila Faria Glaser. Ann Arbor: U of Michigan P, 1994.

De Landa, Manuel. *War in the Age of Intelligent Machines*. New York: Zone, 1991.

Deleuze, Gilles. *Cinema 2: The Time-Image*, trans. Hugh Tomlinson and Robert Galeta. Minneapolis: U of Minnesota P, 1989.

—. *The Logic of Sense*. Trans. Mark Lester. New York: ColumbiaUP, 1990.

—. *Difference and Repetition*. Trans. Paul Patton. New York: Columbia UP, 1994.

—. and Félix Guattari. *Anti-Oedipus*. Trans. Robert Hurley, Mark Seem and Helen R. Lane. Minneapolis: U of Minnesota P, 1983.

Derrida, Jacques. *Spectres of Marx: The State of the Debt, the Work of Mourning, & the New International*. Trans. Peggy Kamuf. London: Routledge, 1994.

Henry, Michel. *Marx: A Philosopher of Human Reality*. Trans. Kathleen McLaughlin. Bloomington: Indiana UP, 1983.

Keohane, Robert O. *Neorealism and its Critics*. New York: Columbia UP, 1986.

Lacan, Jacques. *Seminar VII: The Ethics of Psychoanalysis*. Ed. Jacques-Alain Miller. Trans. Dennis Porter. New York: W.W. Norton, 1992.

—. *Seminar XX: On Feminine Sexuality, The Limits of Love and Knowledge 1972-1973*. Ed. Jacques-Alain Miller. Trans. Bruce Fink. New York: W.W. Norton, 1998.

—. *Écrits*. Trans. Bruce Fink. New York: W.W. Norton, 2006.

Lambert, Gregg. *Report to the Academy (RE: The NEW Conflict of the Faculties)*. Aurora, CO: Davies Group, 2001.

Lyotard, Jean- François. *The Postmodern Condition: A Report on Knowledge*. Trans. Geoff Bennington and Brian Massumi. Minneapolis: U of Minnesota P, 1984.

—. *Libidinal Economy*. Trans. Iain Hamilton Grant. Bloomington: Indiana UP, 1993.

Marx, Karl. 1992. "A Contribution to the Critique of Hegel's Philosophy of Right. Introduction" *Early Writings*. Trans. Rodney Livingstone and Gregor Benton. London: Penguin, 1992.

New York Times. "Military Predicts Robot Soldiers in Decade." February 20, 2005.

Virilio, Paul. *The Vision Machine*. Trans. Julie Rose. Bloomingon: Indiana UP, 1994.

—. *The Art of the Motor*. Trans. Julie Rose. Minneapolis: U of Minnesota P, 1995.

—. *Desert Screen: War at the Speed of Light*. Trans. Michael Degener. London: Continuum, 2002.

Walz, Kenneth N. *Theory of International Politics*. New York: McGraw-Hill, 1979.

Žižek, Slavoj. *Tarrying with the Negative: Kant, Hegel and the Critique of Ideology*. Durham, NC: Duke UP, 1993.

—. *The Puppet and the Dwarf: The Perverse Core of Christianity.* Cambridge, MA: MIT, 2003.
—. *The Parallax View.* Cambridge, MA: MIT, 2006.

~ 13 ~

The Weakness of God:
A Theology of the Event

John D. Caputo

"For the foolishness of God is wiser than human wisdom,
and the weakness of God is stronger than human strength...
But God chose what is weak in the world to shame the strong;
God chose what is low and despised (*ta agene*) in the world,
things that are not (*ta me onta*), to reduce to nothing the things that are (*ta onta*).
> – I Cor.1:25, 27-28

I have a weakness for theology, the way one has a weakness for sex or money; it is what I secretly desire, or maybe not so secretly, even as it desires everything of me. I would never lay claim to actually be theological, but, with all due deference, like Kierkegaard's Johannes Climacus speaking of being a Christian, I would say that at best I am involved in becoming theological. Theology delineates the logos of a passion, the logos of a desire for God. *I have taken God, the name of God, what is happening in the name of God, as my subject matter.* With or without religion, with or without what ordinarily passes for theology, the name of God being too important to leave in the hands of the special interest groups. That is why I freely own up here to a certain theological gesture, to a theological desire and a "desiring theology," as Charles Winquist would have put it, which is undeniably a desire for God, for something astir in the name of God, a desire for God knows what, for something I know not what.

Name and Event

The modest proposal I make in this paper is that the name of God is an *event*, or rather that it harbors an event, and that theology is the hermeneutics of that event, its task being to release what is happening in that name, to set it free, to give it its own head, and thereby to head off the forces that would prevent this event. My subject is theology and the event, a theology of the event. Obviously, then, everything turns on explaining what I mean by an "event" and how it is related to a "name."

(1) *Uncontainability*. Names contain events and give them a kind of temporary shelter by housing them within a relatively stable nominal unity. Events, on the other hand, are uncontainable and they make names restless with promise and the future, with the result that names contain what they cannot contain. Names belong to natural languages and are historically constituted or constructed, while events are a little unnatural, almost eery and ghostly things that haunt names and see to it that they never rest in peace. Names can accumulate historical power and worldly prestige and have very powerful institutions erected in or under their name, getting themselves carved in stone, while the voice of events is ever soft and low and may be dismissed, distorted or ignored.

There is always something uncontainable and unconditional about an event, while names, like "God," belong to conditioned and coded strings of signifiers. The event is the unconditional promise contained within a name, but a promise that the name can neither contain or deliver. No name–the name of God is the particular case in point in this study–can enjoy more than a contingent privilege relative to the event, a privilege generated by the particular historical circumstances of a language and a culture.

Names set off chains of promise and aspiration or chains of memories that outstrip themselves, in the face of which the name itself is stressed, being unable to sustain the promise it itself engenders. A name is a promissory note that it itself cannot keep. In the "democracy to come," for example, "democracy" is a name that may someday collapse under the strain of the "to come," which is the force of the event that will force the name beyond itself. In the "democracy to come," the "to come" is more important than the "democracy." A name is conditioned, coded, and finite while the event it shelters is unconditional and infinite in the sense of being capable of endless linkings. One is a nominalist about names because of one's respect for the event.

(2) *Beyond Being*. An event refers neither to a being or entity nor to being itself, but to an impulse or aspiration simmering within both the names of entities and the name of being, something that groans to be born, something that cannot be constricted to either the ontic or ontological order at all. Rightly understood, the event overflows any entity; it does not rest easily within the confines of the name of an entity, but stirs restlessly, endlessly, like an invitation or a call, an invocation ("come") or a provocation, a solicitation or a promise, a praise or benediction ("good, very good"), whether or not the occurrences on the plane of being are promising or good, whether or not they are the match for what is stirring in the event of the call. An event is not an ontico-ontological episode on the plane of being but a disturbance within the heart of being, within the names for being, that makes being restless.

The Weakness of God

Let us turn then to God (a life long task!) and to the name of God.

Is not the name of God a dream of power aplenty, of omnitude and plenitude and plenipotentiarity, of exnihilatory and annihilatory power, and is not "theology" the very name, the very model, of the love of God's power?

Can one imagine anything or anyone more sovereign power than God's? Can one imagine anything more supportive of the established order. *Pro deo et patria*: is that not a lethal combination, literally a call to arms in whose ungodly name more blood has been spilled than just about anything else we can imagine? Is not the sovereign Father Almighty, Creator of Heaven and Earth, the very model of every earthly patriarchy? How often has the "reign of God" meant a sovereign reign of theocratic terror? What has been more violent than theocracy? What more patriarchal, more hierarchical? What more authoritarian, inquisitorial, misogynistic, colonialist, militaristic, terroristic?

Suppose–and this is the working hypothesis of a theology of the event–we raise the possibility of a "God" who belongs not to the fixed order of presence but to the (dis)order of the deconstruction of presence? Suppose we abandon the top down schema of one Sovereign God in heaven, one Father Almighty, one King to rule the land (another father), in favor of a paradigm where such sovereign power slips out of favor? Suppose we say that the event that is sheltered in the name of God does not belong to the order of manifestation, power and presence, but rather withdraws from the world in order to station him or herself (Godself is the gender neutral word, if you can get used to it) with everything that the world despises? Suppose we think of God not on the model of kingly power but as someone who prowls the streets (a *voyou*) and disturbs the peace? Suppose we imagine God as a street person with a definite body odor? Suppose our thought of God is not domesticated by Sunday sermons by His Reverence or coopted by ecstatic visions of the supereminent power of the supreme creator of heaven and earth? Suppose instead we take our lead in thinking about God from images of the most powerless remnants and marginalized bodies and nobodies, the little *me onta*, the obscure pockets and folds and hovels of the world? Suppose God most especially pitches God's tent among the homeless, so that God would be the last and least likely one to say "*pro deo et patria?*" since he has no place on which to lay his head?

Suppose further that "religion" and "theology," which are human all too human and not to be confused with God, tend systematically, structurally, regularly, to forget this, and to associate themselves with a discourse of power, which is what we mean by strong theology? Suppose that the God of religion and theology, which is also our invention, might almost be defined by its prevention of the event that is sheltered by the name God, by its oblivion of this event, so that the first step that would be required, as Meister Eckhart said, is to pray God to rid us of this God? To which we might add, "I pray God to rid us of religion," since, according to Isaiah (*Is*.1:11-17), Amos (*Amos*. 5:21-24), and Hosea (*Hos*. 6:6), God can do *without* religion if religion means cultic sacrifice and ritual, but not without the event of justice, which is not always what religion means, which is also a point that Karl Barth was fond of making from time to time.[1] Suppose indeed that "God," that the event that is astir within the name of God, is stationed not on the side of the *arche* and the *principium*, or of timeless being and unchanging presence, of the true, the good and the beautiful, but on the side of the an-archic and subversive, as the driving force of a divine subversion? Suppose God is the prime mover unmoved not of physical movement but of justice, and that God moves not by force but by attraction, like a call, by drawing us on and luring us? Suppose the name of "God" harbors an event of solicitation?

Suppose God is not to be conceived as the overarching and sovereign governor of the *ordo universi*, of the *cosmos*, but as what disorders such orders, de-worlds such worlds, and subverts and poly-verts such universes, all for the "chaosmic" ends of justice? Suppose God is not conceived theo-cratically and onto-theo-logically as the rock solid ground upon which the onto-theo-political edifice of sovereignty is erected, but is systematically associated with the different, the marginal, the outsider, the left out, the beggars on the temple steps not the high priests in long robes in the sanctuary within, with the least among us, the destitute, the *anawim*, those who are plundered and ground under (*Amos* 8:4), and hence as a subversive and "revolutionary" impulse?

Suppose the event that is sheltered by the name of God is not identified with timeless infinite power invested in an *omnipotens deus*, but with the powerless who suffer the ravages of time? Suppose the sense of "God" is to interrupt and disrupt, to confound, contradict and confront the established human order, the human all too human way and sway of doing business, the authority of man over man–and over women, animals, and the earth itself–human possessiveness and dominion, to pose, in short, the contradiction of the "world?" Suppose God has no time for the hierarchical power structures that human beings impose upon one another and even less time for the power of God over human beings, which is actually the power that human beings exert "in the name of God"? Suppose the event that simmers in the name of God, if it were to be written out, would read "No God, No Master?"

Suppose the idea behind calling God a father is not to set up an oppressive patriarchal model of sovereign power but the relativization of worldly power: "Do not call any man on earth father, for you have one Father, and he is in heaven...the greatest among you must be your servant." (*Matt.*23:8-12). Then repeat and update that with a sexual difference, and say that you have one mother in heaven, and for the same reason (which should make us worry about some of these mothers here on earth). Then generalize it in terms of parents and human authorities.

Suppose we associate God with disseminating tongues and deconstructing towering edifices, with confusion and profusion, the way God interrupted the plans of the Shemites (*Genesis* 11:1-9), who wanted to build the tower of Babel and then disseminated their language into a profusion of mutually unintelligible tongues so that they could no longer build up a consensus and no longer build their transcendental tower?[2]

Suppose "God" stands for an event that confounds, confuses, contradicts, and scandalizes the crusts of power and privilege, this order of presence, *not*, I hasten to add, in order to throw us to the wolves of lawlessness but in order to let the lamb lie down with the wolf (*Isa.* 11:6), not in order to level institutions and structures, but precisely in order to keep them open, to open them up, to keep them just, to let justice reign? Suppose then the international politics that accompanies the theology of this event is a community of nations without individual sovereignty?

Suppose we cross out the name of God in order to release the event this name contains? Suppose we do this just in order to save the name of God, saving the event sheltered by the name of God, from the God of religion and theology, which is an idol, a graven image, an instrument of institutional power, of moral melancholy, of top down authoritarianism, and confessional divisiveness? Suppose we cross out the name of God not in the spirit of a mystical theology, where God is the *nomen innominabile* of a *hyperousios*, where it signifies the mystery of the great power of Being, but in the name of a weak theology, which is composed of graffiti that defaces standard theological writing, like a body that is scratched, scarred and defaced, marred by lines of hunger or persecution, wounded and bleeding? Suppose we imagine weak theology as a meditation upon God crossed out, cut and bruised, bleeding and bent in pain, like the crucified God of which Moltmann speaks?

Suppose we imagine God not as a prime mover unmoved but as removed from the order of cosmic movements and cosmological explanations, removed from the onto-causal order altogether, from being, presence, power and causality? Suppose we think of God as something "unconditional," an unconditional appeal or call or claim, that is nevertheless without "sovereignty?" Suppose we imagine that God makes an unconditional claim upon us without exercising unqualified force or power? Suppose we imagine God otherwise, not as seated in the height of power, not really having a seat in being at all, but below being and beings, as the heart of a heartless world, the heart of an unconditional claim? Suppose we think of God not so much in terms of everything that we desire, which seems a little acquisitive, but in terms of everything that desires us, everything that draws us out of ourselves and calls upon us, calling from below being to what is beyond, that summons up what is best in us, that asks us to go out of our creaturely way of being and live generously, to live and love, to live and let live, to love and let love, to live by loving, unconditionally? Suppose we hold that whatever has being can come to be only under certain conditions while the unconditional would somehow be free from being, otherwise than being, a kind of demi-being, almost like a ghost, a very holy one no doubt, and almost nothing?

Suppose, then, in short, and contrary to the expectations of religion, mainstream theology and the vested interests of His Reverence, the name of God harbors an event that is at best a "weak force" (*force faible*), and that the "weakness of God" is, nonetheless, the only thing that is strong enough to save us, which is why we want to save this name?

What then?

Then we would have sparks, or anarchy on our hands, sacred sparks and a sacred anarchy. In the New Testament, the "world" means the holding sway of the real power of this world, the *strong force* of the power of the present age, of the *aion*, to which the weak force of the Kingdom is opposed. The "world" is what really exists, in the order of being, whereas the Kingdom *calls for* something else. The world stands for the business as usual of the powerful and privileged, the oppressive order of presence that builds wealth on the backs of the poor and the outcast, that builds privilege on the backs of the despised and the different, while the Kingdom contradicts the world, which means it calls for something contrary to the world. The Kingdom belongs to a different order, a different plane, than that of being or presence. Make no mistake, there is only one world, in the sense of what Heidegger calls "being-in-the-world," but the Kingdom and the "world" are its tensions.

The Transcendence of God

But let us not shirk our duty and run from the hard questions: what can it possibly mean to speak of the "weakness of God" and to say that the event that is sheltered in the name of God is a "weak force"? If we save the name of God as a weak force, how is God able to save us? If God is weak, how is God strong enough to save us? Indeed, if God is weak, how can God still be God at all? It is time to face the music, time to pay the piper for all this impudence and impiousness. Let us try to do so by asking how, on such anarchical terms, we can speak of what has always been called the "transcendence" of God?

One quite classic way to explain the transcendence of God in strong theology is to adapt the Platonic way of eminence, of the Good beyond being, the Good for which being is not good enough. God is "without being" where "without" signifies an excess beyond not a lack, that than which nothing that is can be greater. But that is not good enough for a weak theology, because the Good in the *Republic* (509) is the ultimate sovereign power, a king (*kurios*) in its own kingdom (*basileia*), the very knowledge of which entitles the philosopher to be a king, a real king not an ironic one, because knowledge rules. The Good in the *Republic* is the most powerful and superlative power, which imposes a hierarchical order upon lower being, just in accord with the model of sovereignty, which is not what I mean by the power of powerlessness. The Good is the father of all, the *arche*, the *hyperousios*, the hyper-being beyond being, the Godhead beyond God (*Gottheit über Gott*), not the power of powerlessness, not the weak force of a powerless solicitation or promise or provocation. Strong theology loves the order of the *Republic*, whereas a theology of the event, as we will see, is happy down below with *khora*.

The admitted perversity of my hypothesis in these pages is that I treat God not as an eminent omnipotent onto-power capable of leveling tall buildings and reducing his enemies (no need for gender neutral language here) to ashes, but as the weak force of a call. If I am pressed by the Lord Cardinal, His Eminence the Grand Inquisitor, to say what then God "is," I would nervously defer because I prefer to say not that God "is" but that God "calls," that God promises, not from beyond being but from below, without being or sovereignty. If I am then pressed further by His Awful Eminence to say what God's transcendence is, I would again defer because I prefer to say not that God is a transcendent super-essential hyper-being towering over other beings, but that God's transcendence is that of a call, of an address that, while arising from the hinter regions below being, lays us low. On my telling, God's transcendence is clearly a matter of the transcendence of the event that transpires in the name of God. God's transcendence means that we are laid low by a call arising from on high, but whose heights arise from someone who, lacking the wherewithal to lay down his head, pitches his tent among the lowly bodies and nobodies below in the bodily bowels of hypo-being. To invoke the safety of the most classical language of the Scriptures and theology, I am saying that the transcendence of God is not that of a fist that smashes but of a Spirit who breathes, who inspires, and whose gentle breath urges us on.

God, like justice, calls unconditionally from beyond or below the law, the way the needs of the lost one prevail over the safety of the ninety-nine. God calls from amidst the hinter-beings, and the kingdom is what is called for.

God's transcendence is the power of a spirit, not of the sword. The transcendence of God is not at odds with the weak force of God; it *is* the weak force of God. Otherwise it would not be transcendence of God but the transcendence of the world, which is a strong force, one with a real army and the real power to enforce its word. The word of God, the God of the word. The promise of God, the God of the promise. If it is true that we can hardly resist God's promise, it is not less true that this irresistible force is weak–for on our impious premise God can only promise.

The weak force of God is to lay *claim* upon us but not the way a sovereign power in the domain of being invades and then lays claim to territory, overpowers its native population and plants a foreign flag, but in the way of a summons that calls and provokes, an appeal that incites us, a promise that awakens our love. The name of God harbors an unconditional appeal, without the power or sovereign force to enforce it. God is, without being, of unconditional import and the object of an unconditional desire. God lays claim upon us unconditionally without overwhelming us with power. The issue is not so much with what name we are to call God, but what the name of God calls for, what it calls upon us to do. To live "before God" (*coram deo*), as Augustine put it so beautifully, is to live on call, under the call, always already solicited, called upon, pressed by the weak force of the call, called by the call to let the Kingdom come, which is what called for. Let the kingdom come, in the name of God. That is the event that calls in the name of God.

God's transcendence is not to be taken as if God is a super-hero, some super-being who out-knows, out-wills, out-does, out-powers and out-exists every entity here below, a higher super-entity, a hyper-presence dwelling in a higher world. I do not think of God as a first cause, or first unmoved mover, or an omnipotent onto-theo-cosmo-logical power source for the universe, but as the unconditional demand for beneficence that shocks the world with a promise that is not kept, as the heart of a heartless world, as the call from below being that summons us to rise beyond being, beyond ourselves. I think of the world as addressed by a call, not produced by a cause, as an addressee, not an effect, and of God as a call, not a cause, as a beneficence, not a sovereign power.

Another way to put all this is to say that, in my vocabulary, the world is there, being is there, and there we are, there, in world, being right there along with the world. By "God," on the other hand, I do not mean a being who is there, an entity trapped in being, or even as a super-being *up there*, up above the world, who physically powers and causes it, who made it and occasionally intervenes upon its day to day activities to tweak things for the better in response to a steady stream of solicitations from down below (a hurricane averted here, a malignant tumor shrunk there, etc.). That I consider an essentially magical view of the world. I do not mean anything that is *there*, because what is *there* belongs to the order of being and power; to the strong force of the world, where you solve problems by raising money–or an army. I mean a call which solicits and disturbs what is there, an event that adds a level of signification and meaning, of provocation and solicitation to what is there, which makes it impossible for the world, for what is *there*, to settle solidly in place, to consolidate, to close in upon itself. By the name of "God" I mean the event of this solicitation, an event of deconsolidation, an electrifying event-ing disturbance, the solvent of the weak force of this spectral spirit who haunts the world as its bad conscience, or who breathes lightly and prompts its most inspired moments, all the while readily conceding that there are other names than the name of God. I am trying to save the name of God, not absolutize it.

Whether over and beyond what we might call the hermeneutics of the event, the lived experience of the call and of being on call, there is some entitative cause calling, some entity or hyper-entity out there with a proper name, verifiable by a metaphysical argument or certifiable by a divine revelation, is no part of my hypothesis, one way or the other (for or against). I leave that stock to fluctuate on the open market of existence. I leave that question to fluctuate in that domain of undecidability wherein all concrete decisions are made, which has the effect of intensifying this decision, not attenuating it. About that decision I have no inside trader information to pass along. About God, God alone knows. To speak a little Heideggerianese, that is an existentiell matter for each poor existing individual, and no part of the trouble we are buying for ourselves with this experiment. No one has authorized us to settle that question. We are not a party to that dispute. Although I have my opinions, I have not the least first hand information to convey about that.

For as I said, the trouble rouged theology buys for itself is the result of selling the body of theology to power. The very core of the mistake made by onto-theology derives from conceiving God on the horizon of being, power and causality, as if God were a cosmic power supply. In the weak and colorless theology whose cause I am promoting, it is profane magic, thaumaturgy, to think of God as an omnipotent meteorological onto-power who could stop (or start) hurricanes, landslides and floods, or as an omni-historical superpower who can stop or start or wars or prevent holocausts and put an end to pornography, obesity, junk TV, spam emails, crime in the streets and the ruining of the environment. When we see an athlete praying for victory in a game, blame the strong theologians, not the poor coach; the athlete simply makes the logic of this onto-theo-cosmo-interventionism embarrassingly visible, right on national TV, as if God were a party to a Final Four office pool. The thoroughly onto-theological project of "theodicy," of getting God off the causal hook, whether for the vagaries of natural disasters or for the disasters caused by human vagary and malice, is no less profane. The authentically religious way to think about God, on my slightly heretical hypothesis, which keeps holy the idea of the anarchical, is in terms of powerlessness not power, or at most in terms of the power of powerlessness, which is what I mean by the weak force of God.

Conclusion: Confessing the Name of God

My hypothesis is that simmering within this contingent and historical name is a subversive and anarchizing event, which is why this name should set off sparks whenever it makes contact with the settled orders of presence or finds its way inside the inaccessible corridors of power. This name has come to us from our mother's breast, from the dark waters of the womb, from our unconscious, from the hidden depths of our language, from our most ordinary language, as opposed to a formal or contrived one, from the lost roots of our multiple histories, all the forces of which have been run together in a massive simplification and concentrated shorthand called "God." This name is made to bear the weight of that history, which it cannot bear, and to carry the torch of our desire, which it cannot carry, and to contain an event that it cannot contain. Philosophers think that it is philosophy that makes everything questionable while theology puts questioning to sleep, indeed puts everyone to sleep, so that theology, like the sermons delivered in church, is most effective among insomniacs. Philosophers think questioning awakens with the provocative poem of Parmenides, with the interrogatory life of Socrates, with the doubt of Descartes, with Kant's critique, or with Heidegger's question of being.

But we advocates of a theology of the event, we partisans of weak theology, who belong to a different party, advance the hypothesis that theology has the interrogatory force to awaken questioning and to stir thought and this just because the name of God is inscribed in theology. *Theo*logy was named after God and is God's word, God's logos, God's namesake, God's desire, the desire for God. The name of God arises from such bottomless and dark depths as to set off an event of endless provocation. To proclaim the death of God, as Nietzsche realized better than anyone, is to proclaim a stunning and mind-numbing event, compared to which the death of anything else would receive only passing notice, at most two columns in the obituary section. The name of God irrupts with shocking force and power, with violence and bloodiness, as well as with beauty and majesty, even as–and this has been our contentious view–this name is true to itself only as the weak but unconditional force of the call or the promise, which is something that is easily missed and part and parcel of theology's bi-polar condition. The bi-polarity is a function of the

distinction between name and event. The name has accumulated all
the power and prestige of the worldly institutions that have taken it
over, which makes for a strong force, while the event it harbors is the
weak but unconditional force of a poor perhaps.

The desire for God is inscribed deep in our unconscious,
leaping to our lips at times of birth and death, of entreaty and
gratitude, of desperation and separation, of surpassing joy and heart-
rending sorrow, of peace and danger.

> "God knows."
> "Thanks be to God."
> "May God be with you."

It is even a name we invoke ("O God"), if I may be ever so slightly
salacious, in moments of explosive orgasmic joy–and rightly so; that
is also good theology. What do the philosophers have to compete with
such a name? What rival name do they propose for such occasions?
Who can they nominate as an opposing candidate in a general
election? "Being"? "Consciousness"? "Substance"? The "System"?
Are they serious? Is that a joke? The last cloudy streak of evaporating
reality, mummifications, conceptual embalmings, Nietzsche said. "Be
a philosopher, be a mummy," he said, as he pointed at such names in
ridicule, holding his sides, collapsing with laughter. And sitting at a
nearby table, not far off, Kierkegaard has put down his cigar and taken
out his handkerchief to wipe the tears of laughter from his eyes as he
reads the latest issue of *The Daily Encyclopedia*, in which we are
given every assurance that work on the System is expected to be
completed no later than the middle of next week. (The System is like
highway construction–it is never finished!)

I would be the first to concede that a theology of the event is
after all in one sense an unnatural being, because it has taken leave of
the names that grow up in the natural languages and occupied itself
with the underlying or innermost events sheltered by these names. But
our usual practice is to use names, to call and be called by name, not
by an "event," which sounds a little eerie, like being haunted by a
ghost or hearing voices. Still, the name for what is coming must
always and in principle be lacking. It is not so much that names fail us
as that such names simply are not here yet, have not formed yet, have
not yet been forged in the furnace of historical circumstance so as to
have taken shape in (and given shape to) our lives. To speak of an

event is already to have taken up a kind of unnatural, dislocated second order position, to have engaged a slightly ghostly or hauntological operation that instead of simply using names straightforwardly has inserted a kind of ironic distance between itself and the straightforward first order use of the name. By opening up the distinction between the name and the event, we put the name of God at risk, exposing it to a harsh truth, to the possibility of the coming of a name that is at present lacking, or not yet found, not yet formed or forged, a new name that will shelter the event in an unforeseen way. We expose the name of God, not to the coming of a new god, but to the coming of something new in which the name of God may or will be displaced and this just in virtue of the event that this name harbors. That is the risk to which the deconstruction of God, of rather of the name of God, exposes us. Nothing is safe.

The idea of the event explodes the notion that there is a name that is above all other names, in the name of which we can and should make war on rival names to the crown. As long as the event that is desired with a desire beyond desire is contracted to the specific terms of a Proper Name, there will be wars of private property, wars over the copyright, over who owns that name, or who gets to speak authoritatively, with the all the authority of the Name? Disputes break out about the difference between the original language and the language of translation, or about whose language gets to be the sacred one, or whose city gets to be the holy one. How in God's name are we going to settle these wars over the name of God? That belligerence, that mundane militancy, arises from reducing an event to a name, from trapping an event inside a name.

I would go so far as to say that desire itself is a desire for the event. Were I psychoanalyst, of which no one has accused me so far, I would start out with that hypothesis and I would take it as my life's work to keep desire alive and well in my patients, leaving them as happy as the lilies of the field, for which gift I would charge a reasonable hourly sum. There is only a chain of conditioned, substitutable, provisional, preliminary names at the sound of which some knees somewhere should sometimes bend, there is a bottomless desire for such names. If the desire for the event is desire itself, the assignation of a Proper Name to the event would be the death of desire.

Were I–God forbid–to resort to politics to keep desire alive I would tour the country giving a stump speech that would say "the only thing in which we have to hope is hope itself." I think that we are saved more by hope itself than by *what* we hope in, which differs from time to time and place to place and is at best a place holder for something, I know not what, for some more elemental quality of our lives. Hope seems like an irreducible feature of desire, that keeps desire alive, but is capable of assuming many forms and of undergoing constant transformation. There is no single and exclusive, no sustainably determinate "what" in hope, no fixed object of hope, for once something is fixed in place, it collapses under the weight of hope. So just as F.D. R. campaigned on the premise that the only thing we have to fear is fear itself, I will run a more Derridean campaign and say that the only thing in which we always and everywhere have to hope is hope itself, which is not deconstructible. Whatever determinate and identifiable something we hope in, whatever that turns out to be, is and ever will be deconstructible, but hope itself, if there is such a thing, is not deconstructible. My ultimate passion is the passion of non-knowing, the passion that does not know what stirs its passion, the passion for God, for the event that is harbored in the name of God, which means the passion for God knows what, the strong passion of weak theology, for which I live unreservedly.

We do not know whether the name of God is a pseudonym for the event, a fantastic concentration into one name of everything we desire and that desires us, or whether what we say we desire about the event is a pseudonym for the desire of God (which is not even to mention the darkness of unconscious desire). Is the event another name for God or is God another name for the event? Is God the incognito of the event or is the event the incognito of God? Does the event belong to theology or does theology belong to the event? A theology of the event arises from the confession that it is not possible to arrest this play, that it is too weak to decide between these two, to resolve this fluctuation from on high in some final and decisive way. But that negative result is the doorway to an affirmation.

Are we to suppose that life is a puzzle and we are charged with solving it, or a quiz we are asked to take in which the challenge is to discover the identity of a hidden god? Are we to think that life is a gamble in which we had to choose between one name or another, a winner take all contest in which we had better make the right guess or regret it for all eternity? On the contrary, everything turns on keeping the gap between the name and the event open, on keeping the tension between them strong and alive, and then on being carried or transported by that tension into the passion of life. The passion of life, the passion of desire, is fueled by revving up the intensity of this tension to the breaking point. Undecidability fires passion to the limit, feeding the flames of faith by the very fluctuation of names. It is when I truly do not know what I desire that desire is desire, that desire is fired white hot. It is when I truly do not know where I am going that I am really faced with making a move.

But the point is to make the move, to carry out the motion. When the Eleatics argued that motion was impossible, Diogenes refuted them by taking a few steps, which is, in the end, all that I am recommending. What matters with the event is taking a few steps. What matters is the passion, the leap, the witness, while leaving the Eleatics to their Greek games.

Who are we? *Quaestio mihi factus sum.* We are the nameless ones who are driven by the undecidability of the desire for God, made restless by the trembling of an indiscernible event. Seeming for all the world to be mercantile souls we are inwardly unhinged by something unconditional. The works and days of our ordinary life are made to tremble by some extraordinary charge which inflicts upon us an invisible wound from which we cannot and do not wish to be cured. We are incited by the powerless power of some quiet provocation, like the words "good, good...very good" sweeping softly across the surface of the deep, making being restless with the good. We are swept up in the winds of solicitation and invitation, of promise and a prayer for the event, our ears pressed close to the name of God, cupped tightly to the force of the event that is gathering in that name and that keeps the world from closing over. We are tuned to the distant but insistent rumbling of the coming of the Kingdom, the coming of the event.

The world quivers quietly under the weak force of an event, made restless by the silent force of God's divinely subversive call. But is it really God who calls? Who knows who is calling? Is the event a breeze blowing out of paradise, the wind that swept across the darkness of the deep, the *ruach Elohim* or the anonymous rumbling of I know not what? God only knows!

NOTES

---

[1] See Karl Barth's *The Epistle to the Romans*. Throughout this famous book Barth delimits "all ethical and religious illusions" (68), the illusions which are ethics and religion, in favour of the impossible possibility" (79).

[2] See Kevin Hart's *The Trespass of the Sign: Deconstruction, Theology, and Philosophy*, 107 ff; see Jacques Derrida's "Des tours de Babel."

Works Cited

Barth, Karl. *The Epistle to the Romans*. Trans. E.C. Hoskyns. London: Oxford UP, 1968.

Derrida, Jacques. "Des tours de Babel." Trans. Joseph Graham. *Difference in Translation*. Ithaca: Cornell UP, 1985.

Hart, Kevin. *The Trespass of the Sign: Deconstruction, Theology, and Philosophy*. 2nd ed. New York: Fordham UP, 2000.

Contributors

NEIL BROOKS is associate professor and chair of the Department of English at Huron University College. He has published several articles in the areas of African American Literature and the postmodern novel, including recent essays on Thomas Pynchon, Martin Amis, Walter White, and Julian Barnes. With Teresa Hubel, he edited *Literature and Racial Ambiguity* (Rodopi 2002).

JOHN D. CAPUTO is the Thomas J. Watson Professor of Religion and Humanities at Syracuse University and also David R. Cook Professor Emeritus of Philosophy at Villanova University where he taught from 1968 until 2004. His newest books are *The Weakness of God: A Theology of the Event* (Indiana UP, 2006), *Philosophy and Theology* (Abingdon, 2006), and *Augustine and Postmodernism: Confessions and Circumfession* (Indiana UP, 2005), which he edited with Michael Scanlon. Recent publications also include *On Religion* (Routledge, 2001), *More Radical Hermeneutics: On Not Knowing Who We Are* (Indiana, 2000), *The Prayers and Tears of Jacques Derrida: Religion without Religion* (Indiana UP, 1997), and *Deconstruction in a Nutshell: A Conversation with Jacques Derrida* (Fordham UP, 1997). He serves as editor of the Fordham University Press book series "Perspectives in Continental Philosophy" and Chairman of the Board of Editors of Journal of Cultural and Religious Theory.

CLAYTON CROCKETT is Assistant Professor of Religious Studies at the University of Central Arkansas. He is the author of *A Theology of the Sublime* (Routledge, 2001), and a forthcoming book on theology and psychoanalytic theory. He is also an editor of the online *Journal for Cultural and Religious Theory* (www.jcrt.org).

CLAYTON DION has earned degrees in both mathematics and literature and is currently completing his PhD thesis, "Integrating the Two Cultures: Einstein as 20th Century Muse," at the University of Western Ontario. Combining his studies of mathematics with an understanding of 20th century literature, Clayton is examining the aesthetic culture generated in response to Einstein's revolution in physics. The thesis considers, specifically, T. S. Eliot and the authors of the Beat Generation. Clayton has written and presented several papers exploring different aspects of Beat literature.

JANE FLAX is professor of political science at Howard University and a psychotherapist in private practice in Washington, DC. Her books include *Thinking Fragments, Disputed Subjects* (U of California P, 1990), and *The American Dream in Black and White* (Cornell UP, 1998). Currently she is completing a new book, *Shadow at the Heart: Racial Melancholy and Contemporary American Politics*.

TODD GANNON is an architect, educator, and writer based in Los Angeles. He has taught architectural theory and design at Ohio State, UCLA, and Otis College of Art and Design. As series editor of Source Books in Architecture, he has published books on the work of Morphosis, Bernard Tschumi, UN Studio, Steven Holl, Mack Scogin/Merrill Elam, Zaha Hadid, and on the MoMA exhibition "Light Construction." His essays have appeared in *Log, Loud Paper, Dialogue*, and elsewhere. He is currently pursuing a doctoral degree at UCLA.

JENNIFER L. GEDDES is Research Associate Professor of Religious Studies at the University of Virginia, Co-Director of the Institute for Advanced Studies in Culture, and Editor of *The Hedgehog Review: Critical Reflections on Contemporary Culture*. The author of numerous articles, reviews, and interviews and the editor of *Evil After Postmodernism: Histories, Narratives, Ethics* (Routledge, 2001), she is currently working on a book entitled *The Rhetorics of Evil*.

N. KATHERINE HAYLES, Hillis Professor of Literature at the University of California, Los Angeles, won the Rene Wellek Prize for the Best Book in Literary Theory for *How We Became*

Posthuman: Virtual Bodies in Cybernetics, Literature, and Informatics (1999) and the Suzanne Langer Award for Outstanding Scholarship for *Writing Machines* (2001). Her most recent book is *My Mother Was a Computer: Digital Subjects and Literary Texts* (2005, U of Chicago P). She is currently at work on a study of narrative and database.

GAVIN KEULKS is Associate Professor of English at Western Oregon University, where he specializes in contemporary English and Irish literature. He is the author of *Father and Son: Kingsley Amis, Martin Amis, and the British Novel Since 1950* (Wisconsin, 2003), the editor of *Martin Amis: Postmodernism and Beyond* (Palgrave Macmillan, 2006), and the online administrator of the *Martin Amis Web*. He also recently completed his first novel, tentatively titled *Flight*.

WILLIAM G. LITTLE is Associate Professor of English at DePauw University. He is the author of *The Waste Fix: Seizures of the Sacred from Upton Sinclair to The Sopranos* (Routledge, 2002). He writes on modern American literature and film.

PAUL MALTBY is Professor of English at West Chester University. He is the author of *Dissident Postmodernists: Barthelme, Coover, Pynchon* (U of Pennsylvania P, 1991) and *The Visionary Moment: A Postmodern Critique* (State U of New York P, 2002).

DAWNE McCANCE is Professor and Head, Department of Religion, University of Manitoba and Editor of *Mosaic: a journal for the interdisciplinary study of literature*. Her recent book, *Medusa's Ear*, was published by SUNY Press in 2004. She is currently working on two books, one on Jacques Derrida and the other, *A Little History of Hearing*.

ROBERT L. MCLAUGHLIN is Professor of English at Illinois State University. His work on postmodern literature and culture has appeared in such journals and collections as *Critique, Pynchon Notes, Symploke*, the *Review of Contemporary Fiction, On Anthologies: Politics and Pedagogy*, and *American Postmodernity*. With Sally E.

Parry, he is the author of *We'll Always Have the Movies: American Cinema during World War II* (UP of Kentucky, 2006).

ROBERT REBEIN is an Associate Professor of English and Creative Writing at Indiana University Purdue University in Indianapolis. He is the author, among other works, of *Hicks, Tribes, & Dirty Realists: American Fiction after Postmodernism* (UP of Kentucky, 2001).

JOSH TOTH teaches English literature at the University of Manitoba. Most recently, he published an article on Hemingway and "autonarration" in *The North Dakota Quarterly*, and he is currently preparing his PhD dissertation – "The Passing of Postmodernism: A Spectroanalysis of the Contemporary" – for publication. He is also working on an examination of the theory of Jacques Derrida and Jean-Luc Nancy as it applies to the ethics of intrusion in twentieth-century American literature.